Workers' Compensation Practice for Paralegals

Workers' Compensation Practice for Paralegals

Lynne J. DeVenny

J. Griffin Morgan

Carolina Academic Press

Durham, North Carolina

Library of Congress Cataloging-in-Publication Data

DeVenny, Lynne J.
Workers' compensation practice for paralegals / by Lynne J. DeVenny, J. Griffin Morgan.
p. cm.
Includes bibliographical references and index.
ISBN-13: 978-1-59460-264-1 (alk. paper)
ISBN-10: 1-59460-264-6 (alk. paper)
1. Workers' compensation--Law and legislation--United States. 2. Legal assistants--United States. I. Morgan, J. Griffin. II. Title.

KF3615.Z9D48 2008
344.7302'1--dc22

2007044852

Carolina Academic Press
700 Kent Street
Durham, North Carolina 27701
Telephone (919) 489-7486
Fax (919) 493-5668
www.cap-press.com

Printed in the United States of America.
2022 Printing

Table of Contents

Preface

The purpose of this textbook is not to provide a detailed analysis of workers' compensation laws nationwide, but to discuss the practical aspects of managing workers' compensation cases by paralegals working under the supervision of attorneys.

Workers' Compensation Practice for Paralegals

CHAPTER 1

Overview of Workers' Compensation Law

Paralegal Practice Tips

Paralegals in workers' compensation practices should have a working knowledge of the relevant state's workers' compensation act. In order to learn basic workers' compensation law and stay up-to-date with new statutes and requirements, a paralegal should:

- Read and become very familiar with the information provided on the applicable state agency website. Save the state agency website address as a favorite on the web browser.
- Know where to locate key information regarding the state's workers' compensation laws, such as statutes, rules and forms, including on the Internet and/or books.
- Learn the state agency's basic administrative rules, filing requirements and deadlines.
- Stay up-to-date on the state agency's rules and forms by frequently checking its website.
- Read legal periodicals for lawyers and workers' compensation practitioners, such as magazines, newspapers and newsletters.
- Ask the law firm to purchase state-specific workers' compensation law books, read them and use them as references.
- Join statewide legal association listservs for paralegals and/or workers' compensation practitioners.
- Read legal periodicals that report statewide appellate workers' compensation decisions, such as magazines, newspapers and newsletters.
- Attend (in person or online if available) state bar and legal association continuing legal education (CLE) seminars and programs for workers' compensation practitioners.

- Ask questions of supervising attorneys and/or mentors well versed in workers' compensation practice.
- Attend workers' compensation mediations and hearings, as an assistant to a supervising attorney, or as an observer.

1.1 History of Workers' Compensation Legislation

1.1(1) The Industrial Revolution

The Industrial Revolution created a dramatic societal change as western civilization moved from an agrarian to an industrial society. It revolutionized the way families earned a living, and changed the social and cultural relationships between members of a transforming society. The Industrial Revolution (approximately 1770–1910) originated in Great Britain and expanded throughout western civilization. The Industrial Revolution initially replaced an agrarian economy based on manual labor with an industrial economy based on machinery to manufacture goods. Textile production moved to factories with the invention of Richard Arkwright's water powered cotton spinning frame in 1769. In the 1780s, the use of James Watt's steam engine permitted the manufacture of numerous products in locations where waterpower was not available. Improvements in the production of iron and the ability to make metal machines led to a substantial increase in production capacity, as well as the dangers inherent in operating those machines. The Industrial Revolution gained momentum in the mid-1800s, with the use of railroads and steam ships. The development and common use of electricity and the internal combustion engine completed the final phase of the Industrial Revolution.

1.1(2) The Development of Workers' Compensation

As industrial production increased, workplace injuries also increased, in both number and severity. The use of dangerous fast-moving machinery caused crippling injuries and numerous fatalities. At the same time, the common law of Great Britain and the United States was evolving in a manner that significantly decreased the ability of injured workers, or their families, to recover damages for their injuries or death.

To recover damages under the common law, an injured worker was required to show that the accident causing the injury was the result of the negligence of the employer. Simultaneously with the development of the Industrial Revolution, the common law developed three defenses that allowed employers to avoid liability for the injuries suffered by their workers: contributory negligence; the fellow servant exception; and the assumption of risk doctrine.

- **Contributory Negligence**: In 1809, the English case of *Butterfield v. Forrester* recognized the defense of contributory negligence. The defense of contributory negligence provided that even if the negligence of the employer caused the accident, if the employee's own negligence, no matter how minimal, contributed to the accident, the employee could not recover any damages from the employer.
- **Fellow Servant Exception**: In 1837, in a famous English case called *Priestly v. Fowler*, the judge, Lord Abinger, created the fellow-servant exception to the general rule that an employer is liable for injuries caused by the negligence of the employer's employee. The fellow-servant exception stated that an employer was not liable when the negligence of one employee caused an injury to another employee (as opposed to injuring a customer or other non employees). The fellow-servant exception to the general rule of an employer being liable for the negligence of an employee was adopted in America in *Farwell v. Boston & Worcester Railroad*, 4 Metc.49 (Mass. 1842.) In *Farwell*, a locomotive engineer was injured because of the negligence of one of his coworkers, a switchman for the same railroad. Relying on the fellow-servant exception, the *Farwell* court held that the employer, Boston & Worcester Railroad, was not liable for the injuries suffered by the locomotive engineer.
- **Assumption of Risk Doctrine**: The two cases above, *Priestly v. Fowler* and *Farwell v. Boston & Worcester Railroad*, provided the employer with a third defense to liability for injuries suffered by one of its employees. The assumption of risk doctrine was based on the concept that when the employee accepted employment, the employee knew of and assumed any risks inherent with the employment. This faulty concept was based on the fiction that the employee was aware of all the dangers of the job and was free to refuse any dangerous assignment. Using this concept, the courts held that the employer was not liable for injuries suffered by the employee, when it was the employee, who voluntarily and knowingly, determined to work in dangerous conditions.

Injured workers could rarely overcome the defenses of contributory negligence, the fellow-servant exception and the assumption of risk doctrine. As a result, few injured workers, or their families, recovered any compensation for workplace injuries. Of those workers who did recover, most received only a small amount of money, insufficient to support the injured worker's family.

Thus, a significant number of injured workers received no compensation for their injuries while losing their ability, due to their injuries, to earn an income. The cost of supporting these injured workers and their families was not borne by the industry in which the injury occurred. Rather, the burden of support fell on families, churches, neighbors and the community.

In the United States, many states, beginning with the Georgia Act of 1855, passed remedial legislation to diminish the effect of the three defenses discussed above. The legislation often abolished the fellow-servant exception in dangerous occupations, such as railroading. Other legislation weakened the assumption of risk doctrine and the defense of contributory negligence. This legislation did not alter the basic principle that an employer was only liable to an injured employee if the employer's negligence caused the injury. The legislation simply reduced the effect of the employer's defenses in cases where the employer's negligence was the cause of the injury.

However, starting with Germany, followed by England and eventually the United States, legislation was passed that did alter the basic principle that an employer was only liable to an injured employee if the employer's negligence caused the injury. The German Compensation Act of 1884 was the first system of compensation not based on negligence. The German plan was composed of three parts: (1) the Sickness Fund paid benefits for the first 13 weeks of disability due to accident or sickness; (2) the Accident Fund paid for disability that continued after the initial 13 weeks; and (3) the Disability Insurance Fund paid for disability caused by old age. Contributions from working employees made up two-thirds of the Sickness Fund and one-half of the Disability Insurance Fund. Contributions from the employer made up 100% of the Accident Fund, one-half of the Disability Insurance Fund and one-third of the Sickness Fund. The German Compensation Act of 1884 only covered hazardous occupations (mining, railroading, manufacturing). However, the Act was amended on numerous occasions and by 1911 it covered all employment.

Great Britain passed the Workmen's Compensation Act of 1897. Initially, it also only covered hazardous employment, but was amended multiple times, until it covered all employment by 1906. The British system was funded exclusively by the employer and required no employee contributions.

1.2 The Workers' Compensation System in the United States

In the United States, Maryland adopted the first workers' compensation act in 1902. The act only covered miners. It was quickly declared unconstitutional.

See Franklin v. United Rys. & Elect. Co., 2 Baltimore City Rep. 309 (1904). In 1909, Montana passed a workers' compensation act that again only covered miners. The Montana act was declared unconstitutional in 1911. *See Cunningham v. Northwestern Improvement Co.*, 44 Mont. 180, 119 P. 554 (1911).

The first successful workers' compensation act was the Federal Employer's Liability Act (FELA). Congress passed FELA in 1908 at the urging of President Theodore Roosevelt, and in response to the high number of railroad deaths in the late 1800s and early 1900s. It is still in existence today.

New York passed a workers' compensation act that required compulsory coverage for employers engaged in hazardous employments. In 1911, the state court declared the legislation unconstitutional because it violated the due process clause of the state and federal Constitutions. The court ruled that the act took the property of the employers without due process of law. *See Ives v. South Buffalo Railroad*, 201 N.Y. 271, 94 N.E. 431 (1911).

The New York legislature then amended the state constitution to permit compulsory coverage and passed another compensation act in 1913, requiring that employers engaged in hazardous employments provide workers' compensation to employees who were disabled or killed. The United States Supreme Court declared the 1913 New York workers' compensation act constitutional. *See New York Central Railroad Company v. White*, 243 U.S. 210 (1917). In *White*, employee Jack White was killed working for the railroad. His family sought benefits under the new workers' compensation act. The employer challenged the state constitutional amendment, alleging it violated the 14th Amendment's due process clause that prohibits the taking of property without due process of law. The railroad argued that the act required the payment of benefits without regard to the employer's fault or negligence and therefore deprived the employer of property without due process. The Supreme Court held that states were entitled to regulate the contract rights of citizens. The Court held the amendment was constitutional because the freedom of contract was restricted in the area of compensation for human life lost and disability incurred in the course of hazardous employment. The Court stated that the public had a direct interest in this area because it affected the common welfare. The Court concluded that the railroad's constitutional rights were not violated.

The single event that may have expedited the passage of workers' compensation legislation in the United States was the March 25, 1911 Triangle Shirtwaist Factory Fire in New York City. The company employed approximately 500 employees, mostly immigrant women, some as young as 12 and 13 years old. A fire broke out on the eighth floor of the building. Many of the women working on the eighth floor were able to escape, but the women on the ninth floor were not. The employer, fearing employee theft, had previously locked the fire escape. One hundred forty-six women died, many of them jumping to their deaths as flames engulfed the building.

Between 1911 and 1915, thirty-two states passed workers' compensation legislation[1]. This passage of workers' compensation legislation was part of the Progressive Era's social reform. Four Constitutional Amendments passed during the Progressive Era: (1) instituted an income tax; (2) provided for the direct election of senators; (3) gave women the right to vote; and (4) prohibited the manufacture and sale of alcoholic beverages (Prohibition). Other Progressive Era reforms sought to regulate child labor and sweatshops, address health hazards, and improve working conditions. Thus, passing a compensation system for workers who were injured or killed was a natural part of the reform movement of the Progressive Era. Almost every state passed some form of workers' compensation legislation by 1920. The last states to adopt a workers' compensation act were North Carolina (1929), Florida (1935), South Carolina (1935), Arkansas (1939) and finally Mississippi (1948). By 1948 each state had adopted a workers' compensation act, including Alaska and Hawaii, which at the time were territories.

1.3 Workers' Compensation Acts Were Compromise Legislation

1.3(1) Elimination of Fault as a Basis for Liability

The critical principle of workers' compensation legislation was to eliminate fault as a basis for determining whether an employee could recover for injuries suffered at work. Under the common law and even under the remedial statutes, such as the Georgia Act of 1855, an injured worker could only recover damages from the employer if the employer's negligence was the cause of the accident. Under the workers' compensation acts passed between 1911 and 1948, fault or negligence was eliminated as a basis for recovery. Under the

---

1. 1911—New York, California, Illinois, Kansas, Massachusetts, New Hampshire, New Jersey, Ohio, Washington, Wisconsin,

1912—Maryland, Michigan, Rhode Island

1913—Arizona, Connecticut, Iowa, Minnesota, Nebraska, Nevada, Oregon, Texas, West Virginia

1914—Louisiana

1915—Kentucky, Colorado, Indiana, Maine, Montana, Oklahoma, Pennsylvania, Vermont, Wyoming

new acts, the test to determine if the employee could recover from the employer was based on whether the accident was connected to the employment.

Additionally, by linking liability to the employment relationship, rather than fault, the new legislation attempted to place the cost of caring for an injured worker on the industry in which the injury occurred, rather than on the worker's family and public charities.

1.3(2) In Return for the Elimination of Fault as a Basis for Liability, the Potential Recovery of the Injured Worker was Reduced

The elimination of fault as a basis for determining employer liability, made it more likely that the injured employee would receive compensation from the employer. In return, the injured employee's recovery was limited to payment for medical treatment, payment for lost earnings and payment for loss of limb or life. Workers' compensation was and is a social contract between employers and employees. Employers must provide injured workers with medical care and wage loss benefits. In return, workers' compensation is the exclusive remedy for injured workers against their employers.

Injured workers relinquished their right to bring a tort claim, with potential larger monetary damages in the form of pain and suffering and punitive damages, against the employer, even when the employer obviously was at fault. This tradeoff of a more certain recovery for the injured employee and reduced liability for the employer caused the new workers' compensation acts to be known as compromise legislation. The intent of the compromise was to allow the injured employee a swifter and more certain recovery, while letting the employer avoid the risk of a large damages verdict. The employer could then treat the cost of injured humans as a business cost, in much the same way the employer would treat the cost of broken machines.

In 1943, the North Carolina Supreme Court summarized the intent of the compromise legislation, quoting courts from across the nation:

> The primary purpose of legislation of this kind is to compel industry to take care of its own wreckage. It is said to be acceptable to both employer and employee, because it reduces the cost of settlement and avoids delay. *To the employee, it means a certainty of some sort of compensation for an injury* received in the course of business; and *to the employer, it reduces unpredictability of loss and puts it on an actuarial basis, permitting it to be treated as "overhead," absorbed in the sales price*, and thus transferred to that universal beast of economic burden, the consumer. *Allen v. State, 160 N.Y. Supp., 85; Village of Kiel*

> *v. Industrial Commission (Wis.), 158 N.E., 68.* It is said to be humanitarian and economical as opposed to wasteful in the conduct of the enterprise, and is referred to the propriety of keeping loss by accident incidental to employment chargeable to the industry where it occurs. *Kenner son v. Thomas Towboat Co., 89 Conn., 367, 94 A., 372.* It is called "an economic system of trade risk." "Losses incident to industrial pursuits are like wrongs and breakage of machinery—a cost of production." *Macklin v. Detroit-Liken Axle Co., 187 Mich., 8, 153 N.E., 49*; *Village of Kiel v. Industrial Commission, supra.* It should be charged against the industry responsible for the injury. *Klawinski v. Lake Shore & N.S. Ry. Co., 185 Mich., 643, 152 N.E., 213*; Schneider, Workmen's Compensation Law, Permanent Edition, s. 1.

Barber v. Minges, 223 N.C. 213, 216–217, 25 S.E.2d 837, 839 (1943) (emphasis added).

1.4 Benefits Payable to the Injured Worker

The workers' compensation acts of all states provide medical compensation and wage loss benefits for non-fatal injuries and death benefits for fatal injuries.

1.4(1) Medical Benefits

The purposes of medical benefits, including rehabilitation, are to provide treatment to the injured worker that affects a cure or reduces the extent of the disability, and provides relief and treatment for permanent injuries. Generally, there is no preset limitation on medical treatment the employer is to provide[2]. However, this was not always the case.

For example, the original New Jersey Workers' Compensation Act adopted in 1911 limited the employer's obligation to provide medical treatment, hospital services and medicines to a two-week period; such services not to exceed one hundred dollars. In 1919, the Act was amended to extend the time period to seventeen weeks and the monetary amount to two hundred dollars. The Legislature again amended the Act in 1922 to require the employer to provide all medical, surgical, hospital and other treatment necessary to cure and relieve the injured worker of the effects of the injury. *See Squeo v. Comfort Con-*

2. Arkansas, California, Florida, Hawaii, Ohio, and Montana have some statutory limitations on the provision of medical care ranging from requiring co-payments in certain situations to requiring an examination by the state agency medical section after compensation has been paid for 90 days.

trol Corp., 99 N.J. 588, 494 A.2d 213 (1985). Under the medical benefits provision of the Workers' Compensation Act, the *Squeo* court ordered the employer to construct an apartment that would allow a single 25 year old quadriplegic to live independently.

Medical and hospital services can include nursing care provided in the home by a nurse or a family member[3], modifications to vehicles to allow them to be driven by paraplegics[4], life care plans[5], medically prescribed equipment, including home exercise equipment, membership in a gym, installation of a home swimming pool with modifications to make it accessible to the injured worker[6], transportation costs to and from the offices of a medical provider[7], medically prescribed weight-loss programs[8], and cosmetic surgery and cosmetic devices[9] (wigs) necessary to correct or minimize injury related disfigurement.

State workers' compensation laws vary on whether the employer or the employee selects the initial treating physician. The majority of states allow the employee to select the initial treating physician. Two states require that the employee choose the physician from a list approved by the state agency.[10] Five states require that the employee choose the physician from a list maintained by the employer.[11] A minority of states allows the employer to select the treating physician, with many of those states providing some mechanism for the employee to request a change in treating physician.

For an analysis of medical benefits provided by each state, see Table 5—Medical Benefits and Methods of Physician Selection Provided by Workers' Compensation Statutes in the U.S. at www.dol.gov/esa/regs/statutes/owcp/stwclaw/stwclaw.htm.

1.4(2) Wage Loss (Indemnity) Benefits

Wage loss benefits can generally be categorized into three categories. Two of the categories, total disability and partial disability, are based on the actual

3. *Levens v. Guilford County Schools*, 152 N.C. App. 390, 567 S.E.2d 767 (2002).
4. *Terry Grantham Co. v. Industrial Commission*, 154 Ariz. 180, 741 P.2d 313 (1987).
5. *Timmons v. N.C. Department of Transportation*, 351 N.C. 177, 522 S.E.2d 62 (1999).
6. *Haga v. Clay Hyder Trucking Lines*, 397 So.2d 428 (Florida 1981).
7. *Sigman Meat Co. v. Industrial Claim Appeals Office*, 761 P.2d 265 (Colorado 1988).
8. *Braewood Convalescent Hospital v. Workers' Compensation Appeal Board*, 34 Cal.3d 159, 666 P.2d 14 (1983).
9. *Akers Auto Salvage v. Waddle*, 394 P.2d 452 (Oklahoma 1964); *Ranson v. Orleans Parish School Bd.*, 365 So.2d 937 (Louisiana 1978).
10. New York and Texas.
11. Florida, Georgia, Tennessee, Virginia, and Pennsylvania.

wage loss suffered by the injured worker. The third category, scheduled injuries, is based on a physical impairment to a body part (such as the loss of an arm or the loss of use of a leg) and presumes a wage loss.

- **Total disability** is the inability to earn any wages after and because of suffering a compensable accident or occupational disease. Total disability may be temporary (such as when an injured employee is recovering from the injury or surgery resulting from the injury) or permanent (if the employee is never able to return to work).
- **Partial disability** is the inability to earn the same wages, after and because of suffering a compensable accident or occupational disease, that the employee was earning prior to suffering a compensable event. Partial disability may be temporary if the injured employee is recovering from an injury and is temporarily limited in the number of hours or type of work that can be performed. Partial disability may be permanent if the employee's work restrictions remain in place, even after the employee reaches maximum medical improvement and the employee continues to be unable to earn the same wages earned prior to the compensable event.
- **A scheduled injury** is a legislative determination that the loss of, or the permanent impairment to, a body part will cause the injured employee to suffer a wage loss for a specific number of weeks. The state legislature assigns the number of weeks of lost wages that each body part is worth. The injured worker is then entitled to be paid a set number of weeks for the anatomical loss or partial loss of that body part. For example, the North Carolina General Assembly determined that the loss of an arm was worth 240 weeks, a hand 200 weeks, a leg 200 weeks, a foot 144 weeks, an eye 120 weeks and hearing in one ear 70 weeks and two ears 150 weeks. *See* N.C. Gen. Stat. §97-31. Using the North Carolina scheduled injury provision, an injured worker whose arm was amputated would be entitled to receive 240 weeks of wage loss compensation. An employee whose arm was permanently damaged and after reaching maximum medical improvement was rated as having a 50% permanent disability to the arm would be entitled to receive 120 weeks of wage loss compensation. Generally, an injured worker may not receive payment for a scheduled injury at the same time that the worker receives total or partial disability benefits.

The calculation of the weekly workers' compensation disability benefit payment is based on a percentage of the injured worker's weekly wage. Most states pay compensation at the rate of 66⅔ percent of the injured worker's pretax average weekly wage, with a minimum and maximum compensation rate set by each state. Some states, such as Alaska, Iowa, Maine, and Michigan pay compensation at the rate of 80% of the worker's spendable earnings. For an analysis of the wage loss benefits provided by each state, see Tables 6, 7 & 8 at www.dol.gov/esa/regs/statutes/owcp/stwclaw/stwclaw.htm.

1.4(3) Death Benefits

If the injured worker dies because of the compensable accident or occupational disease, the injured worker's dependents are entitled to death benefits and funeral expenses. In most states, death benefits are determined as a percentage of the injured worker's average weekly wage. A few states pay a determined amount for death benefits regardless of the injured worker's average weekly wage. Funeral expenses are a determined amount set by each state with a low of $2,000 in Mississippi and a high of $15,000 in Minnesota and Rhode Island. Several states pay an additional amount for transportation of the body, if the death occurred away from home.

Generally, a spouse and minor children living with the deceased worker are presumed to be fully dependent on the deceased worker and entitled to benefits. Other family members are usually required to prove dependency. The method of dividing death benefits among the various family members entitled to receive death benefits varies from state to state. For an analysis of death benefits provided by each state, see *Table 12—Benefits for Surviving Spouses and Children in Death Cases by Workers' Compensation Statutes in the U.S.* at www.dol.gov/esa/regs/statutes/owcp/stwclaw/stwclaw.htm.

1.5 Types of Workers' Compensation Insurance

Every state, except Texas, requires that employers provide workers' compensation insurance to their employees. Texas allows most employers to choose whether to provide workers' compensation. Texas requires public employers, and employers with a building or construction contract with a government entity, to provide workers' compensation insurance.

In the majority of states, private insurance companies are the only providers of workers' compensation insurance. Nineteen states[12] operate a

12. Arizona, California, Colorado, Hawaii, Idaho, Kentucky, Louisiana, Maine, Maryland, Minnesota, Montana, New Mexico, New York, Oklahoma, Oregon, Pennsylvania, Rhode Island, Texas, and Utah.

state insurance fund that provides workers' compensation insurance at the same time that private insurance companies provide workers' compensation insurance within the state. These are known as competitive state insurance plans. They allow employers to purchase their workers' compensation insurance from either private insurance companies or the state insurance fund. In order to prevent nonprofit state operated insurance funds from competing directly with private insurance companies, the state funds are limited to providing only workers' compensation insurance and must provide assigned-risk programs or operate as the insurers of last resort. Private insurers can decline the worst risks and can include workers' compensation insurance within a comprehensive insurance package that also covers personal injury, general liability and other forms of risk.

Five states have a monopoly state fund.[13] A monopoly state fund requires employers to purchase their workers' compensation insurance policies through the state's fund.

Regardless of which of the above three systems a state uses, most states allow an employer to self-insure its obligation to provide workers' compensation insurance, if the employer can meet certain financial solvency requirements mandated by the state.

1.6 Locating State Workers' Compensation Agencies and Laws

1.6(1) Addresses and Home Pages for All 50 States

The following is a list of free websites that provide contact information for all state agencies. This list is not intended to cover all lists of state agencies currently available online, but rather to provide some nationally recognized websites that provide this information (see also the websites listed in 1.6(2)).

- **U.S. Department of Labor Office of Workers' Compensation Programs,** http://www.dol.gov/esa/regs/compliance/owcp/wc.htm
- **International Association of Industrial Accident Boards and Commissions,** http://www.iaiabc.org/links.htm
- **North Carolina Industrial Commission's List of Home Pages and Workers' Compensation Agencies,** http://www.comp.state.nc.us/ncic/pages/all50.htm (contains links to all fifty states' and the District of Columbia's

13. North Dakota, Ohio, Washington, West Virginia, and Wyoming.

home pages and workers' compensation agencies, and is updated daily. The International Association of Industrial Accident Boards and Commissions (IAIABC) has a hyperlink directing users to this website for "an excellent list of workers' compensation agencies")

- **Southern Association of Workers' Compensation Administrators,** http://www.sawca.com/htm/wcusa.htm

1.6(2) Links to State Workers' Compensation Rules and Statutes

The following is a list of free websites that provide overviews, summaries, and links to all fifty states' workers' compensation laws. This list is not intended to cover all workers' compensation legal websites currently available online, but instead to provide some nationally recognized websites which provide this information. In addition, most law firms have subscription-based programs, such as Westlaw and Lexis/Nexis, which also provide access to this information.

- **U.S. Department of Labor Office of Workers' Compensation Programs,** http://www.dol.gov/esa/regs/statutes/owcp/stwclaw/stwclaw.htm (provides a summary of workers' compensation coverage and benefits in each state through 2006. IAIABC and Workers Compensation Research Institute (WCRI) took over this publication effective 2007).[14]
- **Workerscompensation.com,** http://www.workerscompensation.com/workers-comp-research.php. (links to national news, state laws and contact information)
- **Workers Injury Law & Advocacy Group** (WILG), http://www.wilg.org/index.asp (contains links to national news, state laws and contact information)

1.6 Locating Federal Workers' Compensation Agencies and Laws

The practice of federal workers' compensation law is even more specialized than state workers' compensation law. Fewer law firms handle federal workers' compensation cases. Paralegals who work for firms that do not handle

14. "WCRI and IAIABC to Publish Inventory of State Workers' Compensation Laws", http://www.iaiabc.org/news/news

these cases should maintain a referral list of attorneys who handle federal workers' compensation cases statewide.

The following is a list of free websites that provide overviews, summaries, and links to information regarding federal workers' compensation laws. This list is not intended to cover all federal workers' compensation legal search engines currently available online, but instead to provide some nationally recognized websites which provide this information.

- **U.S. Department of Labor Office of Workers' Compensation Programs—Home Page,** http://www.dol.gov/esa/owcp_org.htm.
- **FedWorkersComp.net,** http://www.fedworkerscomp.net (provides assistance to federal workers)

1.7 General Reference for Workers' Compensation Practitioners

Larson's Workers' Compensation Law, published by the Matthew Bender Division of LexisNexis, is a comprehensive twelve-volume treatise on workers' compensation law and an invaluable research resource. The twelve-volume treatise may be too much for a small office, in which case *Larson's Workers' Compensation, Desk Edition* is a wonderful resource. This three-volume set contains the essential information needed to practice workers' compensation and to inform the practitioner of the theories accepted and used in different jurisdictions.

CHAPTER 2

Determination of Compensable Claims

Paralegal Practice Tips

Paralegals in workers' compensation practices should have a working knowledge of the definition of employment and the types of injuries and illnesses covered by the relevant state's workers' compensation act. In order to learn the frequently used legal definitions and concepts applicable to the practice of workers' compensation law, a paralegal should:

- Read and become very familiar with the state workers' compensation act, including the annotations to the provisions.
- Know where to locate the provisions of the state workers' compensation act, including on the Internet (free or subscription-based websites) and/or statute books.
- Stay up-to-date on changes to the state workers' compensation act, by frequently reviewing the state agency website, reading legal periodicals for workers' compensation practitioners, attending continuing legal education (CLE) programs and joining listservs for workers' compensation practitioners.
- Ask questions and discuss case scenarios with supervising attorneys and/or mentors well-versed in workers' compensation practice.

2.1 The Employment Relationship in Workers' Compensation

Workers' compensation laws apply to employers and employees. Generally, workers' compensation laws do not apply outside the employment relationship. In evaluating a potential workers' compensation claim, one of the first determinations is whether the client is within an employment relationship that subjects the client to the state's workers' compensation act.

2.1(1) Employee v. Independent Contractor

Generally, parties that are involved in an independent contractor relationship are not subject to the workers' compensation act. It is often difficult to determine whether a relationship is an employment relationship or an independent contractor relationship. This difficulty has perplexed courts for many decades because no one factor is determinative. Over time, courts have established a series of tests, which when balanced together determine whether the relationship is one of an employer-employee or independent contractor.

An example of one series of tests is found in the *Restatement of Agency (Second) §220.* Paraphrasing the test, the following circumstances should be considered in determining whether a person is an employee or an independent contractor: (1) the extent of control which, by agreement, the employer may exercise over the details of the work; (2) whether or not the worker is engaged in a distinct occupation or business; (3) whether the work is usually done under the direction of the employer or by a specialist without supervision; (4) the skill required in the particular occupation; (5) whether the employer or the worker supplies the tools and the place of work for the person doing the work; (6) the length of time the person is employed; (7) the method of payment, whether by time or job; (8) whether the work is a part of the regular business of the employer; (9) whether the parties believe they are creating the relationship of employer and employee; and (10) whether the principal is in business. *Restatement of Agency (Second) §220.*

An example of another test is the one applied by the North Carolina Supreme Court. There are generally eight factors, with no one factor being determinative, which indicate classification as an independent contractor, namely, the person employed: (1) is engaged in an independent business, calling, or occupation; (2) is to have independent use of his special skill, knowledge, or training in execution of work; (3) is doing a specified piece of work at a fixed price or for a lump sum or upon a quantitative basis; (4) is not subject to discharge because he adopts one method of doing work rather than another; (5) is not in regular employ of other contracting party; (6) is free to use such assistants as he may think proper; (7) has full control over such assistants; and (8) selects his own time. *Hayes v. Bd. of Trustees of Elon College*, 224 N.C. 11, 16, 29 S.E.2d 137, 140 (1944).

Paralegals should be familiar with the series of tests used in the relevant jurisdiction to determine whether the relationship is one of independent contractor or employer-employee. It may be helpful to create a checklist of the factors used, with space below each factor to note the relevant facts of the case. A brief summary at the end of a checklist could contain the paralegal's and attorney's opinion of whether the client is subject to the workers' compensation act and a list of the cases and legal authorities relied upon in making the determination.

2.1(2) Number of Employees

Most states require employers with one or more employees to provide workers' compensation coverage. Colorado requires employers with two or more employees to provide workers' compensation. The following states subject an employer to the requirements of the workers' compensation act only if the employer has three or more employees: Arkansas, Georgia, Michigan, New Mexico, North Carolina, Virginia, and Wisconsin. South Carolina and Florida require coverage of the employer has four or more employees. Alabama, Mississippi, Missouri, and Tennessee only require coverage if the employer has five or more employees. However, for several of these states the above rule is the general rule and the state may have stricter requirements or broader exemptions in certain occupations (for example, construction or seasonal work). Thus, paralegals must be familiar with the statutory definitions of employment in the relevant workers' compensation act.

2.1(3) Exclusion of Certain Occupations or Categories of Workers

Many states have specific laws regarding whether certain nonindustrial occupations are subject to the workers' compensation act. The most common occupations that are treated differently are domestic workers and agricultural workers.

- **Domestic Workers**—The compulsory coverage of domestic workers under the workers' compensation act varies widely from state to state. Many state statutes have a specific reference to the coverage of domestic workers. For example, Connecticut requires coverage of any domestic worker employed more than 26 hours per week by one employer. Utah requires coverage of any domestic worker regularly employed for 40 or more hours per week by the same employer. However, Ohio provides coverage to any domestic worker who earns $160.00 or more in any calendar quarter from a single household.[1]

- **Agricultural Workers**—Twelve states and the District of Columbia do not distinguish agricultural workers from other forms of employment and cover agricultural workers with the same workers' compensation insurance coverage.[2] The remaining states have special provisions regarding the coverage of agricultural workers.
- **Children, Aliens, and Casual Employees**—States are not uniform in the workers' compensation coverage provided to casual employees, or to employees employed in violation of certain laws. If the case involves a special category of employee, it will be important to know how the state treats that category of employment under its workers' compensation act. For example, North Carolina does not allow an employer to escape its obligations under the workers' compensation act even if the employment relationship violated child labor laws or federal laws regarding immigration status. *See Ruiz v. Belk Masonry Co.*, 148 N.C. App. 675; 559 S.E.2d 249 (2002) (The prohibition against hiring illegal aliens did not prevent the employee from meeting the workers' compensation act's definition of employee, nor did federal law prevent employee, based solely on his immigration status, from receiving workers' compensation benefit.); *Lemmerman v. A.T. Williams Oil Co.*, 318 N.C. 577; 350 S.E.2d 83 (1986) (An eight year old, performing odd jobs for a dollar a day at a convenience store where the mother worked, was a covered employee under the workers' compensation act.)

Other states penalize the employer for impermissibly hiring children in violation of the child labor laws by increasing the compensation benefits payable to the minor child.[3] *Larson's Workers' Compensation Law §66.02.*

---

1. *See* http://www.dol.gov/esa/regs/statutes/owcp/stwclaw/stwclaw.htm. Table 4—Jurisdictions Covering Domestic Workers

2. Arizona, California, Colorado, Connecticut, District of Columbia, Hawaii, Idaho, Massachusetts, Montana, New Hampshire, New Jersey, Ohio, and Oregon. *See* http://www.dol.gov/esa/regs/statutes/owcp/stwclaw/stwclaw.htm. Table 3—Coverage of Agricultural Workers.

3. "Alabama (double); Arizona (50%); Arkansas (double, unless age falsified); California (50%, unless age falsified); Connecticut (50% for over 52 weeks for schedule disability if under 18; 100% if under 16); Florida (double); Illinois (50%, if under 16, unless age falsified); Indiana (double, if under 16); Maryland (double); Massachusetts (double); Michigan (double, unless age falsified); Mississippi (double); Missouri (50%); New Hampshire (double); New Jersey (double, if under 14, or between 14–18 without proper permit, unless age falsified); New York (double, unless age falsified); Ohio (double); Oregon (25% if

Most states provide workers' compensation coverage to illegal aliens, either by statutory definition or by court decision. However, a few states[4] include only lawfully employed aliens in their definition of an employee in the workers' compensation act. *See Larson's Workers' Compensation Law §66.03*. Additional problems, outside of coverage, arise when the illegal alien is provided workers' compensation coverage. These problems include returning the injured worker to work, when to do so violates federal law, or providing medical and rehabilitation services when the worker is no longer in the country.

Paralegals need to be familiar with the specific coverage requirements of the jurisdiction regarding specific categories of employees, such as aliens, minors, domestic workers and agricultural workers.

2.1(4) Statutory Definitions of Employment, Employer and Employee

The logical starting place to determine if a client is subject to the relevant state's workers' compensation act is to review the definitions provided in the act. The definitions vary in complexity from state to state, but each attempts to provide the parameters of the workers' compensation act's coverage. Definitions from a few state statutes provide an illustration of the generally broad scope of coverage provided by the compensation act.

Employees—Alabama defines an employee as:

> (5) Employee or Worker. The terms are used interchangeably, have the same meaning throughout this chapter, and shall be construed to mean the same. The terms include the plural and all ages and both sexes. The terms include every person in the service of another under any contract of hire, express or implied, oral or written, including aliens and also including minors who are legally permitted to work under the laws of this state, and also including all employees of Tannehill Furnace and Foundry Commission. Any reference in this chapter to a "worker" or "employee" shall, if the worker or employee is dead, include his or her dependent, as defined in this chapter, if the context so requires.

Ala. Code §25-5-1(5).

---

in bad faith); Pennsylvania (50%); Puerto Rico (double); Rhode Island (treble); Virgin Islands (30%); Wisconsin (double or treble)." *Quoting Larson's Workers' Compensation Law §66.02 fn. 2.*

4. For example, Wyoming and Idaho.

Kansas' definition starts out the same but become more detailed:

> (b) "Workman" or "employee" or "worker" means any person who has entered into the employment of or works under any contract of service or apprenticeship with an employer. Such terms shall include but not be limited to: Executive officers of corporations; professional athletes; persons serving on a volunteer basis as duly authorized law enforcement officers, attendants, as defined in subsection (d) of K.S.A. 65-6112, and amendments thereto, drivers of ambulances as defined in subsection (b) of K.S.A. 65-6112, and amendments thereto, firefighters, but only to the extent and during such periods as they are so serving in such capacities; persons employed by educational, religious and charitable organizations, but only to the extent and during the periods that they are paid wages by such organizations; persons in the service of the state, or any department, agency or authority of the state, any city, school district, or other political subdivision or municipality or public corporation and any instrumentality thereof, under any contract of service, express or implied, and every official or officer thereof, whether elected or appointed, while performing official duties; persons in the service of the state as volunteer members of the Kansas department of civil air patrol, but only to the extent and during such periods as they are officially engaged in the performance of functions specified in K.S.A. 48-3302 and amendments thereto; volunteers in any employment, if the employer has filed an election to extend coverage to such volunteers; minors, whether such minors are legally or illegally employed; and persons performing community service work, but only to the extent and during such periods as they are performing community service work and if an election has been filed to extend coverage to such persons. Any reference to an employee who has been injured shall, where the employee is dead, include a reference to the employee's dependents, to the employee's legal representatives, or, if the employee is a minor or an incapacitated person, to the employee's guardian or conservator. Unless there is a valid election in effect which has been filed as provided in K.S.A. 44-542a, and amendments thereto, such terms shall not include individual employers, limited liability company members, partners or self-employed persons.

Kan. Stat. Ann. §44-508 (b).

Employers—Alabama defines an employer as:

> (4) Employer. Every person who employs another to perform a service for hire and pays wages directly to the person. The term shall include a service company for a self-insurer or any person, corporation, copartnership, or association, or group thereof, and shall, if the employer is insured, include his or her insurer, the insurer being entitled to the employer's rights, immunities, and remedies under this chapter, as far as applicable. The inclusion of an employer's insurer within the term shall not provide the insurer with immunity from liability to an injured employee, or his or her dependent in the case of death to whom the insurer would otherwise be subject to liability under Section 25-5-11. Notwithstanding the provisions of this chapter, in no event shall a common carrier by motor vehicle operating pursuant to a certificate of public convenience and necessity be deemed the "employer" of a leased-operator or owner-operator of a motor vehicle or vehicles under contract to the common carrier.

Ala. Code §25-5-1(4).

However, Michigan's definition of an employer is much more complex:

> 418.115 Employers covered; private employers; agricultural employers; medical and hospital coverage.
>
> Sec. 115. This act shall apply to:
>
> (a) All private employers, other than agricultural employers, who regularly employ 3 or more employees at 1 time.
>
> (b) All private employers, other than agricultural employers, who regularly employ less than 3 employees if at least 1 of them has been regularly employed by that same employer for 35 or more hours per week for 13 weeks or longer during the preceding 52 weeks.
>
> (c) All public employers, irrespective of the number of persons employed.
>
> (d) All agricultural employers of 3 or more regular employees paid hourly wages or salaries, and not paid on a piecework basis, who are employed 35 or more hours per week by that same employer for 13 or more consecutive weeks during the preceding 52 weeks. Coverage shall apply only to such regularly employed employees. The average weekly wage for such an employee shall be deemed to be the weeks worked in agricultural employment divided into the total wages which the employee has earned from all agricultural occupations during the 12 calendar months immediately preceding the injury, and no other definition pertaining to average weekly wage shall be applicable.

> (e) All agricultural employers of 1 or more employees who are employed 35 or more hours per week by that same employer for 5 or more consecutive weeks shall provide for such employees, in accordance with rules established by the director, medical and hospital coverage as set forth in section 315 for all personal injuries arising out of and in the course of employment suffered by such employees not otherwise covered by this act. The provision of such medical and hospital coverage shall not affect any rights of recovery that an employee would otherwise have against an agricultural employer and such right of recovery shall be subject to any defense the agricultural employer might otherwise have. Section 141 shall not apply to cases, other than medical and hospital coverages provided herein, arising under this subdivision nor shall it apply to actions brought against an agricultural employer who is not voluntarily or otherwise subject to this act. No person shall be considered an employee of an agricultural employer if the person is a spouse, child or other member of the employer's family, as defined in subdivision (b) of section 353 residing in the home or on the premises of the agricultural employer. All other agricultural employers not included in subdivisions (d) and (e) shall be exempt from the provisions of this act.

Mich. Stat. Ann. §418.115.

A review of Ohio's definitions of employer and employee show that the Ohio legislature attempted to address many of the problems listed in the earlier sections, such as the distinction between independent contractor and employee, by using lengthy detailed definitions. *See* Ohio Rev. Code Ann. §4123.01.

Well-qualified paralegals will become familiar with the definitions contained in the relevant state's workers' compensation act and with the case law interpretations of those definitions. Workers' compensation practitioners will develop an understanding of which categories of clients are included within the act's coverage and who may be excluded from coverage.

2.1(5) Exclusion from Coverage for Fraudulent Employment Application

Some states exclude an employee from coverage under the workers' compensation act if the employee falsified the employment application. In states that exclude the deceitful employee from coverage, the following three elements are usually required: (1) the employee must have willfully made a false representation as to his or her physical condition; (2) the employer must have substantially relied upon the false representation in making the hiring decision; and (3) there must have been a causal connection between the false representation and the injury. *Larson's Workers' Compensation Law* §*66.04.*

Several states, including Arizona, Colorado, Nevada, New Jersey, North Carolina and Pennsylvania will not bar compensation based on a false application because such a defense is not part of the state's workers' compensation act. *See Hooker v. Stokes-Reynolds Hospital/North Carolina Baptist Hosp. Inc.*, 161 N.C. App. 111, 115, *rev. denied* 594 S.E.2d 192 (2004) (Defendant urged the court to adopt the defense of misrepresentation as a complete bar to workers' compensation benefits. The court refused to adopt such a defense because it was not included within the workers' compensation act). Other states allow the defense only under certain circumstances.[5] *Larson's Workers' Compensation Law* §*66.04.*

Paralegals should be knowledgeable regarding the relevant state's workers' compensation law on the possible exclusion from benefits based on an employee's misrepresentation.

2.2 Injury by Accident Cases

Injury by accident cases and occupational disease cases constitute the two categories of workers' compensation cases. Injury by accident cases generally occur within a definite time and place. The defined time may apply to the event causing the injury (the accident), the actual injury itself (herniated disc, heart attack) or both. Occupational disease cases do not usually have a defined event causing the injury or a defined onset of the disease.

The British workers' compensation system upon which many states based their workers' compensation act required that to be compensable an injury must be (1) by accident, (2) arising out of, and (3) in the course of the employment.

The term "accident" generally refers to an unanticipated, unexpected, unforeseen event, not expected or designed by the person who suffers the injury.

The term "arising out of" refers to the origin of the accident or the causal connection between the accidental injury and the employment. Did the employment cause the accident or injury?

---

5. For example, Louisiana's statute states that an employee will forfeit the rights to benefits if the employee answers falsely when asked about pre-existing disabilities or prior job accidents. However, the employer must give written notice, which complies with the statute, to the employee that a false answer will cause a forfeiture of compensation benefits and show a causal connection between the false statements and the workers' compensation injury. In Michigan and Texas, misrepresentation applies only to occupational diseases.

The term "in the course of" refers to the time, place and circumstance in which the accident occurred. Did the accident happen at work?

In order to determine whether an alleged injury by accident at work is compensable, workers' compensation practitioners must have a firm understanding of the relevant jurisdiction's application of the "injury by accident arising out of and in the course of employment" doctrine. It is critical to remember that the determination of compensability is by the application of this test. Unlike tort damages, negligence and fault do not determine liability. Under workers' compensation law, the critical issue for determining compensability is whether there is a sufficient connection between the injury and the work to make the employer liable, regardless of fault. The "injury by accident arising out of and in the course of employment" test is used to determine the connection between the injury and the job.

2.2(1) Injury by Accident

Thirty-four states' workers' compensation acts contain the phrase injury "by accident" or "accidental injury."[6] Ten states have omitted the requirement that the injury be by accident in order to be compensable.[7] The remaining states have their own definitions and rules requiring that an injury be "by accident."

"Accident" generally means an unanticipated, unforeseen event, neither expected nor designed by the injured worker. There is a difference in interpretation among jurisdictions regarding whether the requirement of an accident refers to the cause of the injury or the injurious result. Jurisdictions that require that the cause of the injury be an "accident" are more restrictive in awarding compensation benefits than are jurisdictions that simply require that the resulting injury be unforeseen and unanticipated.

For example, imagine an employee, whose job consists of loading cases of soft drinks onto a delivery truck, driving the truck to various grocery stores, and then unloading the drinks. The driver performs this job, without any injuries, for 15 years. One day, as the driver is loading the truck, he bends over to pick up a case of drinks and feels a sharp excruciating pain in his lower back. He is unable to

---

6. Alabama, Alaska, Arkansas, Arizona, Connecticut, Delaware, Florida, Georgia, Hawaii, Idaho, Illinois, Indiana, Kansas, Kentucky, Louisiana, Maryland, Mississippi, Missouri, Nebraska, Nevada, New Hampshire, New Jersey, New Mexico, New York, North Carolina, North Dakota, Oklahoma, Oregon, Pennsylvania, South Dakota, Tennessee, Utah, Vermont, Virginia, Wisconsin.

7. California, Colorado, Iowa, Maine, Massachusetts, Michigan, Minnesota, Pennsylvania, Rhode Island, and South Dakota.

straighten up. His employer takes him to the hospital where it is determined that he has herniated a lumbar disc. That evening he undergoes surgery.

In this case, the injurious result (herniated disc) was accidental because it was unanticipated and unexpected, but no accident caused the injury. The driver was simply injured while performing his normal job in the normal fashion. In jurisdictions requiring only an accidental result (the injury is unexpected), the delivery driver will be covered by workers' compensation. However, if the jurisdiction requires that the cause of the injury be accidental (such as an unexpected slip, trip, fall), workers' compensation will not cover the delivery driver. In states that require that the cause of the injury be accidental, there must be an accident (an unexpected event) which causes the injury. The injury itself, even though unexpected, is not enough.

In order to reduce the harshness of denying claims in states that require an accident cause the injury, some states have created special rules for hernias and back cases. For example, North Carolina does not require that an accident cause a hernia or a back injury. It now simply requires that the injury occur because of a "specific traumatic event." Thus, in the illustration above, workers' compensation would cover the truck driver because the driver could point to a specific traumatic event (lifting the case of drinks and feeling a sharp pain) as the cause of his herniated disc.

Generally, whether "injury by accident" is required for coverage under the workers' compensation act is defined by statute, with common law modifications. Similarly, if "injury by accident" is a requirement for coverage under the workers' compensation act, the Act itself will usually provide the initial interpretation of the requirement. Court decisions then modify and refine the definition of "injury by accident." It is important that workers' compensation practitioners learn and remain current regarding their state's current interpretation of the injury by accident requirement.

2.2(2) Injuries Arising out of Employment

The term "arising out of" refers to the origin of the accident or the causal connection between the accidental injury and the employment. Another way of phrasing the question is: Did the employment cause the accident or injury?

2.2(3) Tests to Determine Connection to Work

There are currently three tests which courts use to assist them in determining whether the injury arose from the employment: the increased risk test; the actual risk test and the positional risk test.

- **Increased Risk Test**—The increased risk test is the most conservative of the three tests in terms of providing coverage to the injured worker. It is also the most commonly used test. The increased risk test requires that the employment place the worker at a greater risk of injury than that to which the public is exposed. For example, a taxicab driver would be at an increased risk of being involved in a motor vehicle accident because the driver spends all day driving. A paralegal, occasionally sent to the courthouse to file documents, would not be at an increased risk of being involved in a motor vehicle accident because the paralegal spends most of the day in an office.

  Under the increased risk doctrine, if the taxicab driver and the paralegal ran into each other, the taxicab driver would receive workers' compensation benefits and the paralegal would not. Remember, fault is not an issue. Compensability is determined by the relationship between the employment and the injury. Using the increased risk test, the injury would arise from a taxicab driver's employment but would not be sufficiently connected to the work of the paralegal.
- **Actual Risk Test**—The actual risk test is the most moderate or "middle of the road" of the three risk tests in terms of providing coverage to the injured worker. The actual risk test is growing in usage in the various jurisdictions. The actual risk test requires that the employment place the worker at risk of injury. The risk need not be greater than that to which the public is exposed. It must simply be a risk of the job.

  Using the above illustration, both the taxicab driver and the paralegal would receive compensation for injuries suffered because of their collision. Both of their injuries arose from the actual risk of their jobs, even though the paralegal's job did not place her in a greater risk of having an accident compared to members of the public generally.[8] *Larson*[9] favors the actual risk test over the increased risk test because it best fulfills the purpose of workers' compensation, to compensate an employee for an injury suffered as a result of an employment related risk.
- **Positional Risk Test**—The positional risk test is the most liberal of the three tests in terms of providing coverage to the injured worker. The positional risk test is growing in usage. The positional risk test is a "but for" test. It only requires a finding that the injury would not have occurred "but for" the requirement of the job that placed the employee in

---

8. Even in states that use the increased risk test for most situations, the actual risk test is often used for on-the-job motor vehicle accidents.

9. *Larson's Workers' Compensation Law § 3.04.*

the position where the employee was injured. For example, a stray bullet, of unknown origin, strikes a paralegal working on the sixth floor of an office building. Under the positional risk doctrine, workers' compensation covers the injury.

Using the same example, there would be no compensation under the increased risk doctrine because the paralegal's job does not place her at an increased risk of being struck by a bullet. There likely would be no compensation under the actual risk doctrine because the paralegal's job did not create the risk of being struck by a stray bullet of unknown origin. However, if the bullet came from the gun of a disgruntled law firm client, the actual risk doctrine would provide coverage because the employment created the risk of a disgruntled client.

States are not necessarily uniform in applying the same risk doctrine to all types of accidents. For example, a state may apply the increased risk test to an employee that suffers an insect or spider bite, but apply the actual risk test to the same employee involved in a motor vehicle accident while working. Thus, workers' compensation practitioners must not only learn which risk tests are used but must also learn which test is applied to the various types of workplace accidents.

2.2(4) Categories of Risk

The risk of an injury can be (1) personal to the employee, (2) directly associated with the job, (3) neither personal nor job related, or (4) a mixture of personal and employment related.

- **Risk Personal to That Employee**—Injuries caused by a risk personal to the employee are not compensable even if they occur at work. Examples of a risk personal to the employee include the employee dying from an inherited disease while in the office or the employee's ex-spouse murdering the employee at work.
- **Risk Directly Connected to the Employment**—Injuries caused by a risk directly connected to the employment are compensable. Examples of such risks include having a hand caught in a machine, a mine cave-in, or a scaffolding collapse.

Injuries caused by risks that are clearly personal or clearly connected to the employment are not often the subject of litigation. Litigated injuries are normally those that are not clearly personal or employment related, or that mix both the personal and employment risk.

- **Neutral Risk**—Neutral risks are those that are neither clearly personal nor clearly connected to the employment. Examples of neutral risks are being struck by lightning, being struck by construction site debris or being hit by an out-of-control vehicle. Most commonly, it is to these neutral risk injuries that the courts apply the increased risk, actual risk or positional risk test to determine if there is a causal connection between the employment and the injury.

- **Mixed Risk**—Mixed risks are those that combine both a personal and employment connection. Examples of mixed risk injuries include falling off a ladder at work because the employee is dizzy due to high blood pressure, or an employee with a history of heart disease suffering a heart attack at work on the day when the air-conditioning failed and the temperature rose to 98°.

Generally, if the employment was a contributing or aggravating factor to the seriousness of the injury, the claim will be compensable. If the employment is not found to contribute or aggravate the injury, the claim will not be compensable. When the employee has a personal medical condition, an accident or injury will arise out of the employment if (1) the employment placed the employee in a position that aggravated the injury (falling off the ladder), or (2) the employment through unusual exertion, strain, heat or trauma contributed to the personal condition (heart attack).

Many other tests are applied to unusual circumstances to determine if the injury arose from the employment. For example, the "appreciable benefit test" states that if an employee is injured while providing assistance to a third party, the injury is compensable if the employer benefitted from the employee's actions. If the case being worked on presents unusual facts, the paralegal or the supervising attorney will need to research the relevant law.

2.2(5) Injuries in the Course of Employment

The term "in the course of" refers to the time, place and circumstance under which the accident occurred. Another way of phrasing the question is: Did the accident happen at work?

- **General Rule**—An injury arises in the course of employment, when it takes place: (1) within the period of employment (Time); (2) at a place reasonable for the employee to be (Place); and (3) in the performance of an activity related to the job (Circumstance).

There are a multitude of rules that define when an employee is within the course of employment. Several of these rules will be identified and briefly discussed. The discussions will focus on the standard concepts. The practitioner will need to learn the specific application of these general concepts to the workers' compensation act in the relevant jurisdiction.

- **Going and Coming Rule**—An injury by accident that occurs while an employee travels to or from work is not compensable if it occurs off the employer's premises, but is compensable if it occurs on the employer's premises. The rationale for the going and coming rule is that the risk of injury while traveling to and from work is one common to the public at large and not specific to the employment.

  In many cases, a question arises—what is considered the employer's premise? The general test is whether the employer owned, maintained, provided, controlled or otherwise exercised dominion over the premises. Therefore, if the employer owned and controlled the parking lot where the employee was injured, the employee would have completed the journey to work upon arriving in the parking lot and the claim would be compensable. However, if the employer only leased the right to use the parking lot (a store in a shopping mall), the employee injured in the parking lot would not have completed the journey to work upon arriving in the parking lot and the injury would not be compensable.

  There are two well-established exceptions to the going and coming rule. The **special risk exception** holds that the zone of employment extends beyond the employer's actual premises to include employees present in an area of special hazard adjacent to the employer's premise. This exception is most commonly applied when the off-premises location at which injury occurred lies on the only route, or most usual route, which employee must travel to reach work.

  The second exception is **the travel between two parts of the employer's premises exception.** The general rule, applied in most states, is that travel between two parts of employer's premises is covered as an extension of the employer's premise. For example, an employee walks from an employer owned parking lot across a public street to the workplace. An injury that occurs in the public street is covered as part of the expanded zone of employment.
- **Special Errand Trips**—The injury is compensable if at the time of injury the employee is performing an errand, mission or duty for the employer while traveling to or from work.
- **Dual Purpose Trips**—The injury during a trip that combines business and personal purposes is within the course of employment, if the trip had been taken to perform a service for the employer even without a personal purpose.

- **Travel Is Part of the Employment**—If the making of the trip is an important part of the employee's duties, then the trip itself is within the course of employment. For example, an on-call employee who needs to go to work whenever called, is an employee whose immediate travel to work is part of the employee's duties. If travel is part of the job requirement, then the traveling employee is covered from the time the trip begins until the journey ends.
- **Traveling Employees**—Employees whose work entails travel away from the employer's premises are within the course of employment continuously during the trip, except when making a distinct departure on a personal errand. Examples of traveling employees are traveling salespersons, flight attendants, and truck drivers.
- **Employer Provides Transportation**—If the employer provides and controls the means of transportation to and from work, an injury incurred during the trip is in the course of employment. The reasoning for the rule is that the employer has expanded the zone of employment to include the means of transportation (truck, bus, car, boat). When the employer provides the transportation, injuries going or coming from work are compensable.
- **Rules Focusing on Activity**—In addition to the above rules, there are multiple rules that focus on the activity of the employee, as opposed to the time and place of the accident. The general rule is that an activity relates to the employment if it carries out the employer's purpose or advances the employer's interest, directly or indirectly. An activity also relates to the employment if the activity is an inherent part of the conditions of the job, taking into account the environment, human nature, custom and practice.
    a) **The Personal Comfort Doctrine**—Employees who engage in acts of personal comfort, do not leave the course of employment, unless the departure is so great that intent to abandon the job can be inferred, or the method chosen is so unusual or unreasonable that the conduct cannot be considered an incident of employment. Thus, an employee's use of the restroom or taking a break does not take the employee outside the course of employment. However, the method chosen cannot be unreasonable. For example, a hospital employee was outside the course of employment when he elected to urinate off the hospital roof rather than use the provided restroom. *Deborde v. Forsyth Memorial Hospital*; N.C. I.C. No. 338027 (1995).
    b) **Acts Outside the Employee's Normal Duties**—An act outside the employee's regular duties that advances the employer's interest is within the course of employment. Examples follow:

c) **Acts to Benefit Co-employees:** Activity by one employee outside the employee's normal duties but undertaken to assist a co-employee is within the course of employment.

d) **Acts to Benefit Customer or Stranger:** When the person assisted stands in some business relationship to the employer; and the benefit to the employer is clear, the act is within the course of employment. When the person assisted is a stranger to the employer, the courts divide as to whether the rendering of assistance is within the course of employment or a deviation from the employment.

e) **Acts to Benefit the Employee:** Self-education and self-improvement are normally not within the course of employment, even though self-improvement may benefit the employer. The exception is a course of study that was part of the employment contract.

f) **Inoculation and Health Test:** If the medical service is necessitated by the particular employment it will be within the course of employment.

g) **Horseplay:** An injury to a nonparticipating victim of horseplay is compensable. An injury to a participant or instigator is compensable if the horseplay does not constitute a deviation from the course of employment. Factors considered in determining whether an instigator's horseplay is a deviation from the course of employment include (1) the extent and seriousness of the deviation, (2) the completeness of the deviation, (3) whether horseplay was an accepted part of employment, and (4) whether the job naturally includes horseplay (look especially at idle time). In determining the completeness of the deviation consider whether the horseplay commingled with work or constituted an abandonment of work, i.e. was the employee doing the job in a foolish way or not doing the job.[10]

h) **Recreational and Social Activities**—Recreational and social activities are within the course of employment when: (1) they occur on the premises during lunch or recreation periods as a regular part of employment; or (2) the employer requires participation or makes the activity part of the service of the employees; or (3) the employer derives substantial direct benefit from the activity.[11]

There are other rules involving resident employees, injuries that occur prior to employment or after the employment relationship has terminated. The above listing of concepts involving "course of employment" has been general

---

10. *Larson's Workers' Compensation Law* §23.01.

11. *Larson's Workers' Compensation Law* §22.01.

and may be contrary to the actual rule applied in a specific jurisdiction. Workers' compensation practitioners need to learn the specific application of these general concepts to the workers' compensation act in the relevant jurisdiction.

In summary, the test for whether an injury by accident is compensable does not focus on the negligence or fault of the employer; rather, it focuses on the connection between the injury and the employment. The most common enunciation of the work connection test is that the injury by accident must arise out of and in the course of employment.

2.3 Occupational Disease

The early workers' compensation acts, passed in 1911 and shortly thereafter, only covered injury by accident cases and did not cover occupational disease cases. In 1920, New York passed the first occupational disease amendment to its workers' compensation statute that included a list of compensable occupational diseases. Many states followed New York's lead and passed occupational disease legislation that covered specifically listed occupational diseases within the workers' compensation act. Diseases commonly listed as compensable under a state's workers' compensation act included: silicosis, asbestosis, arsenic poisoning, brass poisoning, zinc poisoning, magnesium poisoning, lead poisoning, benzyl poisoning, and mercury poisoning. It was not difficult to make the causal link between the listed diseases and the workplace exposure to the listed toxic substance.

Subsequently, New York and most other states broadened the coverage for occupational diseases beyond a specific list of diseases to provide general coverage for occupational diseases. The history of the North Carolina Workers' Compensation Act provides a model of how and why many states amended their workers' compensation acts over time to include and then broaden coverage of occupational diseases.

North Carolina adopted its Workers Compensation Act in 1929. The original Act covered workplace accidents but specifically excluded occupational diseases from coverage. The first occupational disease provisions were enacted in 1935 to include a list of covered occupational diseases. *See* N.C. Gen. Stat. §§97-52 through 97-76. The 1935 occupational disease amendments were motivated by the filing of multiple civil cases alleging negligence by the employer for exposing employees to asbestos and silica, causing asbestosis and silicosis. *See McNeely v. Carolina Asbestos Co.*, 206 N.C. 568,174 S.E. 509 (1934); *Swink v. Carolina Asbestos Co.*, 210 N.C. 303,186 S.E. 258 (1936).

In *McNeely,* the North Carolina Supreme Court stretched the definition of accident to find that the employee s inhalation of asbestos dust over five months in a plant, which had failed to install a dust suction system commonplace in other asbestos plants, constituted a compensable injury by accident under the Act. By stretching the definition of a workplace accident, the court was able to dismiss plaintiff's civil claim for negligence. *McNeely v. Carolina Asbestos Co.*, 206 N.C. 568,174 S.E. 509 (1934). Two years later, but after the passage of the 1935 amendments providing compensation for asbestosis as a specifically listed occupational disease, the same court looking at almost identical facts from the same employer, found the inhalation of asbestos dust was an occupational disease and not an injury by accident. *Swink v. Carolina Asbestos Co.*, 210 N.C. 303,186 S.E. 258 (1936). The plaintiff in *Swink* received no compensation because he acquired his occupational disease prior to the passage of the 1935 amendments.

The North Carolina Act was similar to the workers' compensation acts of many other states, covering only the specific diseases enumerated in the statute. For thirty-five years, between 1935 and 1970, there were few appellate court decisions interpreting the occupational disease statutes.

In 1971, North Carolina followed a national trend to expand the definition of occupational disease to provide coverage that was more comprehensive and included occupationally related diseases not specifically set out in the statute. The Act was amended to include the catch all provision that provided compensation for unlisted occupational diseases. The amendment states that a compensable occupational disease is:

> Any disease, other than hearing loss covered in another subdivision of this section, which is proven to be due to causes and conditions which are characteristic of and peculiar to a particular trade, occupation or employment, but excluding all ordinary diseases of life to which the general public is equally exposed outside of the employment.

N.C. Gen. Stat. 97-53 (13).

Since the passage of this amendment, there has been a substantial increase in the number of occupational disease appellate decisions. The passage of this amendment, plus improved medical knowledge, and increased public awareness of the effects of workplace exposure resulted in a substantial increase in the number of occupational disease claims filed in the last three decades. The increases are particularly apparent in cases related to toxic exposures, repetitive motion disorders, and psychological conditions.

The occupational disease statute enacted in North Carolina is substantially similar to the occupational disease statutes, or in the alternative, the case-law definition of an occupational disease, currently in place in most states. For example, Connecticut defines an occupational disease as:

> "Occupational disease" includes any disease peculiar to the occupation in which the employee was engaged and due to causes in excess of the ordinary hazards of employment as such, and includes any disease due to or attributable to exposure to or contact with any radioactive material by an employee in the course of his employment.

Conn. Gen. Stat. §31-275 (15). New York probably has the simplest definition of occupational disease: "'Occupational disease' means a disease resulting from the nature of employment and contracted therein." N.Y. Workers' Comp. §2(15).

The inclusion of a broader definition of occupational diseases brought with it difficulties in determining whether a disease had a substantial enough connection to the workplace to make it an "occupational" disease or whether it is simply an ordinary disease of life. Without a significant workplace connection, the cost of the disease should not be borne by the employer or the industry. With a significant workplace connection, the cost of the disease, like the cost of an industrial accident, should be borne by the employer and the industry.

Most occupational disease litigation focuses on distinguishing occupational diseases from ordinary diseases of life. The critical issue in making this distinction is whether the job significantly increased the exposure to the disease-causing agent to show a work connection between the job and the disease and differentiate the worker's risk of contracting the disease from the risk borne by the public. The issue, as stated by the Connecticut Supreme Court and later adopted in North Carolina, was whether the conditions of employment created a hazard of acquiring the disease that distinguished it from the ordinary exposure experienced by employees generally.

> "The phrase, 'peculiar to the occupation,' is not here used in the sense that the disease must be one which originates exclusively from the particular kind of employment in which the employee is engaged, but rather in the sense that the conditions of that employment must result in a hazard which distinguishes it in character from the general run of occupations ... To come within the definition, an occupational disease must be a disease which is a natural incident of a particular occupation, and must attach to that occupation a hazard which distinguishes it from the usual run of occupations and is in excess of that attending employment in general. *Glodenis v. American Brass Co.*, 118 Conn. 29, 40, 170 A. 146, 150."

Booker v. Duke Medical Center, 297 N.C. 458, 473, 256 S.E.2d 189, 199 (1979).

Another area of significant litigation in occupational disease claims involves cases in which the worker had a pre-existing condition that made the worker more susceptible to acquiring the occupational disease. The general rule is that if an identifiable hazard of the employment combines with a pre-existing condition to produce a disabling disease, the disabling disease is an occupational disease.[12]

Similar to injury by accident cases that have mixed risk (combine both a personal and employment connection), occupational disease cases can have multiple causes, some of which are personal and some of which are employment related. The most common examples involve employees who smoke cigarettes (personal) and breathe toxic dusts and chemicals at work (employment). The general rule is that the employer accepts the employee "as is." If the worker can meet the employee's burden of proving that the workplace exposure to harmful substances was a significant causal factor in the development of the disease, the disease will be compensable. In order for a disease to be compensable, the workplace exposure to harmful substances does not have to be the sole causative factor or even the dominant causative factor in the development of the disease. It must be a significant causative factor in the development of the disease.

Our country has moved from an industrial society to a country where more people work in offices and within the service industry. This transition has created significant downsizing in many industries. It has also required many workers to make one or more career transitions and exposed workers to a growing occupational hazard—workplace stress. As a result, there has been an increase in occupational disease claims for depression, anxiety and other mental illnesses based on the mental health hazards of the workplace.

Some states, through legislation, have simply excluded such claims from their workers' compensation acts. For example, Washington passed legislation that stated: "'Occupational disease'—Exclusion of mental conditions caused by stress. The department shall adopt a rule pursuant to chapter 34.05 RCW that claims based on mental conditions or mental disabilities caused by stress do not fall within the definition of occupational disease in RCW 51.08.140." Wash. Rev. Code § 51.08.142

Other states have allowed claims for mental stress under the occupational disease statute. However, while stating that the same rules apply to mental stress claims as to other occupational disease claims, some courts struggle to apply objectively the elements of an occupational disease claim to a mental stress.[13]

---

12. *Larson's Workers' Compensation Law § 52.06(3)*.

13. *Woody v. Thomasville Upholstery Inc.*, 355 N.C. 483, 562 S.E.2d 422 (2002) (adopting dissent in 146 N.C. App. 187, 202, 552 S.E.2d 202, 211 (2001).

In addition to standard occupational disease claims, some states have special provisions for certain occupational diseases, such as silicosis or asbestosis, or for certain occupations, such as law enforcement officers and firefighters.

Workers' compensation practitioners need to stay abreast of the developments in occupational disease law.

2.4 Disability

Disability is the inability of the injured worker to earn the same wages earned prior to the compensable event because of the occupational disease or a workplace accident. In some cases, disability is based on a permanent physical impairment, which is then translated into a presumption of wage loss for a set number of weeks. A fuller discussion regarding the payment of disability benefits is found in Chapter 1, Section 1.4(2).

2.5 Defenses to Claims for Compensation

Each jurisdiction permits some defenses to claims for workers' compensation. As discussed in the previous chapter, some states provide that a fraudulent employment application will be a bar to a claim for compensation. Other defenses that are recognized include: (1) if the employee intended to injure himself, or (2) if the employee's intoxication was the cause of the accident. Workers' compensation practitioners should become familiar with the defenses permitted in the practitioner's jurisdiction.

2.6 Exclusiveness of Workers' Compensation

The elimination of fault as a basis for determining employer liability, made it more likely that the injured employee would receive compensation from the employer. The injured employee's recovery was limited to payment for medical treatment, payment for lost earnings and payment for loss of limb or life. In return, workers' compensation became the exclusive remedy for workers. Injured workers relinquished their right to bring a tort claim, with potential larger monetary damages in the form of pain and suffering and punitive damages, against the employer, even when the employer obviously was at fault.

There are generally recognized exceptions to the exclusive remedy doctrine. Those exceptions hold that when an employee is injured by the intentional conduct of an employer or co-employee, the victim of the intentional tort, (as opposed to negligence), should not be relegated to the limited remedies provided by workers' compensation. The most commonly occurring workplace intentional torts are assault & battery.

2.7 Third Party Claims

The exclusive remedy does not apply to injuries caused by third parties. Thus, the paralegal injured in a motor vehicle collision with a taxicab driver while driving to the courthouse will have a civil tort claim against the taxicab driver, if the taxicab driver's negligence caused the collision. The paralegal will also have a workers' compensation claim. Generally, the provider of workers' compensation will have a subrogation interest against the proceeds of the third party tort claim. This prevents a double recovery by the injured worker and properly places the cost of the accident on the negligent party.

Summary

The workers' compensation acts apply to the employee-employment relationship. There must be a work connection between the employment and the injury or disease. In accident cases, the test for work connection is often stated as whether there was an injury by accident arising out of and in the course of employment. In occupational disease cases, the work connection is stated as whether the job was a significant causal factor in the development of the disease and whether the employment placed the worker at an increased risk of developing the disease. The exclusion provision of the workers' compensation acts do not apply to third parties whose negligence caused the injury and may not protect employers or co-employees who intentionally harm the injured worker.

CHAPTER 3

EVALUATION AND ACCEPTANCE OF CASE

PARALEGAL PRACTICE TIPS

A knowledgeable workers' compensation paralegal should be able to gather sufficient information for a plaintiffs' firm to evaluate a potential claim and to open a new file if the firm decides to accept the case. In order to fully understand the case, as well as assist the client, a paralegal should:

- Meet the client to establish a comfortable working relationship.
- Use pre-prepared intake forms and releases to avoid missing key information.
- Obtain and review all documentation the client has regarding the claim, injury and employment.
- Gather as many details as possible about how the injury or occupational disease occurred.
- Obtain sufficient information to thoroughly understand the injured worker's job duties.
- Obtain complete background information about the injured worker, including a medical and employment history, criminal record (if any) and prior injury claims and pre-existing conditions (if any).
- Verify the legal name of the employer by reviewing paychecks, paycheck stubs, IRS wage-earning report forms, other employment documents and Secretary of State and Department of Labor websites.
- Return client telephone calls as promptly as possible.
- Decline to give clients legal advice. Instead, refer questions regarding legal issues to the attorney.
- Keep copies (paper or digital image) of frequently contacted medical providers' required release forms.
- Carefully draft and review the contents of all correspondence, including E-mail, prior to sending it, as it may be seen by unintended parties.

- If the paralegal works for a plaintiffs' firm, keep contact information for local agencies which assist individuals and families in crisis.

* * *

This chapter focuses on law firms that represent injured workers, also referred to in workers' compensation cases as "plaintiffs," "employees" and/or "claimants." Law firms that represent injured workers need to make a case by case, client by client decision whether to represent the injured worker. The firm will make the decision based on a variety of factors, including:

- Does the claim appear to be legally viable?
- Will the case present the opportunity to advance the law or make new law?
- Will the case require the firm to expend significant resources?
- Is the worker someone the firm staff will enjoy working with?
- Will representing the worker bring justice to an unjust situation?

Law firms that represent self-insured employers and workers' compensation insurance carriers, sometimes referred to as "defense firms," rarely have discretion in accepting cases. The firm's client is not an individual but a business entity, the self-insured employer or the workers' compensation insurance carrier, which send cases to a defense firm when legal representation is needed, usually in cases with disputed factual or legal issues. However, information contained in this chapter will be helpful to paralegals working for defense firms because the ability to analyze and evaluate a case is equally applicable. Additionally, the gathering of information, the use of forms, releases and case management software applies to paralegals who work for plaintiffs' or defense firms.

A competent paralegal in a plaintiffs' practice can gather most, if not all, of the initial information used by the supervising attorney to evaluate a potential workers' compensation claim and to decide whether the law firm (the "firm") is going to accept the injured worker as a client. Paralegals may use a combination of standard intake forms and thorough interviewing skills to obtain the extensive but necessary data for the attorney's review. The attorney will use the information to:

1) Determine whether the injured worker has a viable claim for workers' compensation benefits;
2) Estimate the value of the injured worker's potential recovery;
3) Evaluate the complexity of the claim and the firm resources necessary to pursue it; and
4) Decide whether the firm wants to represent the injured worker.

3.1 Initial Client Interview

When a potential workers' compensation client contacts the firm for the first time, a proficient paralegal can gather the necessary personal and factual information to allow the supervising attorney to evaluate the case, or help the attorney gather this information. This information will also be used to open a new file and to file paperwork with the state workers' compensation agency if the firm takes the case. The initial intake meeting can be handled in a variety of ways, depending on the firm's preference. An attorney can interview the injured worker and take notes and complete intake forms. A paralegal can also interview the injured worker and then provide the information to the attorney to review. The attorney and the paralegal may prefer to interview the injured worker as a team. Because an experienced paralegal can perform substantive work on a workers' compensation case and often communicates extensively with the client during the course of the firm's representation, it can be very helpful for the paralegal to be introduced to the injured worker and establish a comfortable professional relationship.

Extensive background and factual information is necessary to decide whether to accept a new case, as well as to manage the file and to prepare necessary legal paperwork once the case is accepted. Having a **standard set of workers' compensation intake forms and releases** is an extremely effective method to make sure that all necessary information is obtained at the first visit and that the injured worker does not leave the office without having provided key information necessary to evaluate the claim and to pursue it if the firm accepts the case.[1] The paralegal can use the firm's existing intake forms, or create forms if necessary. Workers' compensation intake forms can be incorporated as part of the firm's case management software, with data entered into the computer while interviewing the injured worker. Paper forms can also be completed, with the data entered into the case management software after the client leaves the office. Many firms manage their cases using a case management software program, because it is fast and efficient. The case management software may also be linked to the firm's billing and time-keeping software programs.

In complex cases, a standard intake form may not be sufficient for all of the information needed to evaluate and file the claim. However, the standard

1. Sometimes complete information may be omitted for a variety of reasons, such as the injured worker or attorney do not have enough time to complete the interview, or the injured worker has difficulty recalling information. The paralegal can contact the injured worker later by telephone, E-mail or letter to complete the intake.

intake form is a good starting point. Additional detailed notes or forms customized for specific kinds of complex cases, such as death cases or asbestos claims, may be necessary.

The following information should be obtained from an injured worker at the initial intake meeting.[2] *See Form 3. 1, Sample Workers' Compensation Client Intake Sheet.* This sample form can be adapted to reflect a specific state's workers' compensation laws, as well as the firm's preferences.

3.1(1) Personal Information

Obtaining **reliable contact information** may seem obvious, but the firm must be able to communicate with its client, often on short notice, as well as accurately identify the clients. (Having to write and ask a new client to call the firm because someone did not get a telephone number at the initial interview does not make a good first impression). Make sure the client provides his or her **full, legal name** to avoid misidentification by the firm and to properly identify the claimant when filing documents with the state agency overseeing the workers' compensation claim. Make a note of any other names the client may have used, such as maiden or married names. Some firms may take the extra precaution of copying the injured worker's drivers license in order to have photo identification for the file.

Obtain the injured worker's street address, as well as his or her **mailing address**, such as a Post Office box, if it is different. Emphasize the importance of having reliable contact information in order to effectively represent the client. Ask the client to call the office to provide updated information if any of the contact information changes in the future. E-mail is a fast and effective way to communicate with clients, if used carefully.[3] Ask if the client would like to use E-mail as one form of communication with the firm and if so, get the E-mail address. In addition to obtaining home, cell and work telephone numbers, get emergency contact information, such as the name and telephone number(s) of a close relative or friend.

---

2. In some instances, an initial personal meeting may not be possible, such as a potential out-of-state client. The firm may mail an intake "package" containing the *Workers' Compensation Client Intake Sheet* and release forms to the injured worker to complete and return and/or obtain information via telephone and E-mail.

3. E-mail is protected by the attorney-client privilege, but the paralegal should keep in mind when drafting E-mail that it (and any other method of correspondence) may be seen by unintended parties. Some states require that the client consent to the use of E-mail and require the law firm to inform the client of the risk of communicating by E-mail.

In addition to reliable contact information, the injured worker's correct **date of birth** and **Social Security number** are key identifying data to obtain at the initial meeting. The date of birth and Social Security number may appear on many documents, including legal filings, medical requests and records, and disability documents. If the client is reluctant to provide this sensitive information, state that it is necessary to have it in order to effectively represent him or her and that the firm will only release this information as required by law. The injured worker's date of birth and/or Social Security number are required by many state agencies, who use this information to identify claimants, as well as by many medical providers, who use it to identify patients and may not release medical records without it.[4] In cases where an injured worker is totally disabled from working or likely to be totally disabled from working, the federal government will not release information regarding Social Security disability benefits or Workers' Compensation Medicare Set-aside Arrangement (WCMSA) requirements without a Social Security number.

Other personal information, such as marital status, spouse's name and employment, and the names and ages of dependents, is helpful to evaluate the injured worker's personal circumstances and individual needs. All this information is used to evaluate the case for settlement and to litigate the case.[5]

3.1(2) Employment Information

Gathering accurate information to correctly identify the injured worker's employer on the date of injury is essential. Obtain the **employer's full legal name** and contact information, and if possible, verify it with a paycheck, paycheck stub, IRS wage earning report form (W-2 or 1099),[6] or other employment documentation from the injured worker. The firm will use this information on all legal filings, as well as to run an internal conflicts check. The correct employer name is also necessary to determine the employer's workers' compensation insurance coverage or self-insured status. Other methods to

4. Many medical practices will accept dates of birth, but some still require the patient's full Social Security number, or the last four digits.

5. In death cases, it is necessary to obtain the full, legal names of the surviving spouse and all known dependents, as well as their dates of birth, Social Security numbers, a copy of the marriage certificate, and a copy of the birth certificates or other legal documentation of dependency, such as adoption orders, consent orders or guardianship agreements.

6. Reviewing employment documentation is especially helpful in cases to determine the correct corporate entity when the injured worker is employed by a subsidiary or the corporation is doing business under a different name.

verify the legal name and status of the employment entity and the nature of the business include (but are not limited to):

- Perform a Google search with the employer's name in the query.
- Review the employer's website, if available.
- Perform a name search through the appropriate state agency, such as the Secretary of State or Department of Labor.
- Obtain a company profile from free, fee-based or subscription-based databases for publicly and/or privately owned companies, such as Edgar-Online, http://www.edgar-online.com/(http://www.edgar-online.com/) or Hoovers, http://www.hoovers.com.[7](http://www.hoover.com). The firm's online legal research service, such as LexisNexis.com or Westlaw.com, may include access to company databases.

Ask the injured worker to estimate how many individuals work for the employer. The number of employees may determine whether the employer is bound by that state's workers' compensation laws. The number of employees will also help the attorney determine if the injured worker has other actionable legal claims arising out of the work injury, such as violations of The Family Medical and Leave Act (FMLA), or violations of state and federal laws pertaining to discrimination and retaliatory discharge.

Get as much information as possible about the injured worker's job title, job duties and employment at the time of the injury. Be thorough and accurate when describing specific job duties. Ask for the correct spellings of occupation-specific terminology, such as machine and tool names and specialized procedures. Get enough details to gain a thorough understanding of the injured worker's job duties and requirements. If available, review and copy any information the client can provide about the worker's job and employment, including (but not limited to):

- Job descriptions
- Employee evaluation forms
- Personnel action forms documenting changes in employment status, such as date of hire, changes in pay, transfers, promotions and demotions (or termination in some cases)
- Correspondence to the injured worker from the employer
- Internal memos to the injured worker from co-workers and/or management

7. This website is not to be confused with Hoover.com for The Hoover Company vacuum cleaners.

- Benefit summaries for health insurance, group disability and/or retirement plans
- Employee handbooks
- Leave of absence forms, including FMLA forms

A job description will be necessary if the injured worker's treating doctor has to evaluate his or her ability to return to work doing the same job.

Determine the injured worker's employment status, especially if he or she has been terminated. The plaintiff's attorney will use this information to decide if the worker has other actionable legal claims besides the workers' compensation claim. The injured worker's employment status will also impact future vocational plans if the injured worker is released to return to work, with or without restrictions. If the injured worker is on a medical leave, ask for a copy of the leave paperwork and remind him or her to comply with the employer's personnel policies and requirements regarding leave time, including a leave under The Family and Medical Leave Act (FMLA), if eligible. For more information regarding FMLA laws, go to the U.S. Department of Labor's website, http://www.dol.gov/esa/whd/fmla.

Confirm the injured worker's earnings at the time of injury with paychecks, paycheck stubs and/or IRS wage reporting forms (W-2 or 1099), if available. Obtaining accurate wage information is crucial because the amount of the injured worker's compensation rate is usually calculated using his or her average earnings for a set period prior to the date of injury.

3.1(3) Carrier/Administrator Information

Employers required by law to have workers' compensation insurance coverage comply with their obligation in one of two ways:

1. by purchasing a policy through the state or an insurance company ("risk carrier"), or
2. by satisfying the state's legal requirements to obtain a **certificate of self-insurance**, with their claims and funds managed by the employer or a third party administrator, often abbreviated as "TPA" on claim documents. (The risk carrier or the self-insured employer or third party administrator will hereinafter be referred to collectively as the "**carrier/administrator**").

If the injured worker has already been contacted by an adjuster (the individual or representative handling the claim for the carrier/administrator), he or she may be able to provide the carrier/administrator's name, address and telephone numbers. Ideally, an injured worker can provide a copy of correspondence received from the carrier/administrator, which will provide all of this information, along with a key identifier, the **carrier/administrator's claim number**. Reference the claim number on all correspondence to the carrier/administrator.

If the injured worker does not have contact information for the carrier/administrator, it can be obtained in a variety of ways, including by contacting the state's workers' compensation agency. In some states, this information is available online at the state agency's website or by simply calling or E-mailing the state agency. The employer can also provide this information.

Ask the injured worker if a **recorded statement** (usually a telephone interview) has already been taken by the adjuster assigned to investigate the claim. Ask if the worker has been contacted by an attorney for the employer in regard to the work injury or received any proposed settlement documents.[8] If the injured worker has received settlement documents, those should be copied and given to the attorney for review and evaluation.

3.1(4) State Agency Information

If a workers' compensation claim has already been filed with the state agency, obtain the **state agency file, case** or **claim number.** The file number will be used on all future pleadings and correspondence. The state agency's file number is different from the carrier/administrator's claim number. The state agency file number can be obtained from paperwork already filed in the case, if the injured worker is able to provide a copy. If not, obtain this information by contacting the state agency via letter, facsimile, telephone or E-mail (usually the quickest and most efficient method). The state agency will release this information only to parties or their attorneys. If a claim has not yet been filed or has only recently been filed, a file number may not be available.

It is important to know **whether the injured worker has timely and properly filed a workers' compensation claim with the state agency in accordance with state law.** If the worker has not properly filed a claim before the **statute of limitations** (the statutory time period the injured worker has from the date

---

8. Occasionally, a potential client will have a copy of signed and approved settlement paperwork which shows that the case has already been resolved. The firm may not be able to assist the injured worker if the case is settled, except in rare cases where the settlement was obtained under fraud, mutual mistake, duress or other circumstances which may violate the relevant state's worker's compensation laws. In some cases an approved settlement may be nullified, voided and set aside upon review by the workers' compensation state agency.

of the injury to file a claim) has expired, the injured worker may have waived or forfeited a claim to workers' compensation benefits. Ideally, the injured worker can provide a copy of the written claim notice with evidence that it was properly filed, such as a file-stamped copy of the form and/or a letter from the state agency acknowledging the claim. If the injured worker does not have this information, it can and should be requested from the state agency.

Another key issue is whether the carrier/administrator has filed paperwork with the state agency **accepting liability for the injury**, or formally agreeing to pay benefits. (Sometimes the carrier/administrator has paid benefits without filing the required paperwork). It is also helpful to know what benefits the carrier/administrator has paid, if any. If the carrier/administrator is denying liability for the injury and refusing to pay benefits, the injured worker may have already received correspondence or paperwork which states the basis or reason for the **denial**. If the injured worker does not have this information, documentation of the denial can be obtained from the carrier/administrator, the employer or the state agency. In some cases, a decision whether to deny or accept the claim may not have been made at the time the injured worker contacts the firm. The carrier/administrator may still be investigating the circumstances of the injury or medical condition and not yet reached a decision regarding whether to accept liability and pay benefits.

If benefits have been paid by the carrier/administrator, deadlines to claim additional benefits may be triggered upon receipt of the last indemnity (disability) check or last payment of medical benefits. Therefore, it is important to determine the date the injured worker last received an indemnity check or medical treatment was paid.

If a hearing or mediation has already been scheduled, note those key dates. The dates may factor into the firm's decision to accept the case.

3.1(5) Injury Information

How the worker was injured or sustained an occupational disease is the crux of the case. A detailed and accurate description of how the worker was hurt or became ill as a result of the employment is necessary to successfully evaluate a claim and then effectively represent the injured worker or the employer.

In a typical injury claim, the worker has to show that he or she was injured by accident arising out of and in the course of employment. *See Chapter 2.* Some injured workers are very articulate and able to provide accurate details about how they were hurt, while others may require a more slow and patient interview process. In cases of catastrophic injury, the injured worker may not remember how the injury occurred, or in a worst case scenario, the worker may have died due to the work injury. The accident facts may have to be reconstructed or corroborated from other sources, including (but not limited to), incident and investigative reports, witness interviews/statements and medical records. If the case has been reported in the media, sometimes media articles and/or reporters will have information regarding the circumstances of the injury. In complex cases, it may be necessary for the firm to hire an expert in the areas of accident reconstruction and/or health and safety issues.

Ask if the injured worker is receiving medical and/or indemnity benefits from the carrier/administrator, or any other source. In accepted cases where benefits are being paid, or in denied cases where benefits are later recovered through litigation, there may be lien, subrogation or employer offset and credit issues to be considered from the following sources:

- Group health insurance, if benefits were paid for treatment arising out of the work injury.
- Medicaid or Medicare, if benefits were paid for treatment arising out of the work injury.
- Disability insurance, if short or long term disability benefits were paid because the injured worker was unable to work due to the work injury.
- Employment Security Commission, if unemployment benefits were paid for the same weeks that workers' compensation indemnity (weekly disability) benefits were paid.

3.1(6) Medical Provider Information

The firm will have to obtain all of the injured worker's medical records related to the injury or occupational disease. The firm may also have to request records for prior medical treatment and/or pre-existing conditions. Ask the injured worker to provide the names of **all medical providers** who rendered treatment for the work injury or occupational disease, including family or primary care physicians, specialists, hospitals, and diagnostic centers. In some cases where the cause of the injury or the existence of a pre-existing condition may be issues in dispute, all medical records for five to ten years preceding the date of the injury or onset of the occupational disease may be needed. In cases that are likely to be contested, it is a good idea to request five to ten years of prior medical records in order to evaluate the injured worker's medical issues thoroughly, avoid unpleasant surprises and prepare for litigation.[9]

9. If the defense firm's client has not accepted the claim or paid benefits, then there may be little or no information in the file regarding the worker's medical providers and

Obtain as much information as possible about the injured worker's **complete medical history:**

- Has the worker had prior serious illnesses, injuries or surgeries?
- Has the worker ever been disabled from working due to prior serious illnesses or injuries?
- Has the worker filed previous workers' compensation claims? If so, what were the diagnoses and who were the medical providers? Did the injured worker receive a prior permanent impairment rating?
- Has the worker made any other claim for benefits arising out of an injury or illness, such as a personal injury claim or disability claim? If so, get as many details as possible.
- What pre-existing conditions, if any, did the worker have?
- What medications, if any, was the worker taking at the time of the injury or onset of the occupational disease?
- Who were the worker's family or primary care doctors for the last ten years?

Obtaining a copy of the injured worker's complete chart from each family practice in the last five or ten years may provide additional details of the medical history that the worker may have forgotten. The family or primary care doctor's chart will often contain referrals to other medical providers and specialists as well as copies of their records, including hospital reports, office notes, correspondence and diagnostic reports.

Ask the injured worker if the carrier/administrator has assigned a rehabilitation consultant, such as a medical case manager, nurse, or specialist to the case. If so, get that individual's contact information from the injured worker. If the worker does not have it, the carrier/administrator can provide it, along with copies of rehabilitation reports submitted to date.

3.1(7) Educational and Vocational Information

The injured worker's **educational and vocational background** is especially important in cases involving serious injury and possible inability to return to pre-injury employment. This information will be used repeatedly in cases which have vocational rehabilitation and/or litigation issues. Obtain as many

---

treatment. The defense firm usually obtains medical information by sending the injured worker or the worker's attorney a letter requesting medical records per state agency rules and/or interrogatories and requests for production of documents requesting medical records and a medical history.

details as possible regarding the injured worker's education, including the dates and institutions where high school, secondary school or technical school certificates, diplomas or degrees, if any, were obtained. If the worker has a general equivalency diploma (GED) in lieu of a high school diploma, get the date and institution where the GED was obtained. If the worker has a military background, obtain the dates and branches of service and the discharge circumstances, such as honorable, dishonorable or other than honorable.[10]

Get enough information to prepare a detailed and accurate summary of the injured worker's vocational background, such as the dates of employment, each job position and duties performed, contact information for each employer, the rate of pay and the reasons he or she left each position. Find out whether the injured worker has a criminal record which may prohibit him or her from certain employment, or adversely impact his or her credibility. Make a note of the injured worker's hobbies. Determine whether the worker has transferable job skills from hobbies, such as graphic design, automobile restoration or carpentry. Ask the injured worker about his or her vocational plans. Does the worker hope to return to work for the same employer, start a different career or go back to school? If the injured worker's "vocational plan" is not to work again, this is key information for the firm to consider, especially if the plan is not realistic.

Also ask the injured worker if the carrier/administrator has assigned a rehabilitation consultant or a vocational case manager to the case. If so, get that individual's contact information from the injured worker. If the injured worker does not have it, the carrier/administrator can provide the contact information and vocational reports. If the injured worker has already started a job search, obtain as much information as possible about the length of the search, the potential employers contacted, and whether any applications have resulted in job interviews and/or job offers. Make a copy of any information the injured worker has retained to document a job search, including job search logs, diaries, calendars, applications and correspondence.

3.1(8) Miscellaneous Information

This section of a client intake form can be customized to reflect the relevant state's workers' compensation laws as well as the firm's individual needs. However, it is very helpful to know if the injured worker has any **third party claims** arising out of the work injury or occupational disease. When an em-

10. Again, the defense firm can send the injured worker or the worker's attorney interrogatories and requests for production of documents to obtain educational and vocational information.

ployee is injured on the job due to the negligence of an outside third party (not the employer), in addition to the claim for workers' compensation benefits, he or she may have a concurrent "third party claim" due to personal injury, wrongful death, medical malpractice or product liability. An example of a concurrent third party claim is when an employee is driving during the course of employment and is injured in a motor vehicle accident caused by someone else's negligence. In situations such as these, it is important to get as much information as possible for the attorney to review. In some cases, the firm may be able to represent the injured worker in the workers' compensation claim, as well as the third party claims. If the firm does not handle personal injury, wrongful death, medical malpractice or product liability cases (or if it does but does not want to handle this one), it is crucial that the firm advise (preferably in writing) the injured worker to contact a lawyer who does handle these matters in a timely fashion, to avoid legal malpractice issues.

Also, it is not unusual for injured workers to have other actionable employment claims arising out of their work injury, such as **discrimination or retaliatory discharge claims**. An employer bound by the Americans with Disabilities Act (ADA) may refuse to accommodate a seriously injured worker's physical restrictions, prohibiting him or her from returning to the pre-injury job or another suitable job within the company with a competitive salary and benefits. An employer may have fired an injured worker simply for filing a claim for worker's compensation benefits. In situations such as these, it is important to get as much information as possible for the attorney to review. If the firm handles employment matters, it may be able to represent the injured worker in the workers' compensation claim, as well as the employment claims. If the firm does not handle employment matters (or if it does but does not want to handle this one), it is crucial that the firm advise (preferably in writing) the injured worker to contact a lawyer who does handle these matters in a timely fashion, to avoid legal malpractice issues.

Some firms track referrals for marketing purposes. If so, ask who referred the injured worker to the firm. Referral sources may include the Internet, television or print ads, a friend or co-worker, a union representative or steward, or other attorneys.

List other legal matters the firm has handled for the injured worker, if any. Ask for the names of other attorneys the injured worker has consulted about the work injury, if any. If the injured worker has had prior representation for this claim, get the name and contact information of prior counsel. The firm will need to know if prior counsel has properly withdrawn from formal representation of the injured worker by filing a written notice or motion to withdraw with the state agency. Ask why the injured worker terminated (or was terminated by) prior counsel. The firm may use this information to decide whether to accept the injured worker as a client, especially in cases where the injured worker has had frivolous reasons for firing attorneys, has unrealistic expectations or has refused to cooperate with prior counsel.

The firm may also want to prepare a brief preliminary evaluation or estimate of the injured worker's potential entitlement to benefits, in order to evaluate whether this is a case the firm wants to accept. Some firms accept cases, no matter how minimal the damages, while others only accept serious or catastrophic injury and/or total disability cases.

3.2 Authorizations

Pursuant to federal law, medical providers cannot release confidential patient information without having a **HIPAA compliant medical authorization** signed by the patient. The Health Insurance Portability and Accountability Act (HIPAA) was initially enacted by Congress in 1996 to provide protection for individuals at risk of losing health insurance coverage. On April 14, 2003 HIPAA's Privacy Rule went into effect to protect the privacy of individual personal health information. "Covered entities" which handle any kind of health care information, including health insurance companies, doctors, hospitals, pharmacies, nursing homes, and Medicare and Medicaid government agencies must comply with HIPAA requirements before releasing health care information. Anyone seen by a medical provider since April 14, 2003 should have been asked to sign a HIPAA notice of privacy practices explaining how patient health information may be shared and used. For additional information regarding HIPAA, the U.S. Department of Health and Human Resources Office for Civil Rights has an excellent website at http://www.hhs.gov/ocr/hipaa/ with a section for frequently asked questions and clearly written overviews for consumers and businesses.

A HIPAA compliant medical authorization allowing the firm to obtain medical information must be signed by the injured worker. *See Form 3.2, Sample Medical Authorization.* Some medical providers will not accept a law firm's medical authorization form and instead require that their own medical authorization forms be signed. If a medical provider that the firm contacts frequently requires its own form, keep one available to copy (hard copy or digital image). Some medical providers and government agencies publish their required release forms on their websites.

Required provisions for a HIPAA compliant medical authorization include (but are not limited to):

- The **legal name of the patient** whose name is on the requested records. Most medical providers require the correct date of birth to identify the patient. Some providers will also request the patient's home address and Social Security number as extra security measures to verify the identity of the patient.
- The **name or categories of persons authorized to release the information.** While a technically valid authorization could simply specify a class such as "any health care provider that has provided services to me," many medical providers require a separate authorization designating the specific provider and will reject an authorization which does not specifically and correctly identify the provider by name.
- A "specific and meaningful" **description of the type of information to be disclosed by the provider.** The description must be specific enough to allow the medical provider to clearly identify the information which the patient is authorizing for release. Valid descriptions include "entire medical record" or "complete patient file." Overly broad, general or vague descriptions may result in a rejected authorization.
- The **name or categories of persons authorized to receive the information.** Most medical providers want the specific name of the entity authorized to receive the information. Many providers also require an address or telephone number for the entity.
- The **purpose of the requested information.** "Pursuing legal remedies/claims" is generally sufficient for an authorization form from the law firm representing the patient.
- A **specific expiration date for the authorization.** Even if an authorization date is specified, some medical providers such as hospitals have their own policies regarding the valid period for authorizations. For example, the firm's authorization may specify that it is valid for 6 months, while a local hospital may only accept authorizations executed within a limited period, such as 60 or 90 days of the request.
- An acknowledgment that the patient has the right to revoke the authorization.
- An acknowledgment that the disclosed information may be re-disclosed by the recipient.
- An acknowledgment that the use or disclosure of the requested information is voluntary and the patient does not need to sign the authorization to ensure access to medical treatment.

The medical authorization must be signed by the patient and dated. A witness signature is optional.

In cases where the injured worker has applied for or is receiving Social Security disability benefits, obtain a signed consent for the Social Security Administration to release information to the firm. The release form can be obtained online at the Social Security Administration's website, http://www.ssa.gov. *See Form 3.3, Social Security Administration Consent to Release Information.* Ask the worker to provide a copy of any Social Security disability documents in his or her possession, including the initial application, award letters, denial letters, requests for reconsideration or requests for hearing. The client's receipt of or pending application for Social Security benefits will be an issue if the workers' compensation case might be settled for a lump sum of money. The injured worker's attorney may need to include Medicare and Social Security offset provisions in the settlement agreement.

3.3 Fee Agreement

When a firm agrees to represent a client in a workers' compensation claim, a **written fee agreement** should be obtained, per the applicable state laws and professional rules of conduct regarding attorney representation of individuals in legal matters. The state agency may require that the fee agreement be filed simultaneously with the firm's notice or letter of representation. Paralegals should know the state agency's legal requirements for entering into a worker's compensation fee agreement. Keep the fee agreements used by the firm in a master form (paper or digital image file) for immediate access. A typical fee agreement:

- Identifies the specific injury or illness claim by date and/or description that the firm has agreed to pursue.
- States how the attorney fees will be paid and whether the fees are subject to approval by the state agency.
- Acknowledges that the client is responsible for any costs advanced by the law firm.
- Provides a method to value disputed fees.
- Allows the firm to withdraw from representation if it determines that the claim does not have a reasonable chance of success.
- Allows the client to end the representation.

3.4 Injured Worker's Documents

Always ask the injured worker to provide **any and all documents** in his or her possession regarding the workers' compensation claim. A client who can provide documentation of the work injury, employment status and medical treatment can save the firm a great deal of time in the initial stages of representation. Basic documents the client may be able to provide are as follows:

- **Medical records** (including disability statements and discharge instructions)
- **Medical bills** (including collection notices and prescription receipts)
- **Group health insurance Explanation of Benefit (EOB) statements**
- **Wage or earnings records** (including paychecks, paycheck stubs, IRS wage reporting forms)
- **Employment records** (including accident reports, correspondence, job descriptions)
- **State agency claim records** (including notices of accident, compensation agreements, denial forms)
- **Any other documentation in the client's possession pertaining to the work injury**

For a more detailed discussion of the information which can be obtained from documents provided by the client, see *Chapter 6.1(1).*

3.5 Firm Guidelines for Injured Workers

In accepting a case, the firm has agreed to guide its client through the workers' compensation process, including answering questions as they arise. Injured workers may ask the same questions repeatedly, especially about payment of indemnity (weekly disability) benefits and obtaining necessary medical treatment. The firm can give its client a written list of basic guidelines (or answers to frequently asked questions) to refer to throughout the course of the claim. *See Form 3.4, Sample Client Guidelines.* Providing these guidelines at the onset of representation helps ensure that the client is informed of his or her responsibilities to maintain contact with the firm and to disclose necessary information. Even if guidelines are provided to the client, the firm should encourage the client to call any time with questions. The paralegal should patiently answer the injured worker's questions, even if the same questions are asked repeatedly.

3.6 Letters of Representation

Once the firm has agreed to accept the injured worker's case and has obtained a fee agreement, written notices or letters of representation should be sent to the carrier/administrator, the state agency and the new client.

3.6(1) Accepting Claims for Investigation Only

There may be situations where the firm is interested in a potential case but needs more information before making a decision. The firm may want to review all of the injured worker's medical records to evaluate causation of the injury or illness and/or pre-existing medical conditions. In cases where the firm has agreed only to investigate the claim prior to making a decision regarding representation, the firm should send a letter to the injured worker confirming it has agreed only to conduct an investigation of the case. The firm should select and enter or "tickle" in its calendaring system a reasonable internal deadline to investigate and review the claim and make a decision. Setting a reasonable deadline to make a decision regarding representation can prevent "investigation-only cases" from being placed on a "back burner" in a busy practice.

3.6(2) Letter of Representation to Client

At the time the firm opens a new case file for the injured worker, the firm should immediately send the injured worker confirmation of its legal representation. The letter may include copies of the fee agreement and/or client guidelines. *See Form 3.5, Sample Letter of Representation to Client.*

3.6(3) Notice of Representation to Carrier/Administrator

A written notice or letter of representation should be sent immediately to the carrier/ administrator, unless the firm knows the employer and its carrier/administrator are represented by counsel. *See Form 3.6, Sample Letter of Representation to Carrier/Administrator.* If that is the case, the firm should send the notice of representation to the defense counsel. If the carrier/ administrator is represented by counsel, the firm may not communicate directly with the carrier/administrator without permission of its counsel.

Many adjusters will not acknowledge the injured worker's legal representative or discuss the case with the firm until a written notice of representation has been received. If the injured worker needs immediate assistance to obtain benefits, the firm should call the carrier/ administrator or its counsel to obtain the current adjuster's or defense attorney's contact information and then send the representation letter via facsimile or E-mail. On rare occasions, the firm may not be able to identify the employer's carrier/administrator or counsel. In those cases, send the representation letter directly to the employer with a request to forward it to its carrier/administrator or counsel.

3.6(4) Request for Information from Carrier/Administrator

The letter of representation to the carrier/administrator should contain a request for all information that can be released from the claim file pursuant to the state's workers' compensation statutes or state agency rules. Carrier/administrator file documents which are required to be released upon request of the injured worker or the worker's attorney may include (but are not limited to) medical records, state agency forms and vocational records. If the carrier/administrator will voluntarily provide an itemized printout of the medical and/or indemnity benefits it has paid to date, if any, this is useful information for the firm to review. If the statutes or rules provide a deadline for the carrier/administrator to provide the requested information, the deadline should be stated in the letter. *See Form 3.7, Sample Letter of Representation to Carrier/Administrator.*

3.6(5) Notice of Representation to State Agency

The firm should immediately send a representation letter and/or required representation form to the state agency, according to the relevant state workers' compensation statutes and/or state agency rules. *See Form 3.8, Sample Letter of Representation to State Agency.* If the state agency will accept correspondence via E-mail or facsimile, those are the quickest and most efficient methods to submit the correspondence.

3.6(6) Request for Information from State Agency

The letter of representation to the state agency should contain a request for all information that can be released from the claim file pursuant to state statutes or state agency rules. The state agency file may include (but is not limited to) the following types of forms and/or documents:

- Employer accident/incident report
- Employee injury report or notice of claim for benefits
- Form compensation agreements accepting the case and setting forth benefits to be paid over a specified period
- Form agreements denying the claim and refusing to pay benefits

- Return to work forms
- Summary or itemization of benefits paid by the carrier/administrator to date
- Requests for hearing and responses to requests for hearing
- Letters or motions requesting relief such as approval of medical treatment, and responsive letters or motions alleging the relief should be denied
- Applications to stop payment of benefits and responses to the applications
- State agency orders regarding compensation or medical issues in dispute
- Mediation orders
- Notices of appearance or withdrawal by the parties' attorneys
- Forms reporting ratings or permanent impairment to body parts
- Notices of hearing

3.7 Case Management Software

A good case management software program allows the firm to enjoy a high level of efficiency and instant access to case data. Staff members can spend more time working on the substantive aspects of cases, and less time generating form documents and hunting for information in paper files. There are numerous case management software programs which can be tailored specifically to workers' compensation cases. Depending on the capabilities of the specific program, a case management software program may be used for a number of purposes, including (but not limited to):

- Obtaining case information with a few keystrokes instead of searching the paper file.
- Generating form documents and/or organizing case documents.
- Calendaring case-related appointments, including mediations, hearings and depositions.
- Providing reminders or "ticklers" of pending deadlines and assignments.
- Recording telephone and electronic communications.
- Tracking attorney and paralegal time spent working on each case.

If the firm already has a case management software program, everyone in the firm should learn to fully utilize its capabilities, either through internal or external training. The firm should stay informed regarding updates and changes to the software program which may further increase its efficiency.

If the firm does not use a software program to manage its workers' compensation cases, obtaining information about available software programs is an excellent project for a paralegal. A good place to start is by networking with other workers' compensation paralegals, in person or via a listserv, to ask what other firms are using and to get feedback on the pros and cons of different programs. Once potential programs are identified, contact the software distributors directly to request further information, including demonstrations of the software and estimates of the costs. The firm can then evaluate the functions of the programs, as well as the expense, to determine if it is ready to utilize case management software and if so, what program is the best fit for the practice.

3.8 Client Relations

Well-trained and experienced paralegals, working under the supervision of an attorney per the state professional rules of conduct, can resolve a number of day-to-day problems for clients and help the firm maintain a high level of client service and satisfaction. One of the top complaints clients have about law firms is that no one returns their telephone calls. A busy workers' compensation practice receives a high volume of telephone calls every day. Paralegals working for plaintiffs' firms can handle many of the routine calls and discuss practical issues with clients including (but not limited to):

- How to obtain authorized medical care in accepted cases.
- What documentation to obtain from their doctors regarding their work status.
- The status of their weekly indemnity (disability) payments.
- How to obtain reimbursement for sick travel or out-of-pocket medical expenses, such as prescriptions.
- The status of their workers' compensation cases.

Paralegals working in plaintiffs' firms can also ask clients for updates regarding medical treatment and/or a job search, as well as remind clients to obtain notes regarding their work status at each medical appointment and that they may be under surveillance by the carrier/administrator.

However, **paralegals cannot give clients legal advice** regarding their entitlement to benefits, or how to settle their claims. Giving legal advice is different from practical advice such as how to get a prescription paid for by the carrier/administrator or how to document work status by asking the doctor for a written work note at each visit. If a client asks for legal advice, the paralegal should say he or she is not an attorney and cannot give legal advice. For example, the client may ask the paralegal whether quitting his or her job will affect the workers' compensation claim. The paralegal should say that the attorney will need to answer that question, and offer to relay the question to the attorney for a response. The paralegal could call the client back with an answer after talking to the attorney, or schedule a time for the client to talk to the attorney over the telephone or in person about the legal issue. If the attorney is available at the time of the call, he or she may agree to answer the client's question at that time.

3.8(1) Maintaining Contact with Clients

Paralegals should promptly return all telephone calls. Even in a busy plaintiffs' practice, scheduling the time to return or accept client telephone calls should be a priority. The injured worker hired the firm to guide him or her through the complex legal process, including answering questions as they arise. Staying in touch with clients is an important part of successful case management. Paralegals can tickle reminders to call clients to get a status report after upcoming medical appointments, or at regular intervals, such as once a month if the firm has not heard from the client. Paralegals should document all telephone calls, per the firm's preference, which may include (but is not limited to) the following methods:

- Entering a telephone note into a case management software program.
- Sending the supervising attorney an E-mail with a summary of the conversation.
- Taking notes during the conversation for the paper file.

3.8(2) Providing Clients with Documents

Clients should know what is happening in their cases. They should be copied on all documents generated by the firm regarding their cases (except for the firm's internal notes and memos). In some instances, an attorney may ask a client to review a draft document for factual accuracy and to obtain the client's approval before it is sent to the state agency and/or opposing party. Workers' compensation forms can be overwhelming and confusing to people who do not use them frequently. Paralegals should be prepared to answer clients' questions regarding the forms and why they are required.

3.8(3) Assisting the Injured Worker

Well-trained paralegals can handle the high volume of typical client needs inherent in a busy plaintiffs' practice. They can assist clients with getting prescriptions filled, verifying that weekly indemnity benefits have been mailed, contacting providers about outstanding medical bills or obtaining mileage reimbursement. They can send documentation of disability and/or medical referrals to the adjuster or defense counsel and request approval of recommended medical treatment. They may do a lot of "hand-holding" and provide reassurance to clients trying to cope with medical issues or financial setbacks. Their assistance may be as basic as reminding clients to call their treating doctors' offices for increased pain, adverse reactions to medication or other medical concerns, or to obtain a doctor's note regarding physical restrictions at each medical visit. They may also be able to assist with more complex needs such as helping clients understand doctors' reports and recommendations, obtaining needed medical treatment or durable medical equipment, or explaining how the workers' compensation system and process work. Some attorneys have paralegals accompany clients to important medical appointments, to assist the clients in asking questions regarding medical issues and to provide information to doctors about the requirements of the relevant state's workers' compensation act.

Clients and their families may also be experiencing financial hardships due to the work injuries. In denied cases, the clients are not receiving indemnity (weekly disability) benefits and their families may not have any other source of income. Although a plaintiff's firm may be handling only the workers' compensation case, and is not representing an injured worker on other legal matters, such as collections or foreclosures, the injured worker may not know where else to go for assistance. An informed paralegal can help by providing the injured worker with contact information for attorneys who handle collections, foreclosures, or bankruptcy, as well as for local agencies which provide assistance to individuals or families in crises, including (but not limited to):

- Employment Security Commission to apply for unemployment benefits (if eligible), vocational counseling and access to the jobs bank.
- Department of Social Services to apply for food stamps, Medicaid or other assistance.
- Consumer Credit Counseling to deal with creditors or make a decision about bankruptcy.
- Legal Aid for assistance with landlord/tenant or domestic issues.
- State division of vocational rehabilitation services to obtain assistance in locating jobs or re-training for a different career.
- City/County health department and/or mental health agencies which provide services to individuals without insurance.
- Various private or church agencies which provide food pantries, meals, emergency assistance with rent and utilities and other privately-funded social services.

Form 3.1—Sample Workers' Compensation Client Intake Sheet

1. Personal Information

Full name: ______________________________
Other names used: ______________________________
Street address: ______________________________
Phones: Home ______________ Work ______________
Pager: ______________ Cell: ______________
Email: ______________ Other: ______________
Social Security number: ______________________________
Date of birth : ______________ Age: ______________
Marital status:
Single_______ Married _______ Divorced _______ Widowed _______
Spouse's name: ______________________________
Spouse's employer: ______________________________
Dependents (names/ages/relationships):______________________________
____
____

2. Employment Information

Employer:______________________________
Employer's address: ______________________________
____
____
____
Employer's phone: ______________________________
Number of employees:______________________________
Nature of business: ______________________________
Claimant's occupation/job title: ______________________________
Job Duties: ______________________________
____
Shift: ______________ Dates of employment: ______________
Last date worked: ______________________________
If terminated, when: ______________ Why? ______________
____
Hourly rate: $______ Hours per Day: ________ /per Week: ________
Average weekly wage: ______________ Compensation rate: __________
Immediate supervisor's name:______________________________

Member of union? Yes _____ No _____
Union name: ________________ Local Number: ______________
Union representative's name: ______________________________
Union address: ____
____
____
Union phone: ____

3. Risk Carrier/Third Party Administrator Information

Name of Carrier/Administrator: _____________________________
Address: ____
Name of adjuster/representative:____________________________
Phone: ____
Statement given by claimant: Yes _____________ No ______________
If so, when: _______________ To whom: ______________________
Mileage/prescriptions reimbursed: Yes ___________ No ____________
Proposed settlement agreement received: Yes ________ No __________
Contact by carrier's attorney: Yes ___________ No __________
If so, name and address: _____________________________________
____

4. State Agency Claim Information

File/claim number assigned: _________________________________
Written claim form filed? ___________________________________
State agency acknowledgment received? ________________________
Compensation agreement filed? _______________________________
Medical benefits paid? ______________________________________
If liability denied, reason given: ____________________________
____
____
Last indemnity check received: _______________________________
Mediation scheduled? _________, if so date:______________________
Hearing scheduled? ________, if so date: ________________________

5. Injury Information

Date of injury: ___/___/___ Time: ________ Place: ________________
City: _____________________ County: ________________________
Accident description: _______________________________________

____
____
____

Witnesses present: ____
Person(s) notified of accident: ____________________________________
____
____
When notified:____
Accident report completed? Yes _____________ No _________________
Nature and extent of injuries: ____________________________________
____
____
Paid for date of injury? Yes _______________ No __________________
Dates absent from work: ____
____
____
Date returned to work: ____
Benefits paid by employer? _______________________________________
Other benefits received: SSD _____ STD ______ LTD _____ ESC ____
Eligible for Medicare? Yes ________________ No __________________
Medicaid recipient? Yes __________________ No __________________

6. Medical Provider Information

Names and addresses of physicians and other health care providers (use additional sheets if necessary): ____________________________
____
____
____
____
____
____
Last doctor seen? _______________ Date? _______________________
If surgery, describe: ____
____
____
____
Maximum medical improvement (MMI)?________ Date? __________
Pre-existing conditions: ____
____

____

____

Prior injuries: ____

____

____

____

Prior ratings: ____

Family doctor: ____

Medical rehabilitation assigned? _______

If so, name/address of specialist: _____________________________

____

____

____

7. **Educational/Vocational Background**

High school diploma?: Yes __________ No __________

Date graduated: __________ High school: ______________________

If not, last grade completed/year attended: ______________________

GED? _________

Driver's license # ____________ Restrictions? __________________

Commercial driver's license? __________________________________

Secondary school: ____

____

____

Technical school/certificate: ____________________________________

____

____

____

Military: ____

Other licenses/certificates: _____________________________________

Prior job experience: ____

____

____

Criminal record? ____

Hobbies: ____

Vocational plans: ____

Vocational rehabilitation/job placement services offered/started? ______

If so, name/address of specialist: _____________________________

____

____

8. Third Party Claim(s)

Third party liability present: Yes __________ No __________
Circumstances: ______________________________
____
____
Potential defendant(s): ______________________
Contact with liability carrier? ______________
Representation by firm? Yes __________ No __________

9. Other Potential Causes of Action:

Discrimination: ______________________________
Retaliatory discharge: _______________________
Common law: __________________________________
Representation by firm? Yes __________ No __________

10. Miscellaneous

Referred by: _________________________________
Other matters handled by firm: _______________
____
____
Other attorneys consulted: ___________________
____
Prior counsel for this claim, if any: ________
____

11. Preliminary Evaluation of Benefits Recoverable

Compensation rate: __________ Wage calculation correct? __________
Mileage/prescriptions: _______________________
Total disability benefits: ___________________
Partial disability benefits: _________________
% Ratings ______________ Body Member(s) ______________
Potential lifetime disability claim: Yes __________ No __________

Form 3.2—Sample Medical Authorization

Authorization to Use or Disclose Health Information

Patient Name: ______________________ Date of Birth: ______________________
Please print full name

1. I authorize the use or disclosure of the above named individual's health information by ______ ______________________ as described below.

2. The type of information to be used or disclosed is as follows (check the appropriate boxes and include other information where needed)

   X Clinic Note
   X Care Line Note
   X Bill for Service
   X Operative/Procedure Report
   X Progress Note
   X Prescription History
   X Laboratory Result
   X Anesthesia/Sedation Record
   X Consultation Note
   X Radiology Report
   X History and Physical Report

X Other: **Any and all medical records, including records in my chart from other providers and correspondence, relating to my care.**

The above information can be released for the period of **ONE YEAR.**

3. I understand that the information in my health record may include information relating to sexually transmitted disease, HIV/AIDS, behavioral or mental health services or alcohol and drug abuse.

4. The information identified may be used or disclosed to the following individuals(s) or organization(s): [**LAW FIRM NAME, ADDRESS, TELEPHONE & FACSIMILE NUMBERS**]

5. The information for which I am authorizing disclosure will be used for the following purpose:
   ___ my personal use ___ sharing with other health care providers
   X other: **pursuing legal remedies/claims**

6. I understand that I have a right to revoke this authorization at any time. I understand that if I revoke this authorization, I must do so in writing and present my written revocation to the medical record department. I understand that the revocation will not apply to information that has already been released in response to this authorization. I understand that the revocation will not apply to my insurance company when the law provides my insurer with the right to contest a claim under my policy.

7. This authorization will expire on ______________________. If I fail to specify an expiration date, this authorization will expire in six months from the date of this authorization.

8. I understand that once the above information is disclosed, it may be redisclosed by the recipient, and the information may not be protected by the federal privacy laws or regulations.

9. I understand the use or disclosure of the information identified above is voluntary. I need not sign this form to ensure access to medical treatment.

______________________ ______________________
Signature of Patient Date

If signed by legal representative, relationship to patient: ______________________

______________________ ______________________
Signature of Witness Date

Form 3.3—Social Security Administration Consent for Release of Information

Form Approved
OMB No. 0960-0566

Social Security Administration
Consent for Release of Information

TO: Social Security Administration/Medicare

Name: __________ Date of Birth ___________ Social Security #:__________

I authorize the Social Security Administration to release information or records about me to:

NAME ADDRESS

I want this information released because:

To establish my Social Security Disability status, date of entitlement to Medicare and the basis for Medicare entitlement (disability or age) for the purposes of my Worker's Compensation claim. (There may be a charge for releasing information)

Please release the following information:

_____ Social Security Number
_____ Identifying information (includes date and place of birth, parents' name)
_____ Monthly Social Security benefit amount
_____ Monthly Supplemental Security Income payment amount
_____ Information about benefits/payments I received at any time
_____ Information about my Medicare claim/coverage at any time
_____ Medical records
_____ Records from my file (specify): Date of Medicare entitlement; Basis for entitlement, and has Medicare paid any medical claims or filed any liens.
_____ Other (specify): Date applied for Disability Benefits; Status of my application; Date SSD benefits started, the amount of the initial benefit paid (excluding subsequent cost of living increases); and has any offset pursuant to 42 U.S.C. §424 been taken.

I am the individual to whom the information/records applies or that person's parent (if a minor) or legal guardian. I know that if I make any representation which I know is false to obtain information from Social Security records, I could be punished by a find or imprisonment or both.

Signature: ____
(Show signatures, name, and addresses of two people if signed by mark.)

Date: ______________________ Relationship: _________________________

Form 3.4—Sample Fee Agreement

Workers' Compensation Fee Agreement

I, [**insert name of client**], hereby employ and retain the law firm of [**insert law firm name**] [**Example: Smith Jones Wallace**] (hereinafter "SJW") to represent me in obtaining workers' compensation benefits for the injuries I received or the occupational disease I developed during the course of my employment with [**insert employer's name**], on or about [**insert date of injury or onset of occupational disease**].

I understand and agree that SJW will charge a fee of [**insert percentage of fee**] of the total amount recovered pursuant to the [**insert name of state worker's compensation act**] [**Example: North Carolina Workers' Compensation Act**], and that this percentage will apply whether the case is settled, whether a hearing is held before the [**insert name of relevant state agency**], whether further appeals are required or whether the employer is entitled to set-offs for payments made under a sickness/accident or other disability plan. In addition, I understand that SJW may file a motion for reasonable attorney fees after six or more months of active representation. The actual amount of the fee must be approved by the [**insert name of relevant state agency**].

I understand that, whether or not a recovery is made, I am responsible for all actual out-of-pocket expenses incurred by SJW in the resolution of this matter, including, but not limited to, long distance telephone calls, travel expenses, depositions and charges incurred to obtain medical records or conferences with medical personnel.

I agree that interest shall be charged at a rate of [**insert percentage interest rate**] per annum for all fees and costs not paid by the last day of the month in which the billing statement was mailed.

I understand that SJW reserves the right to withdraw as my counsel if in their opinion this claim does not have a reasonable chance of success. I understand that I am retaining SJW and any lawyer or legal assistant associated with SJW may handle all or any portion of my case.

I acknowledge that, at my election, any dispute between me and SJW concerning the fees described in the Agreement may be submitted to the Fee Dispute Resolution Program of the [**insert relevant state bar organization**].

This fee agreement is subject to the approval of [**insert name of relevant state agency**].

I understand and agree to what is written above, this the _____ day of _____, 20__.

____

[Name of Client]

Employment Accepted
On the Terms Stated.

By: ______________________________
[Attorney's Name]

Form 3.5—Sample Client Guidelines

WORKERS' COMPENSATION GUIDELINES
for
CLIENTS of [insert law firm's name]

1. <u>Medical Treatment</u>: Please keep your medical appointments, including physical therapy and diagnostic tests, as scheduled. If you cannot keep an appointment for a good reason, call the doctor's office **in advance** and reschedule your appointment. However, you should make every effort to attend medical appointments as scheduled, or the insurance company may accuse you of failure to cooperate in your medical rehabilitation.

   Please keep us informed of all medical treatment. After you see a doctor, please give us a call to update us and to let us know your next doctor's appointment.

   Do not make appointments with doctors not authorized by the insurance company, unless you have gotten approval from our office. If you do see a doctor without prior approval from the insurance company, you risk being responsible for payment of the medical expenses you incur for this treatment.

   If you receive bills for your work-related medical treatment, please forward these to our office immediately.

2. <u>Disability Payments</u>: **Keep your check stubs in a safe place.** Mark on each check stub the date you received the check. If your checks do not have stubs, then you need to 1) photocopy your checks before cashing them, **or** 2) keep a written log of the check number, the period it covered, and the date you received it. **Please have this information readily available when you call our office about late disability payments so that we will know the date you were last paid.**

   Disability payments are not past due unless they are not received within [insert number of days specified by relevant state statute or rule regarding late disability payments] days of the due date. Disability payments are **not paid in advance** of the period due. Most insurance companies process and mail checks at the end of the week the benefits are due. You may not get your check on the same day each week, especially if your check is mailed from a processing center in another state. However, if your check is more than a few days past due, please call our office and we will check on it for you.

3. <u>Surveillance</u>: **It is common for insurance companies to hire private investigators to observe injured workers periodically.** Please be aware that you may be under surveillance at any time. Normally, if you are not doing anything you are not supposed to be doing, the surveillance is only for a short period. The insurance company may use private investigators to attempt to seek evidence that you are not as limited in your activities as you have indicated to your doctors, or that you are receiving temporary total disability benefits at the same time you are earning wages

   If you have told your doctor you cannot perform certain activities, such as yard work, sports, shopping, housework, lifting children, etc., then do **NOT**, under any circumstances, perform these activities. If your doctor has written you out of work, then do **NOT** work "on the side" or "under the table." If the insurance company obtains evidence that you are not as limited in your activities as you have indicated to your doctors, or that you are receiving temporary total disability benefits at the same time you are earning wages, this could have an adverse impact on workers' compensation benefits to which you may be entitled, including immediate termination of benefits you are receiving. The insurance company may accuse you of insurance fraud. Proof of insurance fraud can result in criminal prosecution.
4. <u>Rehabilitation Consultants</u>: The insurance company may hire a rehabilitation consultant, such as a medical case manager or nurse to manage your medical care or a vocational specialist to help you return to work. Please be aware that these consultants' main goal is to help you BUT they have been hired by the insurance company. They write regular reports about their contacts with you. **Please do not discuss anything with them which you do not wish to appear in a report to the insurance company**.

   While it is important for you to cooperate and comply with the reasonable requests of these consultants, you need to address any questions or concerns regarding your contact with them to our office. If you have questions regarding your workers' compensation benefits or rights, you need to discuss this with us and **not** the rehabilitation consultant. If the rehabilitation consultant attempts to discuss these matters with you, please let us know immediately.

   If you are contacted by a rehabilitation consultant who has not previously obtained permission to work with you from our office, please have this individual call our office immediately. Generally, a new consultant will be advised by the insurance company that you have an attorney and will call our office to obtain permission to work with you. We usually schedule the first meeting between you and the consultant in our office.

5. Remember:
   A. **Do not call the insurance company directly, even about late checks.** Call our office if you have problems or questions. You can hurt your case if you talk to the insurance company directly. If the insurance company should send you correspondence or forms directly, do NOT sign them but bring them to our office immediately.
   B. **Notify our office immediately of any changes in your address or telephone number.** Otherwise, we may not be able to reach you when necessary.
   C. **Notify our office immediately of any changes in your medical condition or work status.**
   D. Damages for pain and suffering are **NOT** included in your claim for workers' compensation benefits. We will generally not discuss final settlement of your case until two things have happened: your doctor has released you from ongoing medical care AND you have returned to work (or your doctors have agreed you cannot work).

Form 3.6—Sample Client Representation Letter

[Insert client's name and address]

Re: [Insert case caption and date of injury]

Dear [insert client's name]:

This letter will confirm that you have retained this firm to represent you in your claim for workers' compensation benefits arising out of the above-referenced injury. We are enclosing copies of correspondence we are sending to the employer, your doctors, and the [insert state agency]. You will be copied with all correspondence from our office.

We are also enclosing a copy of our guidelines for our workers' compensation clients. Please read the enclosed guidelines carefully and then put them in a safe place for future reference.

It is very important that you notify us immediately of any changes in your address or telephone number. You should also keep us updated regarding your medical progress and your work status.

We are looking forward to working with you on this important matter. Please feel free to call us with any questions or concerns you may have.

With kind regards, I am

[Signature line]

Enclosures as stated

Form 3.7—Sample Carrier/Administrator Representation Letter

[Address of Carrier/Administrator, Employer or its Counsel]

Re: Client:
Employer:
Date of Injury:
State agency File Number and/or Carrier/Administrator Claim Number:

To Whom It May Concern:

This firm has been retained to represent the injured worker in the above-referenced case. Please direct all future inquiries or correspondence directly to this office. I am enclosing a copy of [the injured worker's notice of injury or claim] for your review and records.

Pursuant to [insert relevant state statute or state agency rules] I request that you or your representative provide us with the following information within [insert time period] of your receipt of this letter:

1. a copy of all approved compensation agreements;
2. a copy of any statement made by the employee;
3. a completed wage verification form;
4. a complete copy of the following which are presently in your possession or which subsequently come into your possession:
   - (a) all medical records,
   - (b) all vocational rehabilitation reports,
   - (c) all medical rehabilitation reports,
   - (d) all nursing rehabilitation reports,
   - (e) all employment records
5. if liability is denied, a detailed statement of the basis of denial; and
6. a print-out of all medical and indemnity benefits paid to date.

If you have any questions, please do not hesitate to contact me.

[Signature Line]

cc: Client
State agency

Form 3.8—Sample State Agency Representation Letter

[State agency address]

Re: Claimant:
Employer:
Date of Injury:
State agency File Number [if known]:

To Whom It May Concern:

This firm has been retained to represent the claimant in the above-referenced matter. I am enclosing the original and one copy of the [written notice of injury or claim and/or attorney form], along with a copy of my retainer agreement.

Please provide this office with a complete copy of the [state agency's] file for this claim, including specifically all forms, pleadings, and compensation agreements.

Thank you for your prompt attention to this matter.

[Signature Line]

cc: Client
Carrier/Administrator or its Counsel

CHAPTER 4

Filing Claims, Requests for Relief, and Responses

Paralegal Practice Tips

Paralegals in workers' compensation practices should know the relevant state agency's rules, procedures and accepted formats for filing claims, responses to claims and other requests for relief and responses, such as motions, letters and applications. In order to learn, as well as stay up-to-date, regarding the rules, procedures, deadlines and forms, a well-qualified paralegal should:

- Know the state statutes and state agency rules regarding proper filing of claims and responses to claims, as well as filing and responding to requests for relief.
- Have immediate access to the state statutes, their annotations and state agency rules via hard copy, software and/or Internet.
- Have immediate access to a set of current state agency claim forms via hard copy, software and/or Internet.
- Obtain and review the entire claim file from the state agency.
- Prepare an index of the state agency claim file.
- Review medical, employment and other documents to verify dates and causes of injury.
- Verify key deadlines to accept, deny and file claims with the supervising attorney.
- Use a reliable calendaring system to enter or "tickle" key deadlines to accept, deny and file claims, as well as file or respond to requests for relief.
- Obtain verification from the state agency that claim forms, requests for relief and responses have been properly filed.
- Send a copy of all claim forms, requests for relief and responses to the opposing party, or the opposing party's attorney, simultaneously with submission to the state agency.

- Use or help the firm create forms for standard pleadings that paralegals can use to draft requests for relief and responses for the attorney's review.

* * *

Properly filing the injured worker's claim for benefits with the correct workers' compensation state agency, before the statute of limitations expires, is crucial. Knowledgeable paralegals may have a great deal of responsibility for drafting the claim forms and entering or "tickling" the reminder dates in the firm's calendaring system for the supervising attorney's review. Failing to file a claim before the statute of limitations expires or filing the claim with the wrong state agency can have serious repercussions for the injured worker and the firm. The injured worker may lose the right to receive medical and indemnity benefits, and the firm will be exposed to a potential legal malpractice lawsuit.

Equally important **is timely filing a response to a claim**, including the employer's defenses, if any. Failure to properly file the correct responsive pleading to a claim for workers' compensation benefits may cost the self-insured employer or the insurance carrier the opportunity to deny compensation or raise all possible defenses. The client may lose its right to contest the claim and the defense firm will be exposed to allegations of malpractice.

Most injured workers hire an attorney because there are issues in dispute between the parties. Disputed issues may include (but are not limited to):

- The carrier/administrator has denied the claim and is refusing to pay medical and indemnity benefits.
- The carrier/administrator is paying indemnity benefits, but the injured worker believes the amount is incorrect (or too low).
- The carrier/administrator has accepted the claim, but will not pay for medical treatment recommended by the treating physician, such as imaging scans, surgery, medications or durable medical equipment.
- The carrier/administrator was paying indemnity benefits but has asked the state agency to stop payment of benefits.
- The injured worker wants to see a different medical provider than the one authorized and paid for by the carrier/administrator.
- The parties disagree regarding the injured worker's ability to earn wages or the extent of the physical restrictions.

The carrier/administrator will generally turn the claim over to its defense counsel when disputes arise between the parties, including:

- The injured worker has requested a hearing in response to the carrier/administrator's denial of the claim.

- The injured worker has filed a motion or request for hearing to request authorization of medical treatment denied by the carrier/administrator.
- The carrier/administrator wants the state agency to order the injured worker to comply with medical and/or vocational rehabilitation services.
- The carrier/administrator believes the injured worker can return to work.
- The carrier/administrator wants to change physicians, or have the injured worker undergo an independent medical examination or another surgical opinion.

Paralegals may be responsible for drafting pleadings or legal documents requesting appropriate relief, or responding to the opposing party's requests for relief. They need to know the state agency's rules, procedures and accepted formats for requesting relief and filing responses.

4.1 Calculating Time Limits to File Claims or Respond to Notice of Claims

To accurately calculate the deadline for filing state workers' compensation claims and responses to claims, plaintiffs' and defense firms must consider the following information[1]:

1) **Jurisdiction**: What agency has the legal authority to oversee the injured worker's claim, or in what state should the claim be filed? The obvious answer may seem to be the state where the injured worker was hurt, but this may not always be the best, or even the correct, jurisdiction. The injured worker may have more than one choice of state jurisdiction and should choose the state with the most favorable workers' compensation benefits. For example, the worker may have the option of filing in the state where the employer is headquartered, the state where the worker was principally employed, or the state where the employment contract was finalized. The supervising attorney will make the final decision regarding in which state to file the

1. There are also federal workers' compensation programs. The Federal Employees' Compensation Act (FECA) covers federal employees. The Longshore and Harbor Workers' Compensation Program covers employees engaged in maritime occupations. The Federal Employees Liability Act covers railroad workers employed by an interstate railroad. The Energy Employees Occupational Illness Compensation Program (EEOICP) covers Department of Emergency nuclear weapons employees. The Black Lung Benefit Act covers employees that have worked in or around a coal mine or coal preparation facility.

claim, based on information gathered during the firm's initial investigation. The attorney will need to know:

- The county and state where the injury or illness occurred;
- The city and state where the employer's principal place of business is located;
- If the company has multiple locations, the state where the injured worker performed most of his or her work; and
- The state in which the employment contract was completed.

2) **Contesting Jurisdiction:** Defense paralegals need to be familiar with the same jurisdictional requirements. The employer or carrier may be able to move the claim from the state where it was initially filed to another state. The reason for moving the claim may be that the preferred state allows the defense better control over medical expenses, or has less generous benefits for certain types of disabling injuries. Additionally, the employer's cost of litigation may be less expensive in certain states.

3) **Type of Workers' Compensation Claim:** Is the injured worker filing an injury by accident claim, an occupational disease claim or a death claim, or even a combination of different types of claims? The date on which the statute of limitations (deadline to file a claim) starts running will depend on the type of claim. For injury by accident claims, the statute usually starts running on the date of the injury. For example, if the statute of limitations to file an injury by accident claim is two years, then the time to file a claim will expire on the two-year anniversary of the date of the accident.

   Generally, the deadline for occupational disease claims does not start running on the date the injured worker likely contracted the illness. The worker may not find out that he or she even has an occupational disease until months or even years have passed. The deadline usually starts running from the date a medical doctor tells a worker he or she has sustained an occupational disease due to the employment, or from the date the worker became disabled from earning wages due to the occupational disease. Again, the supervising attorney will decide the kind of claim that needs to be filed, based on the detailed information gathered during the firm's initial investigation.

4) **Applicable Statute or Rule to Calculate the Statute of Limitations:** Once the plaintiff's firm has made a decision regarding the type of claim being filed and the proper state in which to file it, the applicable state law regarding the statute of limitations or filing deadline can be applied. Although the supervising attorney is ultimately responsi-

ble for calculating statutes of limitations or filing deadlines, paralegals should also know statutes of limitations for the states in which the firm litigates workers' compensation cases. Paralegals need to know where the law dictating the statute of limitations is located, whether in the state statutes and/or state agency rules. If a paralegal is responsible for entering or "tickling" reminders of statutes of limitations or filing deadlines, the paralegal should always verify the dates with the supervising attorney. If the firm fails to properly file its client's claim before the statute of limitations expires, that could be a basis for a claim of legal malpractice against the firm.

Defense paralegals should also know the relevant filing deadlines and statutes of limitations for filing injury by accident claims and occupational disease claims. They should also know if there are time limits for raising a defense to a claim on the grounds that it was not timely or properly filed.

4.1(1) Using Information Provided by Client or Client Representatives

Generally, the client can provide accurate information regarding the date of an accidental injury, as well as where the accident occurred. If the client is the employer and received notice of the accident from the injured worker, the employer can usually provide information from its file. If the employer alleges it did not receive notice of the accident, then its representative may not be able to provide much information to the defense firm.

If the firm's client is the injured worker and a reliable historian, then the client may be able to provide accurate information about the injury. However, sometimes the client may not be able to provide the specific date. The injury may have happened several months or several years ago, or the client may be a poor historian, incompetent, incapacitated or deceased. If the client cannot provide this information during an intake interview, this information may be obtainable from a family member, a legal representative who has power of attorney, a legal guardian or an executor appointed by the court to administer the deceased's estate, as well as from a review of employment records, medical records, accident reports and other documents.

Pinpointing the onset of an occupational disease may not be as straightforward as identifying the date of an accident. The employer may have very little information regarding the alleged occupational disease, especially if the worker did not know about the occupational disease until shortly before filing a claim for workers' compensation benefits. In most cases, the injured worker does not know he or she has an occupational disease until a doctor says that the illness is related to the employment or job duties. The injured worker may not remember the exact date the doctor first discussed a diagnosis of an occupational disease. The worker may have suffered the symptoms for a long time without getting a proper diagnosis or have seen a number of medical providers seeking relief from the symptoms. Depending on the state's laws, the statute of limitations for filing an occupational disease claim may start running from the date the injured worker was told by a medical doctor that the illness is related to the job, or the date the worker was disabled from earning wages due to the alleged occupational disease, or a combination of both factors. The injured worker's medical records will be the key source to verify the date the worker was advised that he or she had an occupational disease, the date he or she became disabled due to the occupational disease, and/or other dates relevant to when the statute of limitations started running.

4.1(2) Review of Medical, Personnel and Other Documents to Verify Dates

Plaintiffs' and defense paralegals should **verify the date, location and kind of injury or occupational disease from other sources**, including medical and employment records. Sometimes clients or their representatives unintentionally (or in rare cases, intentionally) provide incorrect information, including dates or locations of injuries. In cases where the carrier/administrator has received notice of the claim and has filed required state agency forms, reviewing a copy of the state agency file is one way to verify the date, location and type of injury.

Organizing the documents in the state agency file in chronological order and **preparing an index of the state agency documents** can facilitate the file review (as well as help locate the documents quickly). *See Form 4.1, Sample Index of State Agency File.* Obtaining and reviewing the injured worker's employment and personnel records is another good way to verify this information. Finally, **carefully review all available medical records to corroborate the date and type of injury**. A thorough review of key documents prior to filing the claim can prevent the plaintiff's firm from filing inaccurate notices of claims that are not supported by the worker's actual medical or other records. In cases where the deadline to file is pending, there may not be time to collect and review medical records before filing the claim. In most cases, an amended notice of the claim can be filed if necessary.

4.1(3) Attorney Confirmation of Time Limits and Deadlines

While paralegals can gather the information required to calculate filing deadlines and then calculate the deadlines using the applicable state's statutes and/or state agency rules, **the final deadline should always be verified by the supervising attorney.** There may be case facts or exceptions to the standard rules that affect the calculation of the deadline, lengthening or shortening the period of time in which the claim has to be filed. The attorney should review the case reminders or "ticklers" in every case for accuracy.

4.2 Properly Filing Claims or Responses to Notice of Claims

Paralegals may be responsible for drafting written notices of claims, or written responses to a notice of claim. The initial written notice to the state agency and the employer that the injured worker has sustained injuries related to work and is claiming workers' compensation benefits is a key document, similar to filing a complaint in civil court. If the initial claim is not timely or properly filed, the injured worker could lose the only source of medical insurance for the injuries and/or only source of income if unable to work due to the injuries. In addition, the employer or its representatives' failure to file a required written response to the injured worker's notice of claim could have serious repercussions, including losing to right to deny the claim and/or assert defenses to the claim. Paralegals need to know these key deadlines, as well as the required format for the state agency where the claim is filed.

4.2(1) Required and/or Accepted Format or Forms

It is important to know the filing procedure for the applicable state agency. **Verify the proper method for filing claims** by reviewing the statutes, rules and other information provided by the state agency. This information may be available on the state agency's website. Successful workers' compensation practitioners, including paralegals, must stay up-to-date on any changes in deadlines or required format. The state agency generally publishes information regarding any changes well in advance of the effective date of the changes. Read all information published by the state agency to avoid missing crucial news or updates. Subscribing to statewide listservs and/or publications for workers' compensation practitioners is another good way to keep up with any state agency changes.

Determine if the state agency accepts notices of claims via E-mail and/or facsimile. Some state agencies prefer E-mail submissions and have published the requirements for filing claim paperwork via E-mail. Whether the state agency accepts E-mail submissions is particularly important when a document has to be filed immediately.

4.2(2) Acknowledgment by State Agency, Employer and its Representatives

Always verify the state agency's receipt of the required claim form or notice (and any other key documents). This is particularly important in cases where the deadline to file the claim is about to expire. Many firms document receipt of the claim notice by having the state agency return an extra copy of the claim form with the agency's filing stamp on it. However, if the firm discovers that the claim form was never received or filed by the state agency, this information does not change or extend the filing deadline. **The time is still running if the state agency did not receive the claim form or notice.** In cases involving very short or immediately pending deadlines, verify receipt of the claim form *before* the statute of limitations expires, in case another claim form needs to be sent prior to the deadline. There might not be time to resubmit the claim form if it is lost in the mail or misplaced at the agency. Know whether the state agency accepts claim forms via other methods, such as E-mail or facsimile. This can be very helpful if the claim needs to be filed immediately. If time is running out and no acknowledgment of the claim notice has been received by mail, E-mail or facsimile, call the claims section of the state agency and verify receipt. Verification can also be obtained by mailing the claim form certified mail, return receipt requested, tracking with an overnight carrier, or receiving fax transmission confirmation sheets.

The firm should also obtain confirmation that the other parties to the claim, such as the employer or its representatives, received a copy of all required claim forms pursuant to state laws and state agency rules. If the employer is represented by an attorney, then a copy of all documents filed with the state agency should be sent to the defense attorney of record.

4.3 Accepted Claims

Accepted claims are usually easier to manage than denied cases. Generally, if the carrier/administrator is paying medical and indemnity benefits, the case has been accepted. However, it is crucial to **verify that the case has been ac-**

cepted in the manner required by state law and state agency rules, particularly regarding filing of specified forms. Failure to file required compensation forms could cause problems for the injured worker later, if the carrier/administrator suddenly stops payment of benefits or tries to reverse its decision to accept liability. Similarly, failure to properly file a denial of a claim may prevent the employer from denying the claim at a later date. The firm should request and carefully review a copy of the entire claim file to date from the state agency.

4.3(1) Filing Proper Acceptance Forms with State Agency

A case can be informally accepted without all of the paperwork required by the state agency being filed. Sometimes carrier/administrators pay medical or indemnity benefits without filing required paperwork. Often the failure to file required acceptance forms is not deliberate, but simply an oversight on the part of the carrier/administrator. Even if the injured worker is receiving benefits, a written claim notice should still be filed, as well as forms or compensation agreements documenting that the carrier/administrator has accepted the claim and has agreed to pay benefits for specified periods.

The plaintiff's firm should quickly obtain a copy of the entire claim file to date from the state agency. The supervising attorney and the paralegal should review it carefully to see if additional forms need to be filed. The supervising attorney will make the final decision regarding which forms, if any, need to be filed. This could include filing a written claim notice on behalf of the injured worker, or contacting the carrier/administrator to request that a form agreement for payment of benefits be filed. The paralegal should enter or "tickle" reminders on the firm's calendar to follow up on outstanding requests for form agreements. In some cases, the firm may need to file a motion and/or request a hearing with the state agency if the carrier/administrator fails to file required documents accepting the claim.

4.3(2) Determining Time Limits to Accept or Deny Claims

The applicable state's workers' compensation statutes and/or state agency rules may state that the employer or its representatives have a specific deadline to investigate a claim, reach a decision whether to accept or deny the claim, and then file the required forms accepting or denying the claim. These deadlines are intended to prevent carrier/administrators from taking an indefinite period of time to decide whether to pay medical or indemnity benefits. The injured worker may be without an income and/or unable to obtain medical treatment while the carrier/administrator investigates the claim.

Paralegals should know the carrier/administrator's deadlines to file acceptance or compensation forms. If the case has not been formally accepted at the time the injured worker hires the firm, the paralegal should enter or "tickle" reminders on the firm's calendar to review the file and follow up with the carrier/administrator regarding the required forms. In some states, if the employer or its carrier/administrator take no action within a specified period of receiving notice of the claim, the case is then deemed accepted by the state agency, and the employer waives its right to contest liability and/or deny the claim at a later date. However, sometimes deadlines are missed by oversights on either party's side, and this issue may be litigated if the employer denies liability after the deadline to deny the case expires.

4.4 Denied or Contested Claims

Denied claims, or even accepted claims with contested issues such as authorization and payment of recommended medical treatment, are more difficult to handle than accepted claims. In denied claims, injured workers usually contact a plaintiffs' attorney because they are not receiving medical treatment and/or weekly disability checks. Injured workers may be experiencing extreme financial hardship or need medical treatment they cannot afford. There is usually a degree of urgency with denied claims. Quickly determining the basis of denial and then deciding on the firm's plan of action to pursue the claim or raise defenses is crucial.

4.4(1) Denial Letters or Forms

Paralegals for both plaintiffs' and defense firms should be very familiar with the relevant state's statutes and state agency rules for denying workers' compensation claims. There is generally a specified time period for the carrier/administrator to investigate the claim, reach a decision, and if that decision is not to accept the claim and pay benefits, then file a written notice of denial with the state agency, with a copy to the injured worker. If a carrier/administrator decides it is not liable for the work injury or illness, a denial letter may be sent to the injured worker. However, the letter may not clearly state the basis for denial. The state agency may require the carrier/administrator to file a specific denial form and/or detailed statement of the basis of denial.

4.4(2) Deadlines to Appeal Denied Claims and/or Request Hearings

Paralegals for plaintiffs' firms should know if the state law or state agency rules limit the amount of time the injured worker has to appeal a denied claim and/or request a hearing before the state agency. Even if there is not a specified deadline to appeal a denied claim and/or request a hearing, the firm should still adopt a plan of action to pursue the injured worker's claim as quickly as possible. Most state agencies have a backlog of cases and it may take as long as a year to get a hearing date. During this period, the injured worker may have no income or means of obtaining medical care.

4.5 Requests for Relief and Responses

An accepted claim does not always mean that the parties are also in agreement regarding payment of various kinds of benefits, including payment of medical expenses and weekly disability checks. Many parties choose to request hearings when there are complex issues regarding liability and causation of the injured worker's medical condition. However, when the claim has been accepted and benefits are being paid, disputed issues may still arise which need more immediate attention, without having to request a hearing and wait for the case to appear on a hearing calendar. State agencies may have administrative procedures in place which allow them to review requests for relief without a formal hearing. The requests for relief may be submitted via motion, letter and/or state agency form, and the state agency can review the documents submitted by the parties and render administrative decisions or orders quickly. If the parties disagree with the state agency's administrative decision or order, they may have the option of appealing and/or requesting a hearing to resolve the dispute.

4.5(1) Types of Relief Requested

Injured workers usually hire attorneys because they need help to obtain the benefits to which they are entitled under the state's workers' compensation act. They may need help requesting some form of relief, including (but not limited to):

- Obtaining or reinstating indemnity (weekly disability) benefits.
- Correcting the amount of the average wage being used to calculate their indemnity benefits.

- Obtaining medical benefits, including care recommended by treating doctors.
- Obtaining assistance with a vocational plan, such as payment of tuition for enrollment in a local community college for retraining.
- Obtaining reimbursement for out-of-pocket expenses allowed by law.
- Removal of a rehabilitation consultant who is violating the state agency rules or providing inadequate services.

Types of relief frequently requested by carrier/administrators, usually through their defense attorneys, include (but are not limited to):

- Suspension or termination of the injured worker's indemnity benefits.
- Compliance with recommended medical treatment (even if the injured worker does not wish to undergo the treatment).
- Compliance with vocational rehabilitation services, such as engaging in a job search.
- Changing the treating physician.
- Obtaining additional medical treatment, such as an independent medical exam or second (or even third) surgical opinion.

4.5(2) Format for Requests for Relief or Responses

All state agencies have their own rules, procedures, deadlines and accepted formats for filing and responding to requests for relief. Well-qualified paralegals know the rules and requirements for the applicable state agencies, as well as how to prepare and/or respond to basic requests for relief, whether as a motion, letter and on a state agency form. Regardless of the state agency or format, standard pleadings[2] requesting relief, as well as responses, contain the following information:

- The case caption.
- The state laws and/or state agency rules which pertain to the relief requested.
- A short summary of the employment relationship, and how the alleged injury or occupational disease occurred.
- Whether the claim has been accepted or denied.
- A clear, chronological recitation of the facts which justify or support the relief requested, or the reasons the other party's request should be denied.

---

2. Legal documents requesting action or relief, or defending the case

- Supporting exhibits for the request or response.
- A plea that the state agency will grant the requested relief, or deny the other party's requested relief.
- The date and attorney signature and contact information.
- A certificate of service that the request for relief, or the response, has been served on all parties.

If the state agency only accepts requests for relief and responses on agency forms, then the parties should submit the request for relief or response on the required form. However, if the state agency does not have specified forms and accepts requests for relief and responses in other formats, such as motions or correspondence, a knowledgeable paralegal who is familiar with the case and has good writing skills can prepare draft pleadings for the attorney's review. If the firm has forms for standard requests for relief and responses, a paralegal should use them as a basis for drafting these documents. If the firm does not have forms for standard pleadings, a paralegal should help the firm create them, especially for the kinds of relief frequently sought, such as state agency approval of medical treatment. The state agency may also require the parties to submit a proposed order with any requests or responses to requests for relief. *See Form 4.1, Sample Request for Approval of Medical Treatment.*

4.5(3) Exhibits to Requests for Relief and Responses

Paralegals can assemble proposed exhibits for a draft request for relief or response as the document is being drafted. The exhibits should support any facts stated in the request for relief or response, and assist the state agency in its review of the pleadings to make its decision. Exhibits to requests for relief or responses may include (but are not limited to):

- Medical records
- Correspondence between the parties
- State agency paperwork or pleadings filed to date
- Rehabilitation reports
- Opinion letters from doctors or other experts
- Wage verification documents such as paycheck stubs and IRS wage reporting forms
- Educational materials, such as program descriptions, degree requirements and fee schedules

4.5(4) Deadlines to Respond to Requests for Relief

Upon receipt of a request for relief, the opposing party may have a specified period per state agency rules, such as 10 or 30 days, to file a response. The state agency will not make a decision until the time has passed for the parties to respond to each other's pleadings. Filing a timely response is crucial to protect the client's rights and defenses. In particular, a successful motion to suspend or terminate an injured worker's weekly disability benefits could have serious financial repercussions for the injured worker, and could save the carrier/administrator substantial money if benefits should be terminated.

Paralegals should know the deadlines for filing responses to requests for relief and make sure they are entered as reminders or "ticklers" in the firm's calendaring system. The state agency may also require the parties to submit a **proposed order** with any requests or responses to requests for relief. A knowledgeable paralegal can draft a response and proposed order for the attorney's review.

Form 4.1—Sample Index of State Agency File

[Insert State Agency Caption]

Pleadings Index

Tab	Description	Date Filed/Served
1	**Form** [insert state agency form number] Employer's **Report** of Injury	11/16/04
2	**Form** [insert state agency form number] **Notice** of Accident to Employer By Employee, State Agency **Acknowledgment**	06/01/05 06/29/05
3	Plaintiff's *Pro Se* **Letter** Requesting a New Doctor	04/22/05
4	Plaintiff's 2nd *Pro Se* **Letter** Requesting a New Doctor	08/09/05
5	Medical Motion **Notice** from State Agency to Carrier	08/10/05
6	Carrier **Response** to Plaintiff's Request for New Doctor	08/22/05
7	[Insert firm initials] **Letter** of Rep to State Agency, State Agency **Acknowledgment** of Rep Ltr and **Copy of Claim File**	08/31/05 09/14/05
8	Initial **Letter** of Rep for Defendants' Counsel	11/21/05
9	Plaintiff's **Motion** for Approval of Medical Treatment	11/28/05
10	Defs' **Response** to Pltf's Motion for Approval of Medical Treatment	12/06/05
11	**Order** (designating Dr. Hart as treating physician)	01/24/06
12	**Form** [insert state agency form number] Employer's Admission of Employee's Right to Compensation	05/25/06
13	**Form** [insert state agency form number] Return to Work Report (effective 9/14/2006)	09/14/06
14	**Form** [insert state agency form number] Statement of Days Worked & Earnings of Injured Employee	11/15/06
15	**Form** [insert state agency number] Agreement for Compensation for Disability State Agency Approval	12/12/06 01/26/07

Form 4.2—Sample Motion for Approval of Medical Treatment

[Insert Case Caption]

MOTION FOR APPROVAL OF MEDICAL TREATMENT

Plaintiff, pursuant to [insert applicable state law and/or state agency rules], moves the [insert name of state agency] for an Order approving plaintiff's request to change her treating physician to Dr. Robert Hart and ordering defendants to pay for treatment recommended by Dr. Hart. In support of this motion, plaintiff respectfully shows the [insert name of state agency] the following:

FACTS

1. On September 1, 2005, the plaintiff Sally Carter (hereinafter "Ms. Carter") was employed as a machine operator at Big Corporation in Raleigh, North Carolina, earning approximately $1,000.00 per week (subject to wage verification). On September 1, 2005, she sustained a compensable injury when her shoulder was struck by a steel bar while she was cleaning a cylinder. As of the date of this motion, Ms. Carter has not been temporarily totally disabled for more than seven calendar days due to the compensable injury. Defendants accepted this claim on a [insert state agency form agreement] dated October 1, 2005.
2. Ms. Carter was initially seen on September 1, 2005 by Big Corporation's plant nurse, who gave her over-the-counter Aleve. She was subsequently seen by Big Corporation's company doctor, Dr. Allen Mason, on September 2, 2005, and diagnosed as having sustained a shoulder sprain. Dr. Mason prescribed an anti-inflammatory medication and moist heat. Dr. Mason continued to follow Ms. Carter and offer conservative treatment through January 1, 2006. Ms. Carter did not feel that Dr. Mason's treatment provided relief, effected a cure or lessened her disability. *See attached Exhibit A, Medical Records of Dr. Mason.*
3. Dr. Mason scheduled an evaluation with Dr. John Beck of City Orthopaedics. Ms. Carter was initially seen by Dr. Beck on January 13, 2006. Dr. Beck diagnosed her as having "right shoulder impingement syndrome following work related injury". He continued to follow Ms. Carter and offered conservative treatment including a cortisone injection, physical therapy and prescription medication through February 15, 2006. In his last office note dated February 15, 2006, Dr. Beck noted that Ms. Carter's symptoms had not responded to conservative treatment. He did not recommend additional treatment but suggested that Ms. Carter rest her shoulder and follow up with him in six weeks, "hopefully for a rating and release."

At this point, Ms. Carter was very concerned that it appeared nothing further was being offered by Dr. Beck to relieve her pain, effect a cure or lessen her disability. *See attached Exhibit B, Medical Records of Dr. Beck.*

4. Dr. Beck's office scheduled a return appointment for March 24, 2006, but his office called Ms. Carter and cancelled the appointment, stating that Dr. Beck was out of the office until April 2006. His office offered to reschedule the appointment with another doctor, or with Dr. Beck when he returned in April. Ms. Carter was still suffering from shoulder pain, to the point that it interfered with her sleep at night. She was not satisfied with the treatment that Dr. Beck had offered to that point. On April 22, 2006, she wrote the [insert state agency name], *pro se*, and requested an evaluation by a different physician. *See attached Exhibit C, Correspondence of Ms. Carter.* On June 15, 2006, the [insert state agency name] filed an Order, allowing Ms. Carter to have a "one-time evaluation" with the physician of her choice. *See attached Exhibit D, Order of [insert state agency name].*

5. While waiting for a response from the [insert state agency name] regarding her request to see a different physician, Ms. Carter sought relief of her ongoing shoulder pain on her own. She was evaluated by Dr. Robert Hart at Hart Orthopedic Specialists on May 24, 2006. Dr. Hart diagnosed her as having "post traumatic AC synovitis and early DJD" and "mild impingement syndrome". He performed a subacromial injection. He indicated that if her symptoms did not improve following the injection that he would recommend a subacromial decompression and distal clavicle excision. *See attached Exhibit E, Medical Records of Dr. Hart.*

6. Per the [insert state agency name]'s June 15, 2006 Order, Ms. Carter asked to be seen again by Dr. Hart. On August 1, 2006, Dr. Hart examined Ms. Carter's right shoulder again. He diagnosed her as having "persistent post traumatic impingement going back to injury September 2005". Dr. Hart noted his concern regarding her continuing pain and inability to sleep due to pain. He requested an updated shoulder MRI and recommended "exam under anesthesia, arthroscopy, subacromial decompression and distal clavicle excision." Dr. Hart saw Ms. Carter again on October 17, 2006 and stated "exhaustive conservative treatment has not improved things. Follow-up MRI showed continued irritation but fortunately not a progression to a full thickness rotator cuff tear. It is my recommendation based on these findings and after discussion with the patient that we should proceed with operative intervention including subacromial decompression and distal clavicle excision." The defendants authorized and paid for these two office visits and the updated MRI. *See attached Exhibit E, Medical Records of Dr. Hart.*

7. After receiving Dr. Hart's October 17, 2006 office note, Ms. Carter, through counsel, requested that defendants authorize Dr. Hart to perform the surgery. The adjuster stated that Dr. Hart was not in the carrier's network but that she would call his office to see what his charges for the surgery are. *See attached Exhibit F, Facsimile to adjuster.* On November 16, 2006, defendants, through counsel, stated that the defendants will not approve Dr. Hart to perform the surgical procedure he recommended, but will approve any physician at City Orthopaedics to perform the procedure. *See attached Exhibit G, Correspondence from adjuster.*
8. Ms. Carter desires to have the surgery performed by a doctor she trusts. Ms. Carter completely trusts Dr. Hart, because she believes he has fully addressed her ongoing shoulder symptoms and has recommended the surgical procedure. She feels that Dr. Beck at City Orthopaedics dismissed her shoulder pain and has nothing to offer her. She is not comfortable undergoing surgery with Dr. Beck or his partners at City Orthopaedics. She does not feel comfortable using any other physician at City Orthopaedics. She understandably wants to use Dr. Hart, who took the time to obtain an MRI and recognizes that the previous conservative treatment provided by Dr. Mason and Dr. Beck has not relieved her pain, provided relief or lessened her disability. Ms. Carter's request to have Dr. Hart be her treating physician and perform the surgical procedure he recommended is fair and reasonable, given her experience with the other physicians who have treated her to date for this injury. Despite her ongoing shoulder pain, Ms. Carter has continued to work for defendant-employer Big Corporation. Ms. Carter is a hardworking, credible employee who simply wants to be treated by Dr. Hart, the only doctor that she feels has fully addressed her ongoing symptoms arising out of her compensable shoulder injury.

RELIEF REQUESTED

Pursuant to [insert applicable state law and/or state agency rules], plaintiff respectfully requests that the [insert state agency name] approve plaintiff's request to change treating physicians and order defendants to pay for the medical treatment directed by Dr. Robert Hart.

Wherefore, plaintiff respectfully requests that an Order be entered approving plaintiff's request to change her treating physician to Dr. Robert Hart.

This the _____ day of _____, 20___.

____

Attorney Name (State Bar #________)
Attorney for Plaintiff
[Firm name & address]
Telephone:

CERTIFICATE OF SERVICE

The undersigned hereby certifies that he/she is an attorney at law licensed to practice in the state of [insert state name], is attorney for the plaintiff and is a person of such age and discretion as to be competent to serve process.

That on __________, 200__, he/she served a copy of the attached *Motion for Approval of Medical Treatment* by placing a copy in a postpaid envelope addressed to the person(s) hereinafter named, at the address(es) stated below, which is the last known address(es), and by depositing said mail envelope and its contents in the United States Mail at Winston-Salem, North Carolina.

Addressee:

[insert address of carrier/administrator and/or its counsel]

____
Attorney Name (State Bar #_________)
Attorney for Plaintiff
[Firm name & address]
Telephone:

CHAPTER 5

Medical Records and Evidence

Paralegal Practice Tips

Well-qualified paralegals who are responsible for obtaining and reviewing medical records in workers' compensation practices should:

- Know the relevant state statutes, case law and/or state agency rules regarding obtaining and disclosure of medical records, as well as contact with medical providers.
- Know how frequently contacted medical providers accept medical record requests.
- Keep medical record release forms or authorizations for frequently contacted medical providers in a form file (paper or digital image).
- Obtain an itemized billing statement from each medical provider to compare with the medical records and verify that no records are missing.
- Have a working knowledge of basic medical abbreviations used by many medical providers.
- Prepare a medical record summary for each client.
- Know where to look up CPT and ICD-9 diagnosis and billing codes.
- Contact medical providers regarding the injured worker's unpaid medical expenses.
- Prepare a medical expense summary when medical expenses have been paid by group health insurance, Medicare or Medicaid, or the injured worker.
- Know if state statutes and/or state agency rules prohibit medical providers from dunning or pursuing collection actions against patients who have workers' compensation claims pending.

- Know if the state agency requires that an itemized statement of medical expenses be attached to any clincher or settlement agreement submitted for approval.

* * *

5.1 Obtaining Medical Records

Paralegals for both plaintiffs' and defense firms play a key role in the management of workers' compensation cases by obtaining, organizing and summarizing medical records. They are not only responsible for gathering all medical records related to the work injury or illness, but also for gathering prior and unrelated records for discovery and litigation purposes. They are responsible for organizing and locating the records as needed during the course of the firm's representation. They need to know how to obtain records, when to disclose records, how to read and understand the records, and how to organize the records for easy and quick access by the firm.

5.1(1) Ethical Considerations

Paralegals should be familiar with the applicable state statutes, case law and state agency rules regarding who can obtain medical records and under what circumstances. They should also be familiar with HIPAA requirements when contacting medical providers. The injured worker can obtain his or her own medical records[1] or sign a HIPAA compliant medical authorization allowing the plaintiff's firm to obtain the medical records and communicate with medical providers. The employer and its representatives, such as the carrier/administrator or defense attorney, may also obtain medical records and communicate with medical providers, if the injured worker has signed a HIPAA compliant medical authorization allowing them to do so, or if the workers' compensation act allows employers access to medical records even without an authorization. Once an injured worker retains the plaintiff's firm to represent the worker in a workers' compensation case, the firm should state in corre-

1. Usually the firm prefers to obtain medical records directly from the medical provider for evidentiary reasons, including verifying directly with the provider that the chart is complete. However, the injured worker may already have his or her own records, or in a situation where the plaintiff's firm has agreed to review a case with a statute of limitations immediately pending, the firm may allow the injured worker to personally make arrangements with the providers to pick up the records to save time.

spondence to medical providers that the firm's medical authorization revokes all previous authorizations signed by the worker.

In cases where an injured worker has not signed a HIPAA compliant authorization allowing the employer or its representatives to obtain medical records, they may still be able to do so if permitted by state statute, case law and/or state agency rules. They may be limited in the scope of their request for information, be required to use specific language and/or state agency forms, and/or have to copy the injured worker or the worker's attorney on all requests as well as the information obtained. State statutes, case law and/or state agency rules may also require the injured worker or the worker's attorney to copy the employer and/its representatives on all information obtained. One of a paralegal's case management tasks may be to make sure that all parties are properly and timely copied when medical records are received.

5.1(2) Contacting Medical Providers

There are a variety of ways to request medical records. The method of the request may vary, depending on the medical provider's preferred method of contact. If the firm does not already have a form medical request, a paralegal can help create a form. Some medical providers will only accept releases signed within certain time frames, such as within 90 days or 6 months of the request, or on a date after (not before) the medical services were rendered. In those cases, paralegals should know the time frames accepted by frequently used medical providers. See Forms 5.1 and 5.2, *Sample Medical Record Requests.*

Some medical providers, particularly hospitals, require that all medical requests be sent via the United States Postal Service and contain either an original release or the provider's original form release signed by the patient. However, rising overhead costs, including postage and paper, may make other methods more attractive if medical providers will accept them. Many medical providers will accept a medical request via facsimile with a copy of a HIPAA compliant medical release attached. Faxing the request may reduce the turnaround time to receive the records and can be very helpful if the request is urgent. Some firms are using online medical record retrieval companies and download the medical records as image files, instead of receiving paper files.

5.1(3) Organizing Medical Records

Organizing medical records in client files is crucial. Everyone in the firm who accesses the files should be able to find specific medical records easily and quickly. There is nothing more frustrating than being unable to find a medical record while the opposing party is holding on the phone, while trying to assemble exhibits to request emergency relief for the client, or while preparing for a hearing or mediated settlement conference. While there is more than one way to organize medical records, the firm should agree on a consistent method which will be used on all of its files.

One method is to organize the medical records by medical provider. This is helpful because the copy of the medical provider's chart stays together and contains a copy of all the records the firm received from that provider. Some firms may file each medical provider's records chronologically, with the initial date of service appearing first and the most recent date of service appearing last. Other firms may file the records in reverse chronological order, with the most recent date of service on top. However, medical records may be Bates-stamped or numbered for use as pleading, deposition, hearing and/or brief exhibits, and may be cited by page number. Medical records organized chronologically are easier to cite when drafting a history of events because the services occur in a natural order, like events in a time line. Court documents may be more challenging to draft if the records are organized "backwards," or even worse, in no particular order at all.

Another method of organizing records is to arrange them chronologically, regardless of provider. This method makes it harder to review the treatment by one provider, but easier to follow the injured worker's overall course of treatment. Sometimes doctors reviewing other medical providers' records prefer to review documents that have been organized in this manner.

Injured workers' medical records should be indexed so they may be quickly located by anyone in the firm. The index may include the name of the medical provider, the dates of service in the records and the page numbers, if any. A medical record index may also be used as a cover sheet for medical exhibits at a state agency hearing. *See Form 5.3, Sample Medical Records Index.*

5.1(4) Verifying Complete Set of Medical Records

There is a simple rule (applicable not just to workers' compensation cases but to any kind of case where paralegals have to gather medical records and expenses, such as personal injury or medical malpractice cases) for assembling a complete set of medical records:

> **Every medical record should be matched to a date of service on an itemized billing statement from the medical provider, and every date of service on an itemized billing statement should be matched to a medical record, with a corresponding date of service.**

Even if the carrier/administrator has accepted the claim and paid all of the medical expenses to date, a paralegal should still request an itemized billing statement from each medical provider and compare the dates on the medical records to the dates of service on the bill, to make sure that no records are missing. Paralegals can also use the carrier/administrator's printout of medical benefits paid to make sure there are medical records for all dates of service on the printout. Paralegals should carefully review all other available documentation of medical treatment, such as rehabilitation reports and group health insurance benefit statements, paying close attention to all dates of service referenced to ensure that all necessary medical records have been requested. Paralegals can also contact their firms' clients with questions about medical treatment.

5.2 Reviewing and Summarizing Medical Records

Simultaneously reviewing and summarizing injured workers' medical records is well worth the time and effort. Reading and summarizing each record upon receipt may seem time-consuming at first, but is actually more efficient in the long run. No one can memorize all of the medical records for multiple plaintiffs, and without some kind of reference or index, it can be difficult to find medical records later, even if the attorney and/or paralegal read them thoroughly upon receipt. Preparing a medical summary for each plaintiff is an excellent way to show the chronological history of treatment and also to have immediate access to medical information, especially when the firm has a high volume of cases to manage. *See Forms 5.5 and 5.6, Sample Medical Record Summaries*

A medical summary can be used to:

- **Evaluate claims and defenses.** A careful chronological summary of the injured worker's medical records, with the facts regarding the occurrence of the injury or onset of the illness included, can help identify any causation problems and reporting inconsistencies by the worker. For example, the worker may have told the employer that he hurt his back lifting heavy equipment at work when his medical records show that he told his doctors that he hurt his back moving furniture at home.
- **Calculate statutes of limitations and avoid missing other actionable injury claims** which may be reported in the medical records, but not by the injured worker to the plaintiff's firm. Some injured workers are poor

historians. During an intake, they may provide incorrect dates of injury or even forget they had more than one date of injury at work, especially if they have had a lot of medical treatment in the past few years. In those cases, a medical summary is crucial to identify all dates of injury referenced in the medical records and help the plaintiff's firm determine what injuries, if any, should be filed as workers' compensation claims.

- **Reference while talking to the client about medical issues.** A paralegal or attorney can quickly access the summary from a desktop computer, review the most recent entries and intelligently discuss the injured worker's medical issues, without having to leave the desk to find the hard file and then hunt through the medical records for the most recent date of treatment. The medical summary can even be updated while the client (adjuster or injured worker) is on the telephone, by asking if the injured worker has had treatment since the last date on the summary and entering the dates and providers in the summary, with a reminder to request the records. If the client has the dates for upcoming appointments, they can be added to the summary, with a note and/or tickler that the records need to be requested at the appropriate time.
- **Review medical providers' itemized billing statements** and compare them to the medical summary to verify whether the dates of service listed on the bill are for medical conditions related to the work injury.
- **Reference when drafting correspondence, discovery responses, requests for medical relief or any other document** which discusses the worker's medical treatment. Text from the summary can be quickly copied and pasted into the document, without having to locate pages in a bulky medical records file.
- **Use to prepare for and during a mediation, deposition or hearing.** A chronological summary of the worker's medical history provides a quick reference when medical information is needed on short notice.

5.2(1) Medical Summary Format

Paralegals can prepare medical summaries using the firm's available word processing or spreadsheet software. A case management software program can be used if it has features to enter medical data and show a chronological history of medical treatment. Whatever method the firm chooses, the main purpose of a medical summary is to provide a chronological overview of key medical issues and to answer frequently asked questions such as:

- What medical treatment has the injured worker received to date?

- What are the injured worker's most recent restrictions?
- What medications were last prescribed for the injured worker?
- When is the last time the injured worker saw a doctor?
- What is the injured worker's current treatment plan?
- Has the injured worker reached maximum medical improvement (MMI)?
- Has the doctor provided impairment ratings?

One clear and easy way to summarize medical records is to use the same medical reporting format that most medical providers use to organize information in their charts or records: **Subjective, Objective, Assessment** and **Plan** or **"SOAP."** Medical records organized in the "SOAP" format contain the following information:

S = **"Subjective"**	The patient's self-reported complaints and history regarding the cause of injury, body parts affected, extent of pain, limitations on daily or work activities
O = **"Objective"**	The doctor's clinical or physical exam findings, including but not limited to, visible injuries, tenderness upon palpation, ranges of motion, reflexes, muscle spasms, and diagnostic test results.
A = **"Assessment"**	The doctor's diagnosis or differential diagnoses if there is more than one possible cause of the injury or illness, medical findings and causation if applicable
P = **"Plan"**	The doctor's recommended course of treatment including conservative non surgical measures, surgery, physical therapy, prescriptions, functional capacity evaluation (FCE), injections, diagnostic studies, work restrictions, whether the patient has reached maximum medical improvement (MMI), and permanent impairment ratings, if any.

The purpose of preparing a medical summary is not to have a document containing a retyped or verbatim version of the medical records in their entirety, but to provide a chronological overview of key medical issues related to the work-related injury or illness. A successful medical summary will highlight and emphasize typical medical issues in workers' compensation cases, such as:

- Causation of the injury or illness reported by the patient
- Diagnosis (or differential diagnoses if there are multiple possibilities for the cause of the injury or illness)
- Treatment plan, including recommended diagnostic reports, referrals and prescriptions
- Likelihood of recovery or "prognosis" (good, fair or poor)
- Permanent impairment or ratings of body members, if any
- Maximum Medical Improvement ("MMI")

- Future medical needs, if any

Paralegals should keep medical summaries continuously updated, as additional information regarding the worker's medical status becomes available. Paralegals can use the following sources of information to identify and insert the names of medical providers, dates of service, the type of services, and/or the treatment plan:

- Medical records
- Medical bills
- Client history and updates, including telephone calls, medical provider receipts and disability statements
- Rehabilitation consultant updates, including phone calls, correspondence and reports
- Carrier/administrator claim file, including printout of medical benefits paid
- Explanation of Benefit (EOB) statements from the worker's group health insurance provider

Paralegals should carefully review all available documentation of medical treatment to ensure that medical summaries are complete and accurate. Medical records may reference treatment by other medical providers. Progress reports or updates from rehabilitation consultants generally discuss medical providers, dates of service and kinds of treatment. Itemized billing statements identify the medical provider, the dates of service and the type of treatment. If the firm does not already have the medical records for treatment referenced and identified in other documents, a paralegal can summarize as much information as is available from the document, such as entering dates of service or the names of providers, and then request the records.

If the software used to prepare the medical summary has a word or text search/find feature, the feature can be used to quickly find medical records by locating key words in the summary, such as "MRI," "tendinitis" or a certain treating doctor's surname, "Jones." For example, a paralegal may need to request copies of the injured worker's MRI scans for the last ten years. Instead of reading and reviewing voluminous pages of records trying to find all of the MRI reports, the search/find feature can be used to locate all of the times the word "MRI" appears throughout the medical summary in a few seconds. The paralegal can use the identified dates and providers of MRIs from the medical summary to locate the corresponding medical records in the chronologically organized file.

5.2(2) Prior and Unrelated Medical Treatment

While reviewing and summarizing medical documentation as it becomes available, paralegals should also pay close attention to references to prior and/or unrelated medical treatment and procedures. At initial evaluations in a new doctor's office and/or histories and physicals (H&P) for surgeries, most medical providers request the patient's medical background via interview, intake forms and/or patient questionnaires. Paralegals should include information regarding prior medical treatment at the beginning of the medical summary. Unrelated medical treatment should be included in the summary on the dates of treatment. However, unless the prior and/or unrelated medical treatment is relevant to the current case, it does not have to be summarized in as much detail as related medical records. This information may be used to:

- Respond to interrogatories regarding prior and/or unrelated medical treatment.
- Determine if the injured worker has unrelated medical conditions which need to be factored into a determination of the worker's life expectancy for settlement purposes.
- Determine if there are other possible causes of the worker's current condition that are not covered under the workers' compensation claim.
- List unrelated and/or pre-existing medical conditions when asking Medicare to approve a Workers' Compensation Medicare Set-aside Arrangement (WCMSA).
- Prepare the worker to testify at a hearing or deposition.
- Prepare to cross-examine the worker at a hearing or deposition.
- Provide to a treating doctor or other medical expert who has been asked to give a medical opinion.

5.2(3) Deciphering Medical Abbreviations, Terms and Codes

If the firm specializes in injury cases and has experienced staff, they will be familiar with basic medical abbreviations used frequently by medical providers. Some firms may even have a current or former licensed nurse on staff whose main responsibility is to review medical records. **Paralegals who review medical records should have a working knowledge of at least the basic abbreviations** or the "shorthand" used by many medical providers to record their handwritten notes. *See Appendix A: List of Frequently Used Medical Abbreviations.* If everyone who will use the summary knows basic medical abbreviations, then the abbreviations can be used to save time while summarizing the records. If the medical summary will be used by individuals who are not familiar with basic medical abbreviations, the full word or phrase should be used instead of an abbreviation.

The definition of medical terms can be included in a medical summary for quick reference. There are numerous online sources to look up medical abbreviations and definitions (see below). However, sometimes a medical provider may use nonstandard abbreviations (or have his or her own shorthand which only his or her staff can decipher). If an abbreviation (or handwriting) cannot be deciphered from the context of the medical record, the medical provider can be contacted directly for clarification. Occasionally, the firm may ask a doctor to dictate his handwritten notes into a typed record in order for them to be legible.

Paralegals frequently have to review medical billing statements from providers and medical expense printouts from group health insurance carriers, workers' compensation carrier/administrators, or Medicare and Medicaid. In many cases the only information regarding the diagnosis on a treatment date is a medical billing code, such as a CPT or ICD-9 code. Current Procedural Technology or "CPT" *billing* codes are used by medical providers to classify medical, surgical and diagnostic procedures and are maintained and copyrighted by the American Medical Association (AMA). International Classification of Diseases or "ICD-9" *diagnosis* codes are used by medical providers to describe diseases, conditions and related issues, and are published by the World Health Organization. CPT codes are used to identify and document the services or treatment for the diagnosis indicated by the ICD-9 codes. Paralegals do not need to become medical billing/coding experts or specialists, but they do need to know how to look up CPT and ICD-9 codes to decipher medical bills or medical expense summaries. Sometimes simply googling "CPT" or "ICD" plus the code number in question will provide a quick answer.

Prior to the availability of the Internet, researching medical terms, definitions and codes was much more challenging and time-consuming for paralegals working in practices that specialized in injury cases, such as workers' compensation, personal injury and medical malpractice. Paralegals had to rely on expensive medical dictionaries and textbooks, and sometimes even go to medical libraries in person to locate medical textbooks or articles. Now the majority of this information is available on the Internet, via free, fee-based or subscription-based websites. Information that may previously have taken hours to locate can now be found in seconds. Sometimes simply googling a medical abbreviation, term, code or procedure can result in an instant definition or explanation. There are also many online sources which provide access to medical information. Some of the free websites include (but are not limited to):

- **AMA CPT Code/Relative Value Search**, https://catalog.ama-assn.org/Catalog/cpt/cpt_search.jsp (CPT codes and Medicare's relative value payment for a code)
- **Flash Code**, http://www.icd9coding1.com/flashcode/freeicdnavigation.do (ICD-9 codes)
- **MedicineNet**, http://www.medterms.com/script/main/hp.asp (Medical dictionary)
- **MediLexicon**, http://www.medilexicon.com/ (Medical abbreviations, definitions, ICD-9 codes)
- **Medline Plus: Medical dictionary**, http://www.nlm.nih.gov/medlineplus/mplusdictionary.html

5.3 Identifying Key Medical Issues

Workers' compensation paralegals may spend significant time reviewing voluminous medical records, especially for seriously injured workers or cases with complex medical issues. Much of the information contained in a standard medical report is required by medical providers to diagnose and treat the medical condition, but not necessarily helpful to evaluate injured workers' claims to workers' compensation benefits.[2] While reviewing and summarizing medical records, paralegals should be aware of key medical issues that may directly affect injured workers' entitlement to workers' compensation benefits as follows:

5.3(1) Causation

Causation is the basis of a workers' compensation case. Injured workers are entitled to workers' compensation benefits only if the injury or illness occurred during the course of their employment or because of their job duties. Paralegals must pay close attention to what an injured worker reported to all medical providers regarding the illness or injury, such as:

- How was the worker injured?
- Was the worker injured at work or elsewhere?
- Did the worker have more than one injury?

---

2. However, these details may be important to document relevant issues in third party personal injury or medical malpractice cases, such as pain and suffering or medical provider violations of the standard of care.

- Are the worker's reports of injury consistent or inconsistent?
- Did the worker tell one provider one story and another provider a different story?
- Did the worker report no injury at all?

These are important questions for paralegals to answer while reviewing and summarizing medical records.

Medical providers generally record the patient's account of the injury or "history" at the beginning of their reports, in the "complaint" or "subjective" part of the records. The patient's history may be reported in more than one place in the medical chart, including the office notes, patient questionnaire and/or nurses' notes. A paralegal should check to see how the injury is reported in all of the documents in the medical chart, not just the first page or the beginning. Key records can be flagged or highlighted for the supervising attorney's review, especially if the injured worker's report of injury in the medical records is inconsistent with the history given to the attorney or the employer and its representatives.

5.3(2) Pre-Existing Conditions

If an injured worker has pre-existing conditions, such as osteoarthritis, bulging discs or prior surgeries or injuries to a relevant body member, this does not mean that the worker is not entitled to workers' compensation benefits, if the affected body part or member is injured or re-injured during the course of employment. A worker may be entitled to workers' compensation benefits if an injury occurred at work, and a non disabling pre-existing condition is exacerbated, aggravated or becomes disabling due to the work injury. However, pre-existing injuries or conditions, especially to the same body part involved in the workers' compensation case, might cause the carrier/administrator to prolong its initial investigation to determine liability. The carrier/administrator may want to review prior medical records as part of its investigation. The carrier/administrator might even deny the claim (with or without justification) on the basis that the injured worker had a pre-existing medical condition.

5.3(3) Disability or Work Restrictions

The carrier/administrator will not pay indemnity or disability benefits without evidence or documentation from the treating doctor that the injured worker cannot perform his or her job, with or without restrictions, or cannot work at all, due to the work injury or illness. The employer should require and the injured worker should request a disability statement or "work note" at each medical visit, including to hospital emergency rooms. The note should state whether the patient cannot work at all due to the injury, can work with restrictions, or can return to work with no restrictions. If the injured worker does not have disability statements or work notes, then a paralegal can review the medical records to see if the doctor addressed the injured worker's ability to work. If the doctor does not discuss work restrictions in the office notes, the paralegal may have to send the doctor a written request for an opinion regarding the injured worker's current ability to work or ability to work during a certain time period.

5.3(4) Permanent Injury

An injured worker may be entitled to compensation for permanent injury or impairment to specific body members as a result of the work injury or illness. Often, when an injured worker is released by the treating doctor as having reached maximum medical improvement (MMI), the doctor will assign a percentage of permanent injury to each injured body member, such as a leg or the back, or the whole body. A paralegal should review the medical records carefully to see if any opinions regarding permanent injury or impairment are stated. If the doctor has discharged the injured worker but not addressed the permanent impairment or ratings (if any), the firm may have to send the doctor a written request for an opinion on the percentage of permanent injury or impairment to the injured body part. Paralegals should know if the state agency has its own guidelines or forms for reporting or documenting permanent impairment. If so, the required forms and guidelines can be sent to the treating doctor to complete.

5.3(5) Future Medical Needs

The employer and the injured worker need to know what future medical needs the worker may have over the course of the worker's anticipated lifetime because of the work injury or illness, including (but not limited to): office visits, physical therapy, surgeries, durable medical equipment (DME) and/or prescriptions. This information is used to evaluate the injured worker's entitlement to future medical benefits over the worker's anticipated lifetime and to estimate the cost of future medical services. If an injured worker has the option of resolving the case for a lump sum of money and wants to pursue it, future medical needs need to be estimated and valued. Workers' compensation practitioners should be able to:

- Discuss the estimated value of these benefits with the client and get settlement authorization.
- Discuss future medical costs with the opposing party in informal settlement discussions.

- Prepare a settlement letter with realistic estimates and values for future medical costs.
- Present a realistic summary of future medical costs at mediation.
- Possibly submit an estimate of the worker's future medical needs to Medicare if the injured worker's case requires a Workers' Compensation Medicare Set-aside Arrangement (WCMSA).

Paralegals should carefully review medical records to see if treating doctors address injured workers' future medical needs in reports and/or in correspondence to the parties. If not, requests for written opinions regarding future medical needs can be sent to treating doctors. Paralegals should know if the state agency has its own guidelines or forms for reporting or documenting future medical treatment. If so, the required forms and guidelines can be sent to the treating doctor to complete.

5.4 Medical Research

Paralegals can perform medical research for a variety of reasons, including to:

- Educate the firm about the nature of the injury and/or illness.
- Educate the firm about symptoms, treatment and prognosis of the injury and/or illness.
- Educate the firm regarding the general causes of the injury and/or illness.
- Educate the firm about medical terms, tests and procedures.
- Obtain copies of medical and scholarly research articles.
- Locate experts in the subject medical specialty.
- Obtain basic illustrations and diagrams of standard injuries and/or conditions.

One of the best ways to start a medical research project is to google the key terms, such as "carpal tunnel syndrome." A Google search of a medical term will generally provide an overview of the subject matter and provide online sources or links to pursue for more specific information.

There are many online sources for medical research, some free and some subscription-based. Some of the frequently used online sources for medical research include (but are not limited to):

- **eMedicine Emergency Medicine Medical Reference**, http://www.emedicine.com/emerg/
- **Gray's Anatomy of the Human Body**, http://www.bartleby.com/107/
- **MedlinePlus**, http://www.nlm.nih.gov/medlineplus/

- **Medscape,** http://www.medscape.com/home
- **The Merck Manual Online Edition,** http://www.merck.com/mmhe/index.html
- **Physicians Desk Reference,** http://www.pdr.net
- **PubMed,** http://www.ncbi.nlm.nih.gov/sites/entrez/
- **RxList,** http://www.rxlist.com/script/main/hp.asp
- **Wheeless Textbook of Orthopaedics,** http://www.wheelessonline.com/

Some firms may hire medical consultants and experts, such as doctors or legal nurse consultants, to perform medical research. However, this is a costly option due the high hourly fees requested by most medical consultants and experts.

5.5 Medical Provider Contact

Paralegals should be familiar with the relevant HIPAA requirements, ethical rules, state statutes and state agency rules regarding medical provider contact. **They should not contact medical providers directly unless instructed to do so by a supervising attorney.** Attorneys should review and approve all correspondence to medical providers, including facsimiles and E-mails, because these documents may be discoverable depending on the circumstances and applicable state statutes and rules.

When directed to do so by supervising attorneys, paralegals may need to contact medical providers to:

- Request copies of medical records and/or the chart in its entirety.
- Request copies of disability statements.
- Request copies of prescriptions for medications and durable medical equipment.
- Request copies of correspondence.
- Request that the treating doctor complete a medical necessity letter or provide other documentation for the carrier/administrator to authorize medical treatment. *See Form 5.7, Sample Request for Medical Necessity Letter to Doctor.*
- Request that the treating doctor answer written questions regarding whether the injured worker can return to work, with or without restrictions, or perform specific jobs.
- Request that the treating doctor assign or clarify a permanent impairment rating.
- Request that the treating doctor provide an estimate of future medical treatment and expenses.

- Complete the state agency's required medical information forms.

The firm should have its own forms and required state agency forms for routine requests, such as requesting medical records or obtaining a rating. More complex requests, such as whether the injured worker needs home attendant services or is mentally competent to handle his or her affairs, may require a paralegal to draft specialized documents, including affidavits. The supervising attorney should review and approve all documents before they are sent to medical providers.

5.5(1) Obtaining Written Opinions from Doctors

Sometimes the parties' attorneys will want written opinions about specific medical issues from treating doctors. Written medical opinions by treating doctors are usually requested for the following kinds of issues in typical workers' compensation cases:

- Did the work injury as reported by the worker cause or significantly contribute to the injury or condition?
- Did the work injury as reported by the worker aggravate a pre-existing condition?
- Is the condition for which the worker is being treated unrelated to the reported work injury or illness?
- Can the worker perform a specific job, with or without restrictions?
- What are the worker's permanent restrictions?
- Is the worker permanently and totally disabled from earning wages?
- What is the percentage of permanent impairment (or rating) due to the work injury?
- What medical treatment will the worker need in the future?

Paralegals should be familiar with the relevant HIPAA requirements, ethical rules, state statutes and state agency rules regarding any kind of communication with medical providers. The kinds of communications allowed may be different for the injured worker's representatives as opposed to the employer and its representatives. The law may require all the parties to copy each other on any written communication to medical providers as well as on any information received from the medical provider in response to the request. The law may limit written contact by the employer or its representatives to specific issues and/or questions. The law may even specify that the employer's representatives only use specific questions and/or state agency forms or questionnaires to obtain information.

Paralegals should be aware that any written correspondence to medical providers becomes a part of the patient or injured worker's medical chart and may be discoverable or disclosed to the other parties. All correspondence to medical providers should be drafted carefully and under an attorney's supervision because of the legal issues involved, including the knowledge that it may be seen by all parties. *See Form 5.8—Sample Letter to Doctor re: Causation Opinion.*

5.5(2) Providing Documents to Doctors to Review

In order to obtain an opinion from a doctor, the firm may need to provide copies of documents for the doctor's review, especially medical records from other medical providers. A doctor will have access to his or her own chart, but may not have a complete set of the injured worker's medical records to review. If an opinion regarding prior or pre-existing medical conditions is needed from a doctor, he or she will need a copy of the injured worker's medical records prior to the injury. **Paralegals should not provide any medical records to a doctor unless requested to do so by a supervising attorney.** Any documents provided to a doctor, including but not limited to, other medical providers' records, accident reports, deposition testimony and job descriptions, may be discoverable by or disclosed to the other parties. Therefore, all documents submitted to a doctor for review should be selected carefully and reviewed by a supervising attorney prior to being sent to the doctor.

All documentation provided by the firm to a treating doctor should be organized to make the doctor's review of the records as easy as possible. Most doctors charge a significant hourly fee for their time spent reviewing medical records and writing a report with their opinion. A well-organized set of medical records could save the firm and the client time and money. If a doctor requests that certain records be organized in a specific format, then the firm should comply with the request. If a specific format is not requested, then a copy of the medical records may be organized in chronological order and numbered. Page numbering makes it easier for everyone to literally be "on the same page" when discussing issues with doctors over the telephone, in-person, or at depositions. The firm should retain a copy of any documentation provided to doctors, including cover letters.

5.6 Handling Unpaid Medical Expenses

In cases where the carrier/administrator has denied all or part of a claim, the injured worker may have unpaid or unreimbursed medical expenses. In denied cases where the injured worker needed emergent or immediate medical treatment and was covered by the employer's or spouse's group health insurance, all or a portion of the medical expenses may have been paid. However, the group health insurance carrier may have a subrogation lien in the amount of the medical expenses it paid against any recovery of medical benefits in the workers' compensation case.

5.6(1) Requesting Itemized Billing Statements

In denied cases, or accepted cases where the carrier/administrator has refused to pay all or some of the medical expenses, an itemized billing statement must be requested from the medical providers. Even if the injured worker provides bills received at home, the firm should still request a complete itemized statement to verify that no expenses have been omitted. An itemized billing statement should contain the following information:

- The name and contact information for the medical provider;
- The dates of each service;
- The types of service rendered (by description or medical code);
- The amount of the charges for each service;
- Any payments on the account and source of each payment (workers' compensation carrier, group health insurance carrier, Medicare, Medicaid, patient self pay or other);
- Any "adjustments" or amounts subtracted by the medical provider; and
- The unpaid balance on the account, if any.

Paralegals may also request a printout of medical expenses paid by the workers' compensation carrier or group health insurance carrier to compare with the medical providers' itemized billing statements.

5.6(2) Contacting Medical Billing or Collection Departments

Paralegals working for plaintiffs' firms should ask clients to provide the firm with all medical bills and/or collection notices received for medical expenses related to the work injury or illness. Paralegals should carefully review all medical bills and/or collection notices and verify that the medical expenses are related to the work injury or illness. If the medical expenses appear to be related to the work injury or illness, and the injured worker is unable to pay the bills pending resolution of the workers' compensation case, a paralegal should contact the medical providers via telephone and letter, and ask that the provider voluntarily hold the accounts until the case is resolved. Calling *and* writing the medical provider's patient billing department ensures that the paralegal has both talked to the appropriate person about the account and that the medical provider also has received written notice of the pending workers' compensation claim.

Paralegals should know if state statutes and/or state agency rules prohibit medical providers from dunning or pursuing collection actions against patients who have workers' compensation hearings pending on the state agency hearing docket. If medical providers are prohibited by law from pursuing collections against injured workers pending a state agency hearing, the plaintiff's firm should send a letter to the medical provider and/or its collection agent, notifying them of the case status and citing the relevant statute or rule.

5.6(3) Summarizing Medical Expenses

A summary of medical expenses should be prepared in the following situations:

- The injured worker has a claim for unpaid and/or unreimbursed medical expenses.
- Medical providers have an alleged lien or subrogation interest for unpaid medical expenses.
- A group health insurance carrier, Medicare or Medicaid has a claim or subrogation lien for medical expenses paid as a result of the work injury or illness.
- The state agency requires that a summary of medical expenses be filed.

At minimum, the medical expense summary should show:

- The medical provider;
- The dates of each service;
- The amount of the charges for each date of service;
- The amount of payments for each date of service and who made the payments (the carrier/administrator, group health insurance, Medicare, Medicaid, patient self-pay or other);
- Any adjustments made by the medical provider; and
- The amount which remains unpaid or unreimbursed.

See Form 5.4, Sample Summary of Medical Expenses. A medical expense summary may be used to document the amount of unpaid or unreimbursed medical expenses at mediation, voluntary settlement or upon receipt of a state agency order directing defendants to pay the expenses. Paralegals should know if the state agency requires that an itemized statement of medical expenses be attached to any clincher or settlement agreement submitted for approval.

5.7 Preparing for Medical Depositions

The most important task a paralegal can perform to help an attorney prepare for a medical deposition is to verify that the firm has a complete set of medical records, including the chart in its entirety from the doctor to be deposed. The deposed doctor's chart is usually the main exhibit to the doctor's deposition. Most medical providers do not provide every sheet of paper in the patient chart in response to a medical request from a law firm. They will generally provide only their own facility's office notes and refuse to disclose records in the chart from other medical providers. Well in advance of the deposition, a paralegal should review the medical provider's chart to see if it appears to be complete.

A ***complete*** patient chart from a doctor's office may contain the following documents:

- Office Notes
- Diagnostic reports, including laboratory results and films
- Registration/intake form
- Patient questionnaires
- Nurses' notes
- Prescription logs
- Correspondence and/or facsimiles to other providers
- Referral sheets
- Disability or work notes

A paralegal for the plaintiff's firm should verify with the treating doctor's office that the chart is complete, either by:

- Reviewing the chart page by page with a medical records clerk over the telephone;
- If the chart is small, faxing a copy to the medical records clerk to review and verify it is complete or supply missing records; or
- Scheduling an appointment to go to the office and review the chart in person.

Reviewing the chart in person is the best way for a plaintiff's attorney to verify that it is complete, but that may not be feasible in some cases or practices. If an injured worker is receiving ongoing care, records for recent treatment may not have been filed at the time the chart was copied for the firm. If possible, a paralegal for the plaintiff's firm should schedule a meeting at the doctor's office at least thirty minutes prior to the deposition for the attorney and/or paralegal to review the chart in its entirety.

In many cases, it is also important that the doctor to be deposed, whether he is the treating doctor or a hired expert, has a complete set of numbered medical records from every medical provider who has treated the injured worker. The paralegal assembling the medical records should work with her supervising attorney to verify which records the attorney wants the doctor to review prior to his deposition.

Form 5.1—Sample Medical Request Letter to Doctor's Office

[Provider Address]

Re: [Patient name]
[Patient date of birth]
[Date of injury or illness onset]

To Whom It May Concern:

This firm represents the above-referenced patient in a workers' compensation case.

Please send me a copy of the patient's chart in its entirety, including but not limited to, office notes, nurses' notes, diagnostic reports and correspondence to and from your office.

In addition, please send me an itemized billing statement for all services rendered to the above-referenced patient.

I am enclosing a medical authorization signed by the patient, allowing you to release information to this firm. If you have any questions or if you need additional information, please do not hesitate to contact me.

Thank you for your attention to this request.

[signature line]

Enclosure as stated
cc: [Client]
[Adjuster or opposing counsel if required by statute or rule]

Form 5.2—Sample Medical Request Letter to Hospital

[Hospital Medical Correspondence Address]

Re: [Patient name]
[Patient date of birth]
[Date of injury or illness onset]

To Whom It May Concern:

This firm represents the above-referenced patient in a workers' compensation case.

Please send me a copy of the following documents only from patient's chart:

Admission chart(s)
Emergency room record(s)
Diagnostic report(s)
History and physical(s)
Consultant report(s)
Operative notes(s)
Discharge report(s)

In addition, please send me an itemized billing statement for all services rendered to the above-referenced patient.

I am enclosing a medical authorization signed by the patient, allowing you to release information to this firm. If you have any questions or if you need additional information, please do not hesitate to contact me.

Thank you for your attention to this request.

[signature line]

Enclosure as stated
cc: [Client]
[Adjuster or opposing counsel if required by statute or rule]

Form 5.3—Sample Medical Records Index

Medical Records Index of Joe Smith			
Tab	Medical Provider	Dates of Service	Page Number(s)
1	County Ambulance	01/15/2007	1–3
2	State Hospital	01/15–01/24/2007; 02/23/2007	4–15
3	City Orthopaedics	01/30/2007–present	16–35
4	City Radiology	02/15/2007	36–37

Form 5.4—Sample Summary of Medical Expenses

[Insert case caption] Exhibit ____, Medical Expenses						
Provider/Date(s) of Service	Charge	WC Paid	Group Health Ins	Adjustment	Self Pay	Balance
County Ambulance 01/15/2007	$365.00	0	0	0	0	$365.00
State Hospital 01/15–01/24/2007 02/23/2007	 $9,450.00 $1,200.00	 0 0	 $4,500.00 $620.00	 $3,800.00 $380.00	 $1,000.00 $165.00	 $150.00 $35.00
City Orthopaedics 01/16/2007	$3,600.00	0	$1,900.00	$750.00	$250.00	$700.00
City Radiology 01/15/2007	$70.00	0	$40.00	$30.00	$0.00	$0.00
Total	**$14,685.00**	**0**	**$7,060.00**	**$4,960.00**	**$1,415.00**	**$1,250.00**

Form 5.5—Sample Medical Record Summary

<table>
<tr><td colspan="3">Medical Summary of Sally Smith
DOI: 11/01/2005</td></tr>
<tr><td colspan="3">Machine operator for 12 years
Nonsmoker, nondrinker
Hypertension</td></tr>
<tr><td>Date</td><td>Provider</td><td>Treatment</td></tr>
<tr><td>06/01/2004</td><td>County Family Practice</td><td>A: Muscle soreness, strain s/p MVA</td></tr>
<tr><td>06/03/2004</td><td>City Hospital</td><td>Cervical MRI
A: Spondylosis at C4-5 level with prominent osteophytic formation resulting in narrowing of canal and foramina. Tiny central disc protrusion at C3-4 not likely to be of any significance.</td></tr>
<tr><td>01/29/2005</td><td>County Family Practice</td><td>A: Neck Strain ... very small likelihood of any impingement ...</td></tr>
<tr><td colspan="3">12/01/2005 DOI [Denied] - pulling a piece of foil out of machine which was turned off ... then raised her arm & had immediate pain in R shoulder & elbow

Supervisor's First Report of Injury: Reported to Johnny White, supervisor ... EE hurt her arm while removing a core from the unit bobbin ... core was hard to remove and as a result, she hurt her arm.</td></tr>
<tr><td>11/01/2005</td><td>Plant Doctor</td><td>RN
S: EE presented c/o pain to R elbow that extends up into R shoulder. Increased pain noted with extension & abduction of R shoulder. Unable to fully elevate R arm above shoulder height without increased pain. Will not attempt to extend R elbow states "I can't do that".... EE states "I was trying to take off an empty core and it was harder than usual to get off." "When I tried again to take it off the machine, I felt a pain in my R arm." ...
O: Visual inspection of R elbow/shoulder show no sign of swelling/deformity.
P: EE unable to finish her work shift b/c of pain. Given Advil ... use ice pack to help control pain ... call in a.m. if any further problems & for evaluation by dr since she states she is unable to complete shift.</td></tr>
<tr><td>11/02/2005</td><td>City Orthopaedic Center</td><td>William Bones MD
S: ... 47 yo pleasant female ... presents today w/R elbow & shoulder pain. While at work on 12/01/2005 ... pulling a piece of foil out of machine which was turned off ... then raised her arm and had immediate pain in R shoulder & elbow ... pain isolated in lateral aspect of shoulder ...
A: 1. R shoulder strain, possible rotator cuff tear 2. R medial epicondyle strain of elbow
P: ... injected subacromial space w/Lidocaine/Marcaine/Kenalog ... obtained excellent relief of shoulder sx ... had improved strength as well ... Rx for Mobic ... OOW 3 wks ... undergo PT ... f/u after shoulder MRI ...</td></tr>
</table>

Form 5.5, cont'd,—Sample Medical Record Summary

12/07/2005	City Radiology	**R Shoulder MRI** (Bones MD) **A:** Supraspinatus and infraspinatus tendinopathy with deep bursal sided tearing of supraspinatus and infraspinatous tendons. Acromioclavicular degenerative disease. Subscapularis tendinopathy.
01/17/2006	City Orthopaedic Center	**William Bones MD** **S:** ... R-hand dominant ... **she was taking a roll off a machine when it caused her shoulder to twist and felt a pop in the shoulder** ... has had pretty much pain since that time ... able to function in repetitive activities above her shoulder level with no problem prior to injury ... **A:** R shoulder partial thickness rotator cuff tear secondary to OTJ injury as well as acromioclavicular joint arthritis **P:** I discussed with pt that she has almost all of her rotator cuff torn from injury at work ... **she would benefit greatly from an arthroscopic evaluation of her joint as well as arthroscopic subacromial decompression of any open rotator cuff repair and open disk clavicle excision** ... <u>unable to work 01/17 - 01/22 ... able to work 01/23 light work duties ...</u>
02/27/2006	City Orthopaedic Center/City Outpatient Surgical Center	**SURGERY - William Bones MD** **A:** R shoulder rotator cuff tear as well as acromioclavicular joint arthritis, as well as torn biceps tendon **P:** R shoulder arthroscopy with extensive intraarticular debridement of torn biceps. Arthroscopic biceps tenotomy and smoothing of superior labrum. Arthroscopic subacromial decompression and CA ligament release. Open disk clavicle excision, mini open rotator cuff repair, and mini open biceps tenodesis in bicipital groove.
03/07/2006	City Orthopaedic Center	**William Bones MD** **S:** ... recheck R shoulder, 8 days s/p rotator cuff repair, biceps tenodesis and distal clavicle resection ... doing fairly well ... taking Robaxin & Percocet for pain control ... **A:** 8 days s/p R shoulder arthroscopy, doing well **P:** ... con't PT ... denied any need for pain Rx.... f/u 4 wks ... <u>OOW 4 weeks</u>
07/26/2006	City Orthopaedic Center	**William Bones MD** **S:** ... recheck R shoulder ... 21 wk s/p rotator cuff tear & arthroscopy ... some con't weakness ... has been OOW since surgery ... discharged from formal PT ... not taking any pain Rx ... very happy with progress thus far ... would like to RTW. **O:** ... R shoulder shows anterior incision ... forward flexion up to 140 deg. External rotation to 45 deg. Internal rotation to L2. Neurovascularly intact ... strength in internal/external rotators 5/5 bilaterally.. **A:** 21 wks S/p R shoulder rotator cuff repair, arthroscopy, doing very well. **P:** ... <u>recommend RTW full duties ... to ease back into activities, esp. lifting and overhead activities</u> ... denies need for any pain Rx ... **15% PPD RUE** ... return prn.

Form 5.6—Sample Medical Record Summary

Medical Summary of Joe Smith DOI: 01/24/2007						
Date	**Provider**	**Doctor**	**Subjective (Complaints)**	**Objective (Exam) & Diagnostic**	**Assessment (Dx)**	**Plan**
12/15/2006	USA Family Care	Shelton, Jim	Injured low back moving Christmas tree ... still working ... having trouble sleeping due to back pain ...	... tenderness to palpation at L4-5 ... normal ROM	Lumbar strain	Rx = IBU 800 mg qd; alternate ice/heat; <u>RTW no restrictions</u>
DOI: 01/24/2007 [Accepted Claim] Per Dr. Martin 03/06/2007: ... lying on back on ground using legs to push up wing carrier of tractor trailer which collapsed despite use of pneumatic support ... had some lower back pain at that time but about 2 days later had significant increase of back pain and pain down LLE.						
01/28/2007	State Hospital		<u>**ER**</u> Back pain since lifting at work 1/24. Pain to L hip to calf this a.m. increased with moving leg.	... walks with limp ... muscle spasms ... tenderness to palpation lower back ... L SLR positive ...	Musculoskeletal hip pain	IV Morphine/Phenergan; f/u PCP tomorrow as scheduled; Rx= Darvocet; <u>OOW thrul 01/29/2007</u>.
01/29/2007	Small City Urgent Care	Fant, Louise	..had another episode at home over weekend ... bent over to tie shoes at home & had sharp pain in L sciatic notch associated with nausea ...	L sciatic notch minimally tender ... SLR positive 45 deg L ...	L sciatica	Sterapred dose pack; if no progress in 5 days, recommend lumbar MRI & orthopaedic referral. <u>Since he is truck driver & on pain medication/muscle relaxers, unable to drive at this point</u>.
02/02/2007	Small City Urgent Care	Fant, Louise	... doing minimally better ...	... quite a bit of sx to L side with some radicular numbness down LLE ... sore over L SI & sciatic notch ... positive SLR 45 deg ... reflex absent L Achilles		Injection Marcaine/Depo-Medrol; Lyrica samples; Lumbar MRI ASAP; <u>no driving 1 wk</u>.
02/08/2007	City Radiology		<u>**Lumbar MRI**</u>	<u>**Lumbar MRI**</u>	... disc extrusion centrally with extruded fragment extending inferiorly along L side at L5-S1 ...	
02/08/2007	Small City Urgent Care	Fant, Louise	... recheck ...	... still has absent L Achilles reflex ... sciatic notch slightly sore ...		Minimal response with Prednisone shot but try one more time; Flexeril; recommend orthopaedic back surgeon; PT with disc syndrome in mind; con't not driving

Form 5.6, cont'd—Sample Medical Record Summary

03/06/2007	State Neurosurgery	Martin, George	… bulk of pain in L hip & L leg … feels better lying down w/L hip flexed … [no] difficulty sitting … difficulty standing in one spot for any length of time … can walk w/out much difficulty … no increase in pain w/cough or sneeze … no incontinence … 2 rounds of Medrol dose-packs & muscle relaxants [gave] temporary relief … has had no PT, epidural blocks or bracing …	… absent L Achilles reflex …	I think this pt has L S1 radiculopathy due to extruded, L L5-S1 HNP due to work injury.	… given extreme large size of disk, I do not think PT likely to help … epidural blocks would give temporary relief … L L5-S1 lumbar diskectomy best chance of getting back to work in near term …
03/15/2007	Big City Memorial Hospital	Martin, George	**Surgery**		Left L5-S1 herniated nucleus pulposus with L S1 radiculopathy	**Surgery** 1. L L5 decompressive laminectomy 2. L L5-S1 medial 1/3 facetectomy 3. L S1 decompressive laminectomy
03/23/2007	State Neurosurgery	Martin, George	… 1 wk s/p L L5-S1 diskectomy … overall a pretty significant improvement of leg pain … some L leg numbness & some hamstring tightness …		Doing well s/p left L5-S1 lumbar diskectomy	… OOW completely until he completes PT and has FCE unless light duty available; removed staples; f/u after PT.
03/27/2007 – 05/18/2007	Therapy Assoc.		**PT**			**PT** - 15 visits Moist Heat & interferential electrical stimulation preceding stretching & strengthening exercises for trunk musculature/lower extremities … progress to work conditioning as tolerated.
05/21/2007	Therapy Assoc.		**FCE**	**FCE**	Physical Demand Characteristic VERY HEAVY	**FCE** Physical Demand Characteristic VERY HEAVY … no functional limitations … can perform all essential duties & meet all physical demand requirements of job without any identifiable work restrictions.
05/23/2007	State Neurosurgery	Martin, George	… has had dramatic resolution of sx … working incredibly hard in PT/work hardening … some occasional residual L hip pain … overall feeling very well … very pleased with outcome of surgery …		Doing well s/p L L5-S1 lumbar diskectomy … has mild L S1 reflex findings only.	Released from active followup. MMI. May work at previous job without restriction at very heavy physical demand level … **15% PPD lumbar spine**

Form 5.7—Sample Request for Medical Necessity Letter to Doctor

[insert medical provider address]

Request for Medical Necessity Letter

Re: Patient: Sally Smith
DOB: [insert worker's date of birth]
MRN: [insert the provider's medical record number for the worker]

Dear Dr. [insert name]:

As you may know, this firm represents Ms. Smith in regard to her claim for workers' compensation benefits arising out of a May 1, 2005 back injury which occurred during the course of her employment as a registered nurse for City Hospital. Per her treating physician, Dr. Robert Jones, her diagnosis is "multi-level disc disease with significant 4-5 degenerative disc disease with annular tear and radiculitis in the 5 distribution."

City Hospital recently authorized an initial pain management evaluation by you on May 9, 2007. I am attaching a copy of your office note for your quick reference. *See attached note.* You made several treatment recommendations, including a prescription for Ultram, a sacroiliac (SI) joint injection under fluoroscopy and a follow-up visit following the injection. City Hospital has not yet authorized the injection or the follow-up visit, but has asked me to contact you and get your written opinion regarding the following issues:

Is the SI joint injection under fluoroscopy part of medical treatment reasonably required to effect a cure, give relief and lessen Ms. Smith's pain and current disability arising out of the original compensable back injury she sustained on May 1, 2005? ❑ Yes ❑ No

If "no", have you recommended the SI joint injection to treat a medical condition unrelated to Ms. Smith's compensable back injury of May 1, 2005? ❑ Yes ❑ No

Additional Comments, if any: ______________________________

____

____

Thank you for your attention to this request for additional information. You should already have a medical authorization on file allowing you to release medical information to this firm. If you have any questions or need additional information, please do not hesitate to contact me or my legal assistant, [insert name].

With kind regards, I am

[Signature Line]

Attachment as stated
cc: Client
Adjuster

Form 5.8—Sample Letter to Doctor re: Causation Opinion

[insert medical provider address]

Re: Patient: Sally Smith
DOB: [insert worker's date of birth]
MRN: [insert the provider's medical record number for the worker]

Dear Dr. [insert name]:

This firm represents Ms. Smith in a claim for workers' compensation benefits. As you may know, the risk carrier is declining to pay medical or indemnity benefits to Ms. Smith for her shoulder injury.

Ms. Smith has worked for [insert defendant-employer name] for approximately 10 years. On December 1, 2005, during the course of her employment as a machine operator for [insert defendant-employer name], Ms. Smith tried to remove the core off a 364 machine to replace the foil. She had difficulty removing it. The core did not come off easily like it normally did; Ms. Smith did not know pins had been placed on the machine to hold the core down. Ms. Smith was pulling and twisting hard on the core in an effort to remove it and felt a pulling sensation in her right arm and shoulder with the immediate onset of pain.

Assuming this is an accurate description of her work injury and that Ms. Smith did not have a prior history of right shoulder problems, I would appreciate your written opinion regarding her **right shoulder condition** as follows:

1. Diagnosis/diagnoses:______________________________

2. In your opinion, did the work place incident, as described by the patient, more likely than not (please check the one that, in your opinion, best applies):

___ Have/has no relation to the current injury or condition;
___ Cause or significantly contribute to the injury or condition;
___ Aggravate, accelerate, or activate a pre-existing condition; or
___ Combine with other non-work related factors to bring about the current injury or condition.

3. Other medical conditions that are affected/exacerbated by the injury or condition: ______

____

____

4. Reasonable and necessary treatment/treatment plan (to include: labs, medications, diagnostic images, tests, studies, referrals, physical therapy, surgery, etc.): ____________________

____

____

Additional Comments, if any: ____________________________________

____

____

____
[insert doctor's name]
Date:________________

You should have a medical authorization on file allowing you to release this information to us.

Please call me if you have any questions regarding this request. Thank you very much for your attention to this matter.

With kind regards, I am

[Signature Line]

Attachment as stated
cc: Client
Adjuster

CHAPTER 6

Investigating and Obtaining Evidence in Claims

Paralegal Practice Tips

Paralegals can perform investigative tasks in workers' compensation cases. When investigating the case and reviewing evidence, the paralegal should:

- Ask clients to provide any and all documentation in their possession regarding the work injury or illness and employment status.
- Send the carrier/administrator a written request for a copy of its claim file via facsimile or E-mail in order to expedite the request.
- Contact the carrier/administrator to confirm receipt of the firm's request for a copy of the claim file and enter or "tickle" reminders in the firm's calendaring system to follow up.
- Know whether the carrier/administrator is required to provide a copy of the injured worker's recorded statement (if any) within a specified period after receipt of a written request.
- Review the injured worker's employment or personnel records carefully.
- Summarize the injured worker's employment history.
- Know the applicable state's ethics rules for attorney contact with witnesses, including medical providers and management employees.
- Prepare a witness list with the name and contact information for each witness, a summary of the witness' testimony or knowledge, and whether the witness has been interviewed and/or subpoenaed to the hearing.
- Have the supervising attorney review and approve any information to be provided to expert witnesses.
- Draft well-stated and clear discovery requests to be sent to the opposing party.

- Read the other party's discovery requests very carefully and review the client's file thoroughly when drafting responses to verify the facts.

* * *

Experienced paralegals may perform much of the investigative work in workers' compensation cases, including (but not limited to), reviewing documents, contacting witnesses and summarizing facts. Paralegals may be asked to give their opinions regarding the merits of cases. They should be thorough, detail-oriented, organized and ready to provide information to supervising attorneys upon request.

6.1 REVIEWING DOCUMENTS

Documents, including medical and employment records, are one of the primary sources of information in workers' compensation claims. In some cases, an injured worker may have key documents. The carrier/administrator, employer and medical providers will also have essential documents. A careful review of the documents from all available sources can yield much of the necessary evidence to prepare a successful claim or defense.

6.1(1) Injured Worker's Documents

When the plaintiff's firm is gathering documentary evidence, the paralegal can start by asking the injured worker (or the worker's representative if he or she is incompetent, incapacitated or deceased) to provide any and all information in the worker's possession regarding the work injury. The injured worker may have already obtained all or part of the relevant medical records, may have received correspondence or copies of state agency filings in the workers' compensation case, and in cases where medical expenses have not been paid, may have billing statements, Explanation of Benefit (EOB) statements from the group health insurance carrier and even collection notices. Many employees also retain originals or copies of key employment documentation, such employment contracts, correspondence, internal memos, job descriptions, employer policies and handbooks, benefit summaries, paycheck stubs and IRS wage earning forms, and medical leave applications.

Paralegals working for plaintiffs' firms should ask injured workers to provide the following documents (if they have them):

- **Medical records**: In addition to copies of office notes and reports, this includes medical providers' disability statements and discharge reports from hospitals or doctors. Reviewing any medical documentation already in the client's possession is helpful to gain an initial understanding of the medical history and to identify medical providers.

- **Medical bills:** Medical bills are useful to identify or verify dates of service and also to start a summary of the medical treatment and a summary of unpaid medical bills in cases where medical benefits are not being paid. In cases where the carrier/administrator has not paid for prescription medication, ask the injured worker to provide prescription receipts or pharmacy printouts which show the date, the prescribing doctor, the name of the medication and the dosage, and the cost of the medication. Even collection notices can be used to identify medical providers and reconstruct unpaid medical expenses.
- **Explanation of Benefit (EOB) statements from health insurance providers:** These statements, provided to insureds by their group health insurance carriers, list medical providers, dates of services, diagnostic codes, the charge for each service and the amount covered or paid by the health insurance provider. They are useful to identify medical providers and dates of service. They can also be used to prepare a medical treatment summary and a summary of unpaid medical bills in cases where medical benefits are not being paid. In cases where the health insurance company is claiming a subrogation lien against a potential workers' compensation recovery or award, these statements are helpful to corroborate the amount of the alleged lien.
- **Wage or Earnings Records:** Copies of paychecks, paycheck stubs and IRS wage reporting forms are useful to verify earnings and calculate weekly compensation rates, as well as the injured worker's employment status.
- **Employment Records:** Employer policies and handbooks, job descriptions, internal memos or accident reports, correspondence, benefit summaries, evaluations, personnel change forms, leave applications, employment contracts and other documentation from the employer are useful to determine employer contact information, job duties, employment status and how the injury occurred.
- **State Agency Claim Records:** These records are necessary to determine the status of the workers' compensation claim, particularly whether it has been properly filed and whether it is accepted or denied. These documents also provide contact information for the carrier/administrator and state agency.
- **Any other documentation or evidence in the worker's possession pertaining to the work injury**, including but not limited to accident reports, news and research articles, photographs, diagrams, instruction manuals, work materials or tools.

The defense firm can obtain documents pertaining to the injured worker and the work injury from the files of its own clients, the employer and the carrier/administrator. If the defense firm wants to review additional documentation not contained in its client's files, such as medical bills or disability paperwork, the information can be requested via correspondence to the plaintiff's counsel requesting the documents be produced voluntarily or pursuant to state agency rules; and/or by sending interrogatories and requests for production of these documents to the plaintiff or plaintiff's attorney.

6.1(2) Carrier/Administrator Claim File

The carrier/administrator's claim file generally contains essential information to evaluate a claim or defense, and to determine whether the case is properly accepted or denied.[1] If the carrier/administrator is the client, the adjuster will forward a copy of the claim file to its defense attorney. If the firm represents the plaintiff, a paralegal can write the carrier/administrator and request a copy of the carrier/administrator's file, pursuant to the relevant state statute or state agency rule. Send the request via facsimile or E-mail to expedite the request. *See Form 3.7, Sample Carrier/Administrator Representation Letter.*

Many states' workers' compensation statutes and/or state agency rules obligate the carrier/administrator to produce certain information to the injured worker's counsel within a specified period of the written request, such as 30 days. In cases where the carrier/administrator refuses to produce all or part of its claim file, this information may need to be compelled for production via motion or hearing before the state agency. One standard objection to produce claim files is that the materials, usually the employer's internal memos regarding the work injury, were prepared in anticipation of litigation. The carrier/administrator may not voluntarily provide its internal notes or telephone logs. If state law and/or state agency rules allow for disclosure of this information, the parties may have to litigate requests for certain documents before the state agency.

A standard carrier/administrator claim file contains the following information:

- All medical records received by the carrier/administrator to date.
- All state agency form documents filed or received by the carrier/administrator, such as accident notices, compensation forms, return to work reports, wage summaries and denials.

1. If the carrier/administrator alleges that it had no prior notice of a workers' compensation claim, there may be very little documentation in its claim file.

- All correspondence generated by the carrier/administrator to date.
- Medical and/or vocational rehabilitation reports received to date.
- A transcribed recorded statement, if one was obtained from the injured worker.
- A printout of medical and indemnity benefits paid to date, if any.

6.1(3) Recorded Statement

Many carrier/administrators obtain recorded statements from injured workers as part of the initial claim investigation. A recorded statement is an interview of the injured worker, usually conducted by an adjuster via telephone. The purpose of the recorded statement is to obtain the injured worker's account of the alleged injury or illness. The adjuster may also ask questions about medical treatment, pre-existing conditions or activities outside of work. The adjuster should ask the injured worker or the worker's attorney for permission to record the conversation at the beginning of the interview. Sometimes an adjuster will ask to take a statement from the injured worker in person. If the injured worker is represented by counsel, the worker's attorney should be present for the telephone or personal interview.

If the carrier/administrator is the client, the adjuster will provide a transcribed copy of the recorded statement (if one was taken) to the defense firm. A paralegal working for a plaintiff's firm should send a written request for the recorded statement to the carrier/administrator, or its attorney. *See Form 3.7.* Paralegals working for either plaintiffs' or defense firms should know whether the applicable state statutes or state agency rules require carrier/administrators to provide copies of recorded statements to injured workers or their attorneys within a specified period after receipt of a written request.

Sometimes carrier/administrators will deny claims based on information provided by an injured worker during the recorded statement. This does not mean that the injured worker does not have a compensable injury or illness. The plaintiff's firm should request a copy of any recorded statement taken from its client, whether prior to or after representation, and review it carefully for accuracy. The injured worker should receive a copy to review. Any inconsistencies or questions raised by the statement should be discussed with the injured worker.

6.1(4) Personnel Records

Paralegals and attorneys should review all of the injured worker's available employment or personnel records from the employer. The worker's personnel file may contain information about the work injury, employment status and rate of pay, and reliability as an employee. The kinds of records retained in an employee personnel file vary widely, depending on the employer, but may include:

- Job application
- Reference checks
- Job descriptions
- Employee evaluation forms
- Personnel action forms documenting changes in employment status such as date of hire, changes in pay, transfers, promotions and demotions (or termination in some cases)
- Benefit summaries and claim forms for health insurance, group disability and/or retirement plan contributions
- Employee handbook
- Internal memoranda
- Internal accident or incident reports
- Medical records if the employer has a medical department, company doctor or plant nurse
- Leave of absence forms, including Family and Medical Leave Act (FMLA) forms

Defense counsel can request the personnel file and other employment documents, such as company policies, directly from its client. There are a number of ways that plaintiffs' counsel can obtain personnel records and other employment documents:

- Have the injured worker sign a release of confidential information and contact the employer, if it is not represented by counsel, directly to request the records.
- If the state's worker's compensation law or rules obligate the employer and/or its carrier/administrator to provide this information, request the records in writing pursuant to the relevant statute or rule.
- If the case is in litigation, request the records via written discovery, such as a request for production of the worker's personnel documents, and/or subpoena the records to a deposition of a management employee and/or the hearing before the state agency.

Sometimes employers may object to providing all or part of an employment or personnel file as well as other employment documents. One standard objection to produce certain documents, such as investigative reports or internal memoranda, may be that the materials were prepared in anticipation of litigation. This is an issue that the parties may have to litigate in a motion or hearing before the state agency.

Upon receipt of the records, review them carefully and prepare a written chronological summary of employment facts. Depending on the circumstances, the employment facts may be summarized separately and/or included in the medical summary (for a complete chronology of events). Start with the date of employment and for each key date, note and describe the relevant event, such as disciplinary actions, pay increases, promotions, demotions, lateral transfers, prior work injuries or termination.

6.1(5) Medical Records

Obtaining and analyzing medical records is frequently the most time-consuming aspect of managing a worker's compensation case. Determine the most expedient source of obtaining these records, both in terms of efficiency and cost effectiveness for the firm and the client. There are a number of ways to obtain the injured worker's medical records, including (but not limited to):

- Directly from the injured worker;
- Directly from the medical providers via letter and/or subpoena; or
- From the carrier/administrator pursuant to state statute or state agency rules, or during the course of formal discovery such as interrogatories, requests to produce documents or subpoena to a deposition or hearing.

While the injured worker or the carrier/administrator can often provide copies of medical records, do not rely solely on these sources. There is no guarantee that either of these sources has all of the key medical records. The most reliable source of medical records is the medical provider.

For a complete discussion of the importance of carefully reviewing and summarizing medical records and using medical records to evaluate key issues such as causation of the injury or condition, causation, pre-existing conditions and even the injured worker's credibility, see Chapter 5.

6.2 Lay Witnesses

Lay witnesses or non expert witnesses can make or break a workers' compensation claim, depending on their knowledge of the events and their testimony. The typical kinds of lay witnesses in a workers' compensation case may include (but are not limited to):

- Co-workers, former co-workers, and supervisors
- Eyewitnesses or bystanders
- Emergency medical workers, such as emergency medical technicians (EMTs) and paramedics
- Law enforcement officers
- Family members
- Friends
- Private Investigators

A paralegal may be asked by a supervising attorney to contact witnesses to find out what they know about an alleged injury. Witness interviews can assist the attorney in determining the strength of the claim or defense and how best to present the case in court if litigation is required.

6.2(1) Identifying Lay Witnesses

The firm's client, whether it is the injured worker or the employer and its representatives, should provide the names of any witnesses they can recall, including as much contact information as possible. An attorney or a paralegal can contact these witnesses to obtain a statement, which may include the names and contact information for other witnesses. **Paralegals should only contact the witnesses that the supervising attorney has specified.** The state's ethics rules may prohibit an attorney from directly contacting a represented party. For example, the opposing party cannot contact a represented injured worker directly, or a represented employer's current management or supervisory staff. If their testimony is needed, the firm will likely have to subpoena them to appear at a deposition or hearing.

Paralegals can also review the documentary evidence in the case to identify witnesses. The following types of documents may contain the names and contact information of potential witnesses:

- Employers' internal accident/incident reports, forms and memoranda.
- Employee/witness statements.
- External accident/incident reports, such as law enforcement or OSHA.[2]
- Ambulance reports.
- News articles.

Part of a paralegal's investigative duties may be to locate lay witnesses, especially if no contact information is provided by the client or the lay witness no longer lives or works at the last known home or employment address.

2. Occupational Safety and Health Administration

6.2(2) Interviewing Lay Witnesses

Paralegals can review case documents and prepare a list of potential lay witnesses for the supervising attorney to review. *See Form 8.4, Sample Witness List.* The attorney will decide which witnesses can be contacted by the firm, as well as which witnesses the firm cannot contact. Again, paralegals should only contact witnesses specified by the supervising attorney. Lay witnesses can be contacted in a variety of ways, including (but not limited to) by telephone, letter or in person. Many people are reluctant to become involved in any type of matter which may inconvenience them, such as potential litigation with court hearings. Some of them may not return telephone calls or even call in response to letters. If the witness is particularly important, a representative of the firm may have to track down the witness personally to talk with the witness.

6.3 Expert Witnesses

Expert witnesses have advanced education and/or professional experience which allow the courts, including state workers' compensation agencies, to hear evidence regarding their qualifications and then designate them as experts in their area of specialty. In some cases, the firm may need to hire expert witnesses to review all or part of the evidence and then testify regarding their expert opinions at a deposition and/or hearing of the case. For example, the firm may need a doctor to testify that the injured worker's medical condition was or was not caused by the occupation and job duties. Types of expert witnesses in workers' compensation cases may include (but are not limited to):

- Doctors (non treating as well as treating)
- Life care planners
- Accident reconstruction experts
- Vocational and other rehabilitation consultants
- Occupational and health safety experts
- Ergonomic experts

6.3(1) Identifying the Need for Expert Witnesses

The supervising attorney will review the case and decide if expert witnesses need to be hired to review all or part of the evidence and then give expert opinions at their depositions and/or the hearing of the case. In some cases, the supervising attorney may want an expert to only prepare a report, such as a life care plan to be used for settlement purposes. Most experts in any field, medical or otherwise, charge significant hourly rates for all of their services to review the file, including consulting with the attorney via telephone or in person, preparing a report if requested to do so, and testifying at a deposition and/or hearing. Experts may also charge for their travel time and expect to be reimbursed for their travel expenses. They may even charge a significant non refundable retainer fee or advance, which is not returned if their services are not used.

6.3(2) Finding Expert Witnesses

Paralegals can help locate potential experts from the following sources:

- Referrals from other attorneys or medical providers.
- Referrals from free or fee-based expert witness services or directories (online or hard copy).
- Reviewing published legal cases with similar issues where an expert provided helpful testimony.
- Reviewing professional, industry or scholarly articles.
- Performing a Google search.

Many reputable experts are scheduled months in advance to review cases and give expert opinions. They may turn down new cases if their current caseloads are heavy, making it very difficult to retain a highly regarded expert on short notice. Therefore, it is important to determine the need for an expert opinion as soon as possible.

6.3(3) Requesting Information from Expert Witnesses

Once potential experts have been identified and a list of experts to contact has been approved by the supervising attorney, a paralegal can contact the experts directly. **The supervising attorney should indicate what information the paralegal can provide to the experts beforehand.** A brief letter or E-mail describing the case can be drafted and approved by the supervising attorney for the paralegal's use. The content of any written materials should be approved by the supervising attorney as these materials may be disclosed later in the case. Then a paralegal can contact potential experts to ask if they are willing to review the case, and if so, obtain copies of the following documents from the experts:

- The expert's curriculum vitae or "C.V." (professional resume).
- A list of cases for which the expert has provided an opinion via deposition and hearing.
- A list of publications by the expert (if not included in the C.V.).

- A fee or rate schedule for the supervising attorney's review.

6.3(4) Providing Documents to Expert Witnesses

In most cases, any information reviewed by expert witnesses to form an opinion may be discoverable, or disclosed to the opposing party. Paralegals should keep this in mind at all times and receive the supervising attorney's approval of any documentation, including E-mail correspondence, prior to sending it to experts. Information disclosed to experts, as well as information not disclosed to experts, may be scrutinized at some point by the opposing party. Once an expert has been retained, usually by sending a retainer fee or an advance for several hours of work, a paralegal may gather, organize and summarize proposed information for the expert's review and give the information to the supervising attorney to review prior to sending.

The supervising attorney and the paralegal can work together to determine what documents will be provided to the expert for review. Sometimes experts will ask for particular documents as well. In cases involving medical experts who are testifying regarding causation of illnesses or injuries, it is important to provide as complete a set of the injured worker's medical records as possible. The task of obtaining updated records as well as prior medical records may fall to a paralegal. In order to verify that key records are not omitted, the paralegal should review the medical records very carefully, as well as all corroborative documents of medical treatment, including but not limited to, client interviews, medical provider bills and group health insurance Explanation of Benefit (EOB) statements.

Paralegals may also be given the task of obtaining copies of diagnostic films, such as x-rays, MRI or CT scans, for experts to review. If an expert can review films via digital imaging files copied to compact disc (CD), and a medical provider can provide copies of diagnostic films on compact disc (CD), this is by far the most economical and efficient method to use.

6.4 Formal Discovery

Formal discovery is the exchange between the parties of written requests for information during the course of litigation, pursuant to the state rules of civil procedure and/or state agency rules. Written discovery includes (but is not limited to) interrogatories, requests for production of documents and requests for admissions. The state agency may specify, as well as limit, the type and amount of discovery exchanged between the parties. The state agency may require a party to file a motion for approval of additional or other types of discovery. Paralegals should know the state laws and agency rules regarding the types of discovery which may be exchanged between the parties.

Another important role for a paralegal is to recommend revisions to the firm's standard discovery forms to improve their quality. Paralegals are often in the best position to note the need for revisions because they often draft the first set of discovery requests and review the opposing party's responses. Thus, a paralegal may know whether the firm is getting the information it wants from its form discovery.

Paralegals may be in charge of entering or "tickling" reminders in the firm's calendar of due dates for discovery responses. Therefore, they should know the relevant state statutes and state agency rules regarding deadlines to respond to discovery (often 30 days after receipt of the discovery). It is crucial that the due dates for the client's responses be entered accurately, because failure to provide timely responses may cause the responding party to forfeit or waive its right to file objections to all or part of the discovery requests. The deadline for the other party to respond to the firm's discovery requests should be entered as well. In many cases, the parties can obtain extensions of time to respond to discovery, either by agreement or stipulation between the parties, or by order of the state agency. However, there will be times, usually when a mediation or hearing is immediately pending, that the other party and/or the state agency will not grant an extension of time.

6.4(1) Interrogatories

Interrogatories are written questions from one party to the other party or parties, which require written answers under oath. *See Forms 8.1, 8.2 and 8.3, Sample Interrogatories and Requests for Production of Documents.* Workers' compensation practitioners tend to exchange standard or "form" interrogatories during the initial stages of litigation. They may exchange subsequent, more customized interrogatories after reviewing documents from the preliminary exchange of information. The number of interrogatories allowed to be sent may be limited by law. A signed and notarized "verification" or oath by the responding party that the answers are true and correct to the best of that party's knowledge should accompany the response. The rules of civil procedure generally require that interrogatory answers be verified, as well as continuously supplemented upon the receipt of new or additional information.

Paralegals may be responsible for drafting interrogatories and/or answers to interrogatories. When drafting interrogatories to the other party, it is important to keep in mind the limit on the number of questions, if any. If the state agency limits the number of questions, then it is very important that the interrogatories be well-stated, clear and written to elicit the desired information. If a set of the firm's form interrogatories is being used as a template, then it is important for the paralegal to make sure the questions have been customized for the current claim. For example, the firm does not want to send questions about a back injury from a previous case when the current case involves a leg injury.

When drafting the answers to interrogatories, it is important to consider each interrogatory or question carefully and only provide the requested information.[3] In cases where the questions are not well-drafted or even nonsensical, it is not the firm's job to do the other party's work and provide the information they meant to ask for. The best response may be an objection that the interrogatory is unclear. A paralegal should work very closely with the party whose answers are being drafted to ensure that the answers are accurate. All documents in the client file should be reviewed to verify and/or corroborate the answers. The answering party should be reminded that inaccurate information and even omissions could adversely impact that party's credibility and hurt the claim or defense. The supervising attorney should review the final draft of the answers prior to having the client verify them.

6.4(2) Requests for Production of Documents

Requests for production of documents are exactly what they sound like, written requests for a party to produce specific documents. *See Forms 8.1, 8.2 and 8.3, Sample Interrogatories and Requests for Production of Documents.* Parties tend to exchange standard or "form" requests for production of documents during the initial stages of litigation. The parties may exchange subsequent, more customized document requests after reviewing documents from the preliminary exchange of information. Document requests may be limited or specified by law. The rules of civil procedure generally require that responses to document requests be continuously supplemented upon the receipt of new or additional documents.

Paralegals may be responsible for drafting and/or responding to requests for production of documents. When drafting requests to produce documents, it is important to keep in mind the limit on the number and type of requests, if any. If the state agency limits the number or nature of the requests, then it is very important that the requests be well-stated, clear and written to elicit

3. The parties may elect not to answer some questions and instead respond with written objections and briefly state the legal basis for the objections.

the desired information. If form requests are being drafted from a firm template, then it is important for the paralegal to make sure the requests have been customized for the current claim.

When gathering the documents to be produced, it is important to consider each request carefully and only provide the requested documents.[4] In cases where the requests are not well-drafted or may even be nonsensical, it is not the firm's job to do the other party's work and provide the documents they meant to ask for. The best response may be an objection stating that the request is unclear.

6.4(3) Request to Inspect Premises

In some cases, the attorneys may want to inspect the site of the injury and/or the equipment or machinery which caused the injury. While the employer's attorney generally has free access to the work site, the injured worker's attorney may be prohibited from entering the work site. If both attorneys agree that an inspection of the work place would assist in resolving the claim, they may agree or stipulate to a planned trip to the site. They may agree to take a photographer or videographer with them. They may even agree on an ergonomic expert or occupational and health safety expert to go with them, with the intent of obtaining the information to prepare a report in their presence.

However, if the employer's representatives will not voluntarily agree to a site inspection, the injured worker's attorney may have to file a motion with the state agency requesting permission to inspect the work site or equipment involved in the injury. The injured worker's attorney may also have to file a motion requesting that an independent ergonomic expert, or occupational and health expert, be allowed to inspect the premises and gather the information necessary to prepare a report.

6.4(4) Requests for Admissions

Requests for admissions are written questions to a party asking that the party admit or deny the truth of the fact stated in the admission. *See Form 8.4, Sample Requests for Admissions.* For example, a request for admission may ask a party to admit or deny that the injured worker was an employee of the defendant-employer on the date of the alleged injury. They are not used as frequently as interrogatories and requests for production of documents. However, they

---

4. The parties may elect not to produce some documents and instead respond with written objections and briefly state the legal basis for the objections.

may be useful when one or both parties are trying to ascertain in advance of the pre-trial agreement and hearing what information the other party will stipulate or agree to. The responding party must answer the requests for admissions in a timely manner. Otherwise, the party's right to respond may be waived and all of the requests deemed admitted pursuant to the rules of civil procedure. Paralegals should keep this in mind if they are responsible for entering or "tickling" the due date of the responses in the firm's calendaring system.

6.4(5) Depositions

Depositions are the oral testimony of parties, expert witnesses or lay witnesses taken before or after the hearing, under oath and recorded by a court reporter. Paralegals should know the state agency rules regarding depositions prior to or post hearing. Most state agencies do not require doctors to come to the actual hearing and will allow their depositions to be taken in lieu of attending the hearing.

6.5 Private Investigators

Many carriers/administrators will assign private investigators or surveillance consultants to observe and record data regarding injured workers' daily activities. It is fairly common for private investigators to videotape injured workers outside their residences. Paralegals should know the state law and state agency rules regarding the disclosure of surveillance documents, including surveillance videotapes. Carrier/administrators are not required to disclose to injured workers or their attorneys that the worker is under surveillance. Most of the time, an injured worker's attorney discovers that the client has been under surveillance when the employer or its representatives try to stop payment of benefits based on activities documented by private investigators. Occasionally, an injured worker will catch a private investigator "in the act."

6.6 Miscellaneous Evidence

The type of evidence used to prove or disprove an injured worker's entitlement to benefits will vary in each case. Other kinds of evidence which can be helpful include:

- News reports and articles.

- Photographs of the accident site, visible physical injuries, demonstrations of the mechanism of injury, equipment and/or objects which may have caused or contributed to the injury, or before and after pictures of the injured worker.
- Diaries, journals and calendars kept by the injured worker.
- Paycheck stubs, IRS wage reporting forms, and state and federal tax returns.
- Telephone records.

See also Section 8.2(4)

Form 6.1—Sample Injury by Accident Interrogatories to Defendant

[INSERT CASE CAPTION]

Plaintiff's First Set of Interrogatories And Request For Production of Documents to Defendants

Instructions

Pursuant to [cite state agency and/or civil procedure rules], plaintiff serves upon defendants the following Interrogatories.

Each Interrogatory shall be answered separately and fully in writing under oath, unless it is objected to, in which event the reasons for objection shall be stated in lieu of an answer. The answers are to be signed by the person making them and the objection signed by the party making them. A copy of the answers and objections, if any, shall be served on me within thirty (30) days after service of these Interrogatories.

All non-privileged information is to be divulged which is in the possession of you, your attorney, investigators, agents, employees, assigns, or any representative of you or your attorney. If any privilege is claimed as the reason for objecting to an Interrogatory, please state the nature of the privilege claimed and the basis for claiming the privilege.

Definitions

1. "You" and "Your" mean the employer, the carrier, and their agents, attorneys, representatives, employees, assigns, subsidiaries, divisions, departments, units and all other persons or entities working on their behalf.

2. "Person" shall mean natural persons as well as all other entities, including corporations, associations, partnerships, firms, organizations, trade unions, hospital, medical provider, professional corporation, professional association, provider of medical rehabilitation, nursing rehabilitation, vocational rehabilitation, physical rehabilitation, governmental agencies or bodies, or any division, department or other unit thereof.

3. "Identify" with respect to a natural person means to state his or her:

(a) Full name;

(b) Present address, and if present address is not known, the last known address and the date thereof;

(c) Present telephone number, and if present telephone number is not known, the last known telephone number and the date thereof;

(d) If employed by you, the date employment started and all jobs held including specifically the job titles and a description of the job responsibilities during the times relevant to these interrogatories.

4. "Identify" with respect to a corporation, association, partnership, firm, organization, trade union, hospital medical provider, professional corporation, professional association, provider of medical rehabilitation, nursing rehabilitation, vocational rehabilitation, physical rehabilitation, governmental agency or body, or any division or department thereof, shall mean to state its:

(a) Full name;

(b) Principal office address;

(c) All business affiliations relating to the subject of these Interrogatories and the identity of the party or other persons on whose behalf such entity or entities acted at the time in question.

5. "Document" means the original (or exact copy of the original and all non-identical copies of such original) writing of every kind and description, whether inscribed by hand or by mechanical, electronic, computer, microfilm, photographic or other means, and including but not limited to correspondence, letters, E-mails, telegrams, telexes, wires, memoranda, notes, lists, worksheets, diaries, vouchers, calendars, ledgers, records, videotapes, photographs, transcripts or minutes of meetings, conferences or telephone or other conversations or communications, studies, reports, technical manuals, statistical analyses, charts, tables, tabulations, computations, tallies, drawings, graphs, maps, photographs, computer programs, computer tapes and tape layouts or formats, computer print-outs, computer runs, summaries of computer runs, or data compilations from which information may be obtained (translated by defendant through an appropriate device(s) into usable form), and includes (a) documents that have been altered, destroyed, discarded, lost, stolen, or are otherwise no longer in your possession and (b) documents that are not presently in your possession but are retrievable by you.

6. "Identify" with respect to a document, means to state to the extent known:

(a) The general nature or description of such document, (i.e., letter, memorandum, drawing, etc.), and the number of pages of which it consists;

(b) The general subject matter of such document;

(c) The date appearing on such document; if no date appears thereon, so state and provide the date or approximate date such document was prepared;

(d) The identity of the author and each person who made any notation thereon, or has signed or initialed the document or, if it was not signed, the person who prepared it;

(e) The identity of the person to whom such document was addressed and the name of each person to whom such document, or copies thereof, were given or sent; and

(f) The location(s) where the document has been stored and the identity of the person having custody of such document.

7. "Communication" means any forms of conveying information between two or more persons, either orally or by documents, and includes, without limitation, conversations in person or by telephone, wires, telexes, letters, memoranda, and any other oral, visual, or documentary means of conveying information.

8. "Meeting" means any occasion on which two or more persons assemble in physical proximity for the purpose, in whole or in part, of communication.

9. "Identify" with respect to a meeting or communication, means to state the nature, date, time, place, method, duration and substance of, as well as the identity of all participants in, persons present at, or witnesses to, such meeting or communication, and the identity of all documents relating thereto.

Interrogatories

1. Identify the person or persons answering these interrogatories.

ANSWER:

2. State when plaintiff became an employee of defendant-employer and briefly describe each job plaintiff has held during his employment with defendant-employer, whether the change in jobs was a lateral transfer, demotion or promotion, the reason for each job change, and his rate of pay at each job.

ANSWER:

3. For each job identified in your answer to interrogatory number 2, please describe in detail the job duties of each position, including the physical,

mental and educational requirements, and the tools required to be used in each position.

ANSWER:

4. Please state the plaintiff's employment status with the defendant-employer. If he has been terminated, please state the effective date of the termination, the basis for the termination and whether plaintiff is eligible for re-hire.

ANSWER:

5. Please state plaintiff's total gross wages earned during his employment by defendant-employer in the 52-week period prior to date of accident, including the hourly rate or other wage rate paid, the total hours worked by plaintiff, and the plaintiff's average weekly wage for this period of his employment by defendant-employer. In lieu of answering this interrogatory, you may attach a copy of a [state agency wage verification form] to your answer to this interrogatory.

ANSWER:

6. Do you contend that plaintiff did not sustain an injury by accident arising out of and in the course of his employment with defendant-employer on or about [date of accident]?

ANSWER:

7. If you contend that plaintiff did not sustain an injury by accident arising out of and in the course of his employment with defendant-employer on or about [date of accident], is one of the reasons for your denial of liability that:

   (a) there was not an injury by accident on or about [date of accident]

   (b) the accident did not arise out of the employment?

   (c) the accident did not occur in the course of the employment?

ANSWER:

8. If you contend that plaintiff did not sustain an injury by accident arising out of and in the course of his employment with defendant-employer on or about [date of accident], state in detail the basis of your denial of liability. Include in your response a statement of facts, as alleged by you to be true, concerning how the injury occurred or did not occur and any other matters in which you dispute the contention of plaintiff that he suf-

fered an injury by accident arising out of and in the course of his employment with defendant-employer on or about [date of accident].

ANSWER:

9. Identify each and every person known to you who supports your contention that plaintiff did not sustain an injury by accident arising out of and in the course of his employment with defendant-employer on or about [date of accident], and state the substance of his or her knowledge.

ANSWER:

10. Identify each and every document known to you that supports your contention that plaintiff did not sustain an injury by accident arising out of and in the course of his employment with defendant-employer on or about [date of accident], and state the content of the document. In lieu of identifying each document, you may attach a copy of each document, including videotapes, to your answer to this interrogatory

ANSWER:

11. Identify each and every person known to you who has information which either (a) does not support your contention that plaintiff did not sustain a compensable injury by accident arising out of and in the course of his employment on or about [date of accident], or (b) supports plaintiff's contention that he did sustain an injury by accident arising out of and in the course of his employment with defendant-employer on or about [date of accident]. State the substance of each person's knowledge.

ANSWER:

12. Identify each and every document known to you that contains information which either (a) does not support your contention that plaintiff did not sustain a compensable injury by accident arising out of and in the course of his employment on or about [date of accident], or (b) supports plaintiff's contention that he did sustain an injury by accident arising out of and in the course of his employment with defendant-employer on or about [date of accident]. In lieu of identifying each document, you may attach a copy of each document to your answer to this interrogatory.

ANSWER:

13. State your opinion as to the causation of plaintiff's injury, and state in detail the factual basis for your opinion and identify the documents upon which you are relying to support your opinion. In lieu of identifying each

document, you may attach a copy of each document to your answer to this interrogatory.

ANSWER:

14. Identify each and every person known to you and not previously identified who claims to have knowledge of the facts and circumstances regarding plaintiff's injury or disability and state the substance of his or her knowledge.

ANSWER:

15. Please state whether defendant-employer has a group illness or injury disability insurance policy for its employees under which plaintiff was covered as of [date of accident]. If so, please identify the name and address of the group disability carrier, the identification number for the policy, whether plaintiff paid any portion of the premium, the amount and term of the benefit(s), and any exclusions which would prohibit plaintiff from receiving benefits during the pendency of this disputed claim for workers' compensation benefits, during which plaintiff is not receiving a weekly disability check from defendant-carrier.

ANSWER:

16. Identify each person you expect to call as a witness in this case, giving a brief summary of the testimony expected from each.

ANSWER:

17. With respect to any expert witness you expect to call to testify as a witness at the hearing of this matter, identify each such expert and as to each expert named, state:

    (a) The subject matter on which the expert is expected to testify;

    (b) The substance of the facts and opinions to which the expert is expected to testify;

    (c) A summary of the grounds for each such opinion;

    (d) The professional or other expert qualifications or credentials and the specific field of expertise, including formal education, experience and membership in professional organizations or other licensed professional groups; and

    (e) The identity of any written report in draft or final form submitted by each expert to defendant or defendant's counsel.

ANSWER:

18. Describe with particularity each exhibit you or your attorneys have which you will or may introduce at the hearing on this matter. In lieu of identifying each exhibit, you may attach a copy of each exhibit to your answer to this interrogatory.

ANSWER:

19. With respect to any exhibits listed in the answer to the above Interrogatory, please describe with particularity any videotape you will or may introduce at the hearing on this matter. Specifically providing:

    (a) The location or locations where the videotape was filmed;

    (b) The nature and extent of plaintiff's actions which led the employer to obtain said videotape; and

    (b) The name and address of the individual that filmed the videotape.

ANSWER:

20. With respect to any videotape you will or may introduce at the hearing in this matter, please state:

    (a) Whether or not plaintiff's treating physicians were provided with a copy of the videotape; and

    (b) What medical opinion(s) were provided by the treating physicians that reviewed the videotape.

ANSWER:

Request for Production of Documents

Pursuant to [insert state law and/or state agency rule], you are requested to produce the following:

1. All documents identified in your answers to the above interrogatories.
2. A complete copy of any and all personnel files for plaintiff maintained by defendant-employer, including a printout of all wages paid to plaintiff.
3. All medical records, nurses' reports, or vocational rehabilitation records currently in your possession or that subsequently come into your possession.
4. A copy of any and all [insert state agency name] forms or paperwork in your possession regarding any work injury or claim for workers' compensation benefits made by plaintiff during the course of his employment with defendant-employer.

Form 6.2—Sample Occupational Disease Interrogatories to Defendant

[Insert case caption]

Plaintiff's First Set of Interrogatories And Request For Production of Documents to Defendants

Instructions

Pursuant to Rules 605 and 607 of the Workers' Compensation Rules of the North Carolina Industrial Commission, plaintiff serves upon defendants the following Interrogatories.

Each Interrogatory shall be answered separately and fully in writing under oath, unless it is objected to, in which event the reasons for objection shall be stated in lieu of an answer. The answers are to be signed by the person making them and the objection signed by the party making them. A copy of the answers and objections, if any, shall be served on me within thirty (30) days after service of these Interrogatories.

All non-privileged information is to be divulged which is in the possession of you, your attorney, investigators, agents, employees, assigns, or any representative of you or your attorney. If any privilege is claimed as the reason for objecting to an Interrogatory, please state the nature of the privilege claimed and the basis for claiming the privilege.

Definitions

1. "You" and "Your" mean the employer, the carrier, and their agents, attorneys, representatives, employees, assigns, subsidiaries, divisions, departments, units and all other persons or entities working on their behalf.

2. "Person" shall mean natural persons as well as all other entities, including corporations, associations, partnerships, firms, organizations, trade unions, hospital, medical provider, professional corporation, professional association, provider of medical rehabilitation, nursing rehabilitation, vocational rehabilitation, physical rehabilitation, governmental agencies or bodies, or any division, department or other unit thereof.

3. "Identify" with respect to a natural person means to state his or her:

(a) Full name;

(b) Present address, and if present address is not known, the last known address and the date thereof;

(c) Present telephone number, and if present telephone number is not known, the last known telephone number and the date thereof;

(d) If employed by you, the date employment started and all jobs held including specifically the job titles and a description of the job responsibilities during the times relevant to these interrogatories.

4. "Identify" with respect to a corporation, association, partnership, firm, organization, trade union, hospital medical provider, professional corporation, professional association, provider of medical rehabilitation, nursing rehabilitation, vocational rehabilitation, physical rehabilitation, governmental agency or body, or any division or department thereof, shall mean to state its:

(a) Full name;

(b) Principal office address;

(c) All business affiliations relating to the subject of these Interrogatories and the identity of the party or other persons on whose behalf such entity or entities acted at the time in question.

5. "Document" means the original (or exact copy of the original and all non-identical copies of such original,) writing of every kind and description, whether inscribed by hand or by mechanical, electronic, computer, microfilm, photographic or other means, and including but not limited to correspondence, letters, E-mails, telegrams, telexes, wires, memoranda, notes, lists, worksheets, diaries, vouchers, calendars, ledgers, records, videotapes, photographs, transcripts or minutes of meetings, conferences or telephone or other conversations or communications, studies, reports, technical manuals, statistical analyses, charts, tables, tabulations, computations, tallies, drawings, graphs, maps, photographs, computer programs, computer tapes and tape layouts or formats, computer print-outs, computer runs, summaries of computer runs, or data compilations from which information may be obtained (translated by defendant through an appropriate device(s) into usable form), and includes (a) documents that have been altered, destroyed, discarded, lost, stolen, or are otherwise no longer in your possession and (b) documents that are not presently in your possession but are retrievable by you.

6. "Identify" with respect to a document, means to state to the extent known:

(a) The general nature or description of such document, (i.e., letter, memorandum, drawing, etc.), and the number of pages of which it consists;

(b) The general subject matter of such document;

(c) The date appearing on such document; if no date appears thereon, so state and provide the date or approximate date such document was prepared;

(d) The identity of the author and each person who made any notation thereon, or has signed or initialed the document or, if it was not signed, the person who prepared it;

(e) The identity of the person to whom such document was addressed and the name of each person to whom such document, or copies thereof, were given or sent; and

(f) The location(s) where the document has been stored and the identity of the person having custody of such document.

7. "Communication" means any forms of conveying information between two or more persons, either orally or by documents, and includes, without limitation, conversations in person or by telephone, wires, telexes, letters, memoranda, and any other oral, visual, or documentary means of conveying information.

8. "Meeting" means any occasion on which two or more persons assemble in physical proximity for the purpose, in whole or in part, of communication.

9. "Identify" with respect to a meeting or communication, means to state the nature, date, time, place, method, duration and substance of, as well as the identity of all participants in, persons present at, or witnesses to, such meeting or communication, and the identity of all documents relating thereto.

Interrogatories

1. Identify the person or persons answering these interrogatories.

ANSWER:

2. State when plaintiff became an employee of defendant-employer and briefly describe each job plaintiff has held during his employment with defendant-employer, whether the change in jobs was a lateral transfer, demotion or promotion, the reason for each job change, and his rate of pay at each job.

ANSWER:

3. For each job identified in your answer to interrogatory number 2, please describe in detail the job duties of each position, including the physical, mental and educational requirements, and the tools required to be used in each position.

ANSWER:

4. Please state the plaintiff's employment status with the defendant-employer. If he has been terminated, please state the effective date of the termination, the basis for the termination and whether plaintiff is eligible for re-hire.

ANSWER:

5. Identify all documents, including videotapes, in your possession or known to you which describe or illustrate the jobs held or job duties performed by plaintiff during the course of his employment with defendant-employer. In lieu of identifying each document, you may attach a copy of each document, including videotapes, to your answer to this interrogatory.

ANSWER:

6. For plaintiff's job as a [insert job title(s)], describe how many times plaintiff had to [*insert components of a repetitive motion job, twisting, lifting items over ___ lbs, reaching overhead, stooping, pulling, etc*]

ANSWER:

7. Identify every chemical to which plaintiff was exposed during the last five years of plaintiff's employment. In lieu of identifying each chemical, you may attach a copy of the material safety data sheet for each chemical to your answer to this interrogatory.

ANSWER:

8. Describe the extent of plaintiff's exposure to each chemical identified above and the basis for your determination of the extent of exposure.

ANSWER:

9. If no testing was done to determine exposure levels, for each chemical identified above state:

    1. the number of years each chemical was used by defendant-employer at the facility where plaintiff was employed.
    2. the amount of the chemicals purchased.
    3. how the chemicals were used.
    4. any safety devices employed to reduce exposure, and
    5. the method of disposal.

ANSWER:

10. Please state plaintiff's total gross wages earned during his employment by defendant-employer in the 52-week period prior to [Date of Injury], in-

cluding the hourly rate or other wage rate paid, the total hours worked by plaintiff, and the plaintiff's average weekly wage for this period of his employment by defendant-employer. In lieu of answering this interrogatory, you may attach a copy of a [insert state agency wage verification form] to your answer to this interrogatory.

ANSWER:

11. Do you contend that plaintiff did not sustain an injury due to an occupational disease arising out of and in the course of his employment with defendant-employer on or about [Date of Injury]?

ANSWER:

12. If you contend that plaintiff did not sustain an injury due to an occupational disease arising out of and in the course of his employment with defendant-employer on or about [Date of Injury], is one of the reasons for your denial of liability that:

    (a) it is not characteristic of persons engaged in plaintiff's particular trade or occupation.

    (b) it is an ordinary disease of life to which the public generally is equally exposed.

    (c) there is not a causal connection between the employment and the disease.

ANSWER:

13. If you contend that plaintiff did not sustain an injury due to an occupational disease arising out of and in the course of his employment with defendant-employer on or about [Date of Injury]:

    (a) State in detail the basis of your denial of liability. Include in your response a statement of facts, as alleged by you to be true, concerning how plaintiff's injury occurred or did not occur and any other matters in which you dispute the contention of plaintiff that he suffers from an occupational disease arising out of and in the course of his employment with defendant-employer on or about [Date of Injury].

    (b) Identify each and every person known to you who supports your contention that plaintiff did not sustain an occupational disease arising out of and in the course of his employment with defendant-employer on or about [Date of Injury], and state the substance of his or her knowledge.

    (c) Identify each and every document known to you that supports your contention that plaintiff did not sustain an occupational disease arising out of and in the course of his employment with defendant-employer on or about [Date of Injury], and state the content of the document. In lieu of identifying each document, you may attach a copy of each document, including videotapes, to your answer to this interrogatory

ANSWER:

14. Identify each and every person known to you who has information which either (a) does not support your contention that plaintiff did not sustain a compensable occupational disease arising out of and in the course of his employment on or about Date, or (b) supports plaintiff's contention that he did sustain an injury due to an occupational disease arising out of and in the course of his employment with defendant-employer on or about [Date of Injury]. State the substance of each person's knowledge.

ANSWER:

15. Identify each and every document known to you that contains information which either (a) does not support your contention that plaintiff did not sustain a compensable occupational disease arising out of and in the course of his employment on or about [Date of Injury], or (b) supports plaintiff's contention that he did sustain an occupational disease arising out of and in the course of his employment with defendant-employer on or about [Date of Injury]. In lieu of identifying each document, you may attach a copy of each document to your answer to this interrogatory.

ANSWER:

16. State your opinion as to the causation of plaintiff's illness or disease, and state in detail the factual basis for your opinion and identify the documents upon which you are relying to support your opinion. In lieu of identifying each document, you may attach a copy of each document to your answer to this interrogatory.

ANSWER:

17. State your opinion as to whether plaintiff was or is capable of earning wages at any time subsequent to [Date of Injury],. State in detail the basis of your opinion.

ANSWER:

18. Identify each and every person known to you who supports your contention that plaintiff is capable of earning wages and state the substance of his or her knowledge.

ANSWER:

19. Identify all documents in your possession which support your contention that plaintiff is capable of earning wages. In lieu of identifying each document, you may attach a copy of each document to your answer to this interrogatory.

ANSWER:

20. Identify each and every person known to you and not previously identified who claims to have knowledge of the facts and circumstances regarding plaintiff's disease and/or disability and state the substance of his or her knowledge.

ANSWER:

21. Please state whether defendant-employer has a group illness or injury disability insurance policy for its employees under which plaintiff was covered as of [Date of injury]. If so, please identify the name and address of the group disability carrier, the identification number for the policy, whether plaintiff paid any portion of the premium, the amount and term of the benefit(s), and any exclusions which would prohibit plaintiff from receiving benefits during the pendency of this disputed claim for workers' compensation benefits, during which plaintiff is not receiving a weekly disability check from defendant-carrier.

ANSWER:

22. Identify each person you expect to call as a witness in this case, giving a brief summary of the testimony expected from each.

ANSWER:

23. With respect to any expert witness you expect to call to testify as a witness at the hearing of this matter, identify each such expert and as to each expert named, state:

    (a) The subject matter on which the expert is expected to testify;

    (b) The substance of the facts and opinions to which the expert is expected to testify;

    (c) A summary of the grounds for each such opinion;

    (d) The professional or other expert qualifications or credentials and the specific field of expertise, including formal education, experience and membership in professional organizations or other licensed professional groups; and

    (e) The identity of any written report in draft or final form submitted by each expert to defendant or defendant's counsel.

ANSWER:

24. Describe with particularity each exhibit you or your attorneys have which you will or may introduce at the hearing on this matter. In lieu of identifying each exhibit, you may attach a copy of each exhibit to your answer to this interrogatory.

ANSWER:

25. With respect to any exhibits listed in the answer to the above Interrogatory, please describe with particularity any videotape you will or may introduce at the hearing on this matter. Specifically providing:
    (a) The location or locations where the videotape was filmed;
    (b) The nature and extent of plaintiff's actions which led the employer to obtain said videotape; and
    (c) The name and address of the individual that filmed the videotape.

ANSWER:

26. With respect to any videotape you will or may introduce at the hearing in this matter, please state:
    (a) Whether or not plaintiff's treating physicians were provided with a copy of the videotape; and
    (b) What medical opinion(s) were provided by the treating physicians that reviewed the videotape.

ANSWER:

Request for Production of Documents

Pursuant to [insert state agency rule], you are requested to produce the following:

1. All documents identified in your answers to the above interrogatories.
2. A complete copy of any and all personnel files for plaintiff maintained by defendant-employer, including a printout of all wages paid to plaintiff.
3. All medical records, nurses' reports, or vocational rehabilitation records currently in your possession or that subsequently come into your possession.
4. A copy of any and all [insert state agency] forms or paperwork in your possession regarding any work injury or claim for workers' compensation benefits made by plaintiff during the course of his employment with defendant-employer.

Form 6.3—Sample Injury by Accident Interrogatories to Plaintiff

[INSERT CASE CAPTION]

Defendants' First Set of Interrogatories And Request For Production of Documents to Plaintiff

Instructions

Pursuant to [cite state agency and/or civil procedure rules], defendants serve upon plaintiff the following Interrogatories.

Each Interrogatory shall be answered separately and fully in writing under oath, unless it is objected to, in which event the reasons for objection shall be stated in lieu of an answer. The answers are to be signed by the person making them and the objection signed by the party making them. A copy of the answers and objections, if any, shall be served on me within thirty (30) days after service of these Interrogatories.

All non-privileged information is to be divulged which is in the possession of you, your attorney, investigators, agents, employees, assigns, or any representative of you or your attorney. If any privilege is claimed as the reason for objecting to an Interrogatory, please state the nature of the privilege claimed and the basis for claiming the privilege.

Definitions

1. "You" and "Your" mean the employee, his or her agents, attorneys, representatives and assigns, and all other persons or entities working on his or her behalf.

2. "Person" shall mean natural persons as well as all other entities, including corporations, associations, partnerships, firms, organizations, trade unions, hospital, medical provider, professional corporation, professional association, provider of medical rehabilitation, nursing rehabilitation, vocational rehabilitation, physical rehabilitation, governmental agencies or bodies, or any division, department or other unit thereof.

3. "Identify" with respect to a natural person means to state his or her:

(a) Full name;

(b) Present address, and if present address is not known, the last known address and the date thereof;

(c) Present telephone number, and if present telephone number is not known, the last known telephone number and the date thereof;

(d) If employed by you, the date employment started and all jobs held including specifically the job titles and a description of the job responsibilities during the times relevant to these interrogatories.

4. "Identify" with respect to a corporation, association, partnership, firm, organization, trade union, hospital medical provider, professional corporation, professional association, provider of medical rehabilitation, nursing rehabilitation, vocational rehabilitation, physical rehabilitation, governmental agency or body, or any division or department thereof, shall mean to state its:

(a) Full name;

(b) Principal office address;

(c) All business affiliations relating to the subject of these Interrogatories and the identity of the party or other persons on whose behalf such entity or entities acted at the time in question.

5. "Document" means the original (or exact copy of the original and all non-identical copies of such original) writing of every kind and description, whether inscribed by hand or by mechanical, electronic, computer, microfilm, photographic or other means, and including but not limited to correspondence, letters, E-mails, telegrams, telexes, wires, memoranda, notes, lists, worksheets, diaries, vouchers, calendars, ledgers, records, videotapes, photographs, transcripts or minutes of meetings, conferences or telephone or other conversations or communications, studies, reports, technical manuals, statistical analyses, charts, tables, tabulations, computations, tallies, drawings, graphs, maps, photographs, computer programs, computer tapes and tape layouts or formats, computer print-outs, computer runs, summaries of computer runs, or data compilations from which information may be obtained (translated by defendant through an appropriate device(s) into usable form), and includes (a) documents that have been altered, destroyed, discarded, lost, stolen, or are otherwise no longer in your possession and (b) documents that are not presently in your possession but are retrievable by you.

6. "Identify" with respect to a document, means to state to the extent known:

(a) The general nature or description of such document, (i.e., letter, memorandum, drawing, etc.), and the number of pages of which it consists;

(b) The general subject matter of such document;

(c) The date appearing on such document; if no date appears thereon, so state and provide the date or approximate date such document was prepared;

(d) The identity of the author and each person who made any notation thereon, or has signed or initialed the document or, if it was not signed, the person who prepared it;

(e) The identity of the person to whom such document was addressed and the name of each person to whom such document, or copies thereof, were given or sent; and

(f) The location(s) where the document has been stored and the identity of the person having custody of such document.

7. "Communication" means any forms of conveying information between two or more persons, either orally or by documents, and includes, without limitation, conversations in person or by telephone, wires, telexes, letters, memoranda, and any other oral, visual, or documentary means of conveying information.

8. "Meeting" means any occasion on which two or more persons assemble in physical proximity for the purpose, in whole or in part, of communication.

9. "Identify" with respect to a meeting or communication, means to state the nature, date, time, place, method, duration and substance of, as well as the identity of all participants in, persons present at, or witnesses to, such meeting or communication, and the identity of all documents relating thereto.

Interrogatories

1. State your full name, any other name you have used, your date of birth, your Social Security number, your driver's license number and your current mailing and street address.

ANSWER:

2. Describe any and all workers' compensation benefits that you contend you are entitled to as a result of the injuries which are the subject of this claim, including medical and disability benefits. Include the dates you contend you are eligible for benefits and the amount claimed for each type of benefit.

ANSWER:

3. Describe the incident which caused your injuries which are the subject of this claim, including the date and location of the incident, what you were doing at the time of the incident, how the incident occurred and whether the incident involved any equipment malfunctions or safety violation on your part or on the part of defendant-employer.

ANSWER:

4. Identify any and all parts of your body which you claim were injured as a result of the subject claim.

ANSWER:

5. Identify all medical providers, including but not limited to, medical doctors, chiropractors, psychologists, psychiatrists, family doctors and hospitals, that have provided treatment for the injuries which are the subject of this claim.

ANSWER:

6. Identify all medical providers, including but not limited to, medical doctors, chiropractors, psychologists, psychiatrists, family doctors and hospitals, you have seen for any reason during the last ten years, and include the approximate dates of treatment and the conditions for which you were treated.

ANSWER:

7. State any formal schooling, certificates or degrees you have completed, the date of completion and the type of certificate or degrees received.

ANSWER:

8. Please identify all of your employers to date, including the name and contact information for each employer, your job titles and duties, the dates you were employed, your rate of pay and the reason for leaving.

ANSWER:

9. Have you ever been charged with any criminal violations, punishable by more than 60 days incarceration? If so, list each charge, the date of such charge and the outcome.

ANSWER:

10. Have you ever applied for unemployment benefits, Social Security benefits, veteran's benefits or other disability benefits? If so, please identify the agency or plan to which you applied, and state whether your application was approved, the period the benefits were paid, and the amount of the benefits paid to date.

ANSWER:

11. State all sources of income you have as of the date of these interrogatories, or have had since the date of the subject claim.

ANSWER:

12. State whether you were working for any other employer while employed by defendant-employer? If so, for each employer other than defendant-

employer, state the name of the employer, the dates of your employment, your job title and duties and your rate of pay.

ANSWER:

13. Have you returned to work for defendant-employer or any other employer since the date of the injuries which are the subject of this claim? If so, please provide the name and contact information for each employer, your job title and duties, the dates of employment, and your rate of pay.

ANSWER:

14. If you have not returned to work as of the date of these interrogatories, please whether you are medically unable to work or if you have been unable to find employment. If you are medically unable to work, please provide the contact information for the doctor who authorized you to remain out of work.

ANSWER:

15. If you have ever claimed compensation or asserted a claim for damages for personal, bodily or work injuries, other than the subject claim, please state the date of the injury, the nature of the injuries, whether a formal claim was filed with any court, and the amount of compensation you received, if any.

ANSWER:

16. Have you ever received a disability rating from any doctor or other medical provider? If so, please identify the medical provider, the amount of the rating, the date of the rating, and the body part or member rated.

ANSWER:

17. Have you sustained any subsequent injuries to the same body parts or members you are claiming injury to in the subject claim?

ANSWER:

18. At the time of the injuries which are the subject of this claim, list your hobbies and/or extracurricular activities.

ANSWER:

19. Have you filed, or do you plan to file, a claim against a potential third party tortfeasor[5] for damages or compensation due to the injuries which are the subject of this claim? If so, please identify the tortfeasor, the tortfeasor's

---

5. An individual or corporate entity who has committed a civil wrong (not a criminal wrong).

liability insurance carriers, the nature of the claim, the damages or compensation claimed, and the present status of those claims.

ANSWER:

20. Identify all lay and expert witnesses you may call to testify at the hearing of the subject claim, and include a summary of their anticipated testimony.

ANSWER:

Request for Production of Documents

Now come the defendants, through counsel, requesting that the plaintiff furnish the defendants with the following documents within 30 days of this request:

1. Copies of any and all medical, vocational, and rehabilitation reports regarding the injuries which are the subject of this claim

2. Copies of any and all defendant-employer employment records in your possession.

3. Copies of any written notes or statements from doctors or other medical providers indicating you cannot work due to the injuries which are the subject of this claim.

4. Copies of your employment records from any other employer where you worked while also working for defendant-employer.

5. Copies of your medical records for all medical treatment rendered to you, including psychological records, for ten years prior to the date of the injuries which are the subject of this claim.

6. A copy of your Social Security disability file, including but not limited to, applications for disability, medical records in support of the disability and awards.

7. A copy of your unemployment records, including but not limited to, applications for benefits and correspondence approving or denying your claim.

8. A copy of your claim file from any other disability carrier from whom you have received benefits due to the injuries which are the subject of this claim, including but not limited to, applications for benefits and correspondence approving or denying your claim.

9. Copies of any documentation of your search for employment since the date of the injuries which are the subject of this claim, including but not limited to, diaries, job search logs, applications and correspondence.

10. Copies of any pleadings or discovery for any actions or claims filed against any potential third party tortfeasors seeking damages or compensation as a result of the injuries which are the subject of this claim.

Form 6.4—Sample Requests for Admissions

[INSERT CASE CAPTION]

Plaintiff's First Requests for Admissions to Defendant-Employer

Now comes the plaintiff, Joe Smith, by and through counsel and pursuant to [**insert applicable state statute and/or state agency rule**] and requests that defendant-employer [**insert name of defendant-employer**] admit or deny the following statements of fact within 30 days of receipt:

1. Admit that plaintiff Joe Smith was an employee of defendant-employer on July 1, 2007.

RESPONSE:

2. Admit that plaintiff Joe Smith's job duties as an investigator for defendant-employer required him to operate his personal vehicle to travel to various assignments specified by defendant-employer.

RESPONSE:

3. Admit that plaintiff Joe Smith was driving his personal vehicle during the course of his employment with defendant-employer on July 1, 2007.

RESPONSE:

4. Admit that plaintiff Joe Smith was injured in a motor vehicle collision on July 1, 2007 while traveling to an assignment on behalf of defendant-employer.

RESPONSE:

CHAPTER 7

Catastrophic Injuries and Death Claims

Paralegal Practice Tips

Paralegals may perform different kinds of tasks for cases involving catastrophically injured workers, who have specialized needs, or cases involving deceased workers, which require additional documentation. A paralegal working on catastrophic injury or death claims should:

- Know the state agency rules, if any, for reporting catastrophic injuries and requesting rehabilitation services.
- Verify that medical case managers assigned to coordinate medical treatment have experience in the area of catastrophic injuries.
- Obtain treating doctors' written orders for home health care and request written documentation for updated or amended home health care orders as needed.
- Know the state law and state agency rules regarding compensation rates for family members who provide home health care.
- Keep a list of the firm's preferred life care planners, including those who have been highly recommended by other workers' compensation attorneys.
- Review life care plans carefully, including verifying the calculation of future medical costs.
- Know the state agency requirements for forms and documentation to be submitted in death cases.
- Know the state agency requirements for forms and documentation for appointment of a guardian ad litem.
- If the firm represents injured workers, frequently contact clients regarding their medical status and medical needs.

- If the firm represents injured workers, ask clients to obtain written scripts for any referrals and/or prescriptions for durable medical equipment and disability access requirements or modifications at each medical visit.

* * *

7.1 Identifying the Needs of Workers with Catastrophic Injuries

Injured workers who have sustained catastrophic injuries will have more immediate and complex medical needs than less seriously injured workers. Catastrophically injured workers will need more time and attention from their attorneys, especially in the initial stages of recovery. Catastrophic injuries may include amputations, spinal cord injuries, brain injuries, and severe burns. Catastrophically injured workers may spend months in hospitals or rehabilitation centers, and may be injured to the point that they cannot communicate with family and medical care providers.

In many of these cases, the carrier/administrator will assign a medical case manager, usually a registered nurse who specializes in catastrophic injuries, to coordinate complex medical care and provide medical status reports to all the parties. In some states, a seriously injured worker may ask the state agency to assign a catastrophic injury rehabilitation consultant and oversee a rehabilitation plan if the parties cannot agree on a plan. Paralegals should be familiar with the relevant state laws and state agency deadlines for reporting catastrophic injuries, if any, and requesting approval of medical treatment.

If a medical case manager assigned to the case does not have extensive experience in the area of catastrophic injuries, the plaintiff's attorney should consider recommending the assignment of a medical case manager who does have this experience. If the firm has not worked with the medical case manager in the past, in addition to asking for a resume or curriculum vitae, the firm should ask for some attorney references. Injured workers and their families will likely have a great deal of contact with medical case managers and will rely on their experience to guide them through the maze of long hospitalizations, repeated surgeries and home health care. Competent medical case managers with experience in catastrophic injuries can often expedite the authorization of specialized medical treatment and make life easier for injured workers and their families, as well as reduce the costs of medical care for carrier/administrators.

Carrier/administrators may require extensive information prior to approval and authorization of treating doctors' referrals, because of the high cost of many specialized services. The parties may need to obtain information about specific programs, contact the treating doctors for medical necessity letters, or obtain additional medical opinions regarding the need for specific treatment if it is disputed. Specialized medical treatment recommended for catastrophically injured workers may include (but is not limited to):

- Long term hospitalization
- Residential rehabilitation programs
- Home health care (skilled nursing and/or assistance with activities of daily living)
- Outpatient rehabilitation programs
- Home physical and occupational therapy
- Psychiatric care and counseling
- Specialized pain management, including implantation of a spinal cord stimulator or intrathecal morphine pump
- Home delivery of pharmaceuticals and medical supplies
- Cognitive therapy and retraining to perform activities of daily living
- Modifications for disability access to the home and/or vehicle
- Durable medical equipment, including wheelchairs and lifts

7.2 Home Health Care

Seriously injured or incapacitated workers may need home health care services if they are discharged from a hospital or residential program, but are still unable to perform self-care activities without assistance. Treating doctors must write orders for home health care and generally write orders to go in the inpatient chart prior to discharge. Contact with a home health care service to get the services started is usually done by hospital social workers and/or medical case managers for carrier/administrators. Home health care services prescribed may be as simple as helping injured workers bathe and run errands, to more skilled medical tasks such as assessment of vital signs, physical or occupational therapy, wound management and intravenous feeding. Some carrier/administrators may only authorize home health care contractors within their networks.

If the home health care services provided are inadequate, the plaintiff's attorney can assist the worker by contacting the carrier/administrator and/or its medical case manager to request a change in provider or services. The treating doctor may be contacted for additional or revised orders for home health care services, and the records of the home health care service providers may be obtained.

7.2(1) Compensation for Family Members Providing Home Health Care

It is not unusual for spouses, parents or other relatives of seriously injured workers to provide home health care, attendant care or even basic nursing services when patients are released from inpatient programs to home, but are still unable to perform activities of daily living or perform medical self-care without help. Before patients leave a hospital and as a condition of discharge, spouses or other family members may be asked to learn medical tasks which would otherwise have to be performed by licensed and trained certified nursing assistants (CNA), license practical nurses (LPN) or registered nurses (RN), such as dressing changes, suctioning wounds, changing and emptying ostomy bags, administering hydration, medications or liquid nutrition through feeding tubes or PICC (peripherally inserted central catheter) lines, and monitoring temperature or other vital signs at frequent intervals. If a spouse or other family member is unwilling or unable to provide necessary medical services at home, the carrier/administrator will have to pay a trained medical professional to come to the home or authorize an admission to a residential facility where these services can be provided.

If a spouse or family member is providing home health, attendant or nursing care in the home, the injured worker's attorney should determine if the applicable state statutes and case law address compensation for these services when they are provided by family members, which otherwise would be provided by an outside provider. If family members are entitled to compensation for these services, then the amount of the fee, usually an hourly rate, will need to be determined. Some state agencies have a set hourly rate for family members who provide home health, attendant or nursing care. In other jurisdictions, the appropriate fee may be dependent on the complexity of the services provided and on the rates charged and received by CNAs, LPNs and RNs who would otherwise provide such services in the injured worker's community.

If the parties cannot agree how to voluntarily compensate a family member providing home health, attendant or nursing services, a hearing before the state agency may be necessary. Paralegals can help gather the necessary evidence to show what services are necessary and what rates should be paid. The attorney may want to get documentation from the treating doctor regarding the medical necessity of the services. A paralegal working for the plaintiff's firm can also work very closely with the family member to prepare a statement or an affidavit summarizing the exact home health, attendant and/or nursing care tasks performed, the periods during which they were performed (if they varied at different stages during the injured worker's recovery) and the average number of hours per week during each period spent providing these services. The care giver's statement or affidavit should be very specific regarding the tasks performed. A life care planner or other medical consultant may need to be hired to review the facts and testify regarding the hourly rates a licensed and trained home health care attendant, such as a CNA, LPN or RN would have earned for weekday and weekend care (not just the hourly rate the agency charged for the services). The carrier/administrator's medical case manager may also be able to testify regarding the need for the services provided by the spouse.

7.3 Disability Access—Modifications to Residence

In cases of serious or catastrophic injuries or illnesses, injured workers may be unable to walk or perform activities of daily living without modifications to their residences. Upon release from inpatient programs, seriously injured workers may not be able to get into their homes if they have extensive stairs or are located on upper floors without elevator service. Other seriously injured workers might be able to get into their homes, but be unable to access the majority of their residences, including bathrooms and bedrooms. If an injured worker cannot access a residence or stay with family or friends who have accessible homes, the worker's attorney may request that the carrier/administrator rent an accessible residence, until the existing residence can be modified for disability access or a different residence with disability access can be obtained.

Modifications for disability access to an existing or new residence can be minimal, such as installing shower bars and/or a wheelchair ramp (temporary or permanent); or major, such as widening doorways or installing overhead hoists to help the injured worker get out of bed or bathtubs. Obtaining modifications to a residence is usually time-consuming because the carrier/administrator will require considerable documentation to justify the expense, including a letter of medical necessity from the treating physician and a written evaluation of the injured worker's needs at home by a qualified individual such as an occupational therapist. Written estimates or quotes from contractors need to be obtained and reviewed, and an agreement reached between the parties regarding the extent of the modifications. Extensive modifications may also require the city or county to approve the proposed modifications and issue a building permit.

Many carrier/administrators choose contractors from their networks of vendors to provide quotes and then perform the modifications to the residences. However, if there are disputes over the extent of the modifications, the injured worker's attorney may want to obtain an estimate or quote from the contractor of his or her choice, usually an individual or firm who specializes in modifying residences to accommodate individuals with disabilities. If disputes arise over modifying the current residence, modifying a new residence, or which contractor which will perform the modifications, a hearing can be requested before the state agency to resolve the issue.

Modifications for disability access to residences can include (but are not limited to):

- Installing wheelchair ramps (temporary or permanent)
- Installing lifts, hoists or ramps
- Installing handrails or grab bars
- Widening doorways
- Lowering counters
- Modifying bathrooms
- Installing non-skid flooring

7.4 Disability Access—Vehicles

Trying to obtain accessible vehicles for disabled workers who can no longer drive a regular car can be a lengthy process. Because of the considerable cost of modifying vehicles for disability access, many carrier/administrators are reluctant to approve this expense without considerable documentation of medical necessity. A carrier/administrator may require a letter of medical necessity from the treating doctor, as well as a written driving assessment by an occupational therapist or other qualified evaluator. Generally, the injured worker must provide or purchase the vehicle itself, either an existing vehicle that can be modified, or a different used or new vehicle, such as a wheelchair accessible van. The carrier/administrator must pay for the equipment and labor to modify the vehicle for disability access, including maintenance and replacement costs of the disability modifications (not the vehicle). Most carrier/administrators choose the vendors to provide quotes and then perform the modifications to the vehicles. If disputes arise over obtaining an accessible vehicle, converting an existing vehicle, or which vendors will perform the modifications and provide future maintenance and service, a hearing can be requested before the state agency to resolve the issue.

Types of vehicle conversions or driving equipment for disability access can include (but are not limited to):

- Steering wheel devices for amputees and wheelchair bound drivers
- Floor-mounted steering for foot control
- Hand-operated brakes or accelerators
- Tie downs to secure wheelchairs
- Removal of seats to accommodate wheelchairs
- Installation of special seating
- Lifts for wheelchairs or scooters
- Floors raised or dropped for wheelchairs

A National Highway Traffic Safety Publication (NHTSA) publication, ***Adapting Motor Vehicles for People With Disabilities***, discusses the various issues affecting disabled drivers, from licensing to vehicle modifications, and is available at http://www.nhtsa.dot.gov/cars/rules/adaptive/brochure/brochure.html.

7.5 Durable Medical Equipment

Durable medical equipment (often abbreviated "DME") is the medical aids or appliances which injured workers need at home to recover from serious injuries or illness and/or to perform basic activities of daily living, such as walking or bathing. Durable medical equipment is prescribed by a physician as being "medically necessary" and is used for medical treatment and rehabilitation only. It can be rented or purchased. Most items of durable medical equipment are quite expensive, and many carriers/administrators work with their own vendors to obtain a significant bulk discount. Some equipment may be needed on a short term basis, such as hospital beds or crutches, until the injured worker recovers. More seriously injured workers with severe limitations may need the equipment for the remainder of their lives, such as prostheses, lifts, hoists, wheelchairs and shower bars and stools. Any plan or estimate of future medical expenses for seriously injured workers should include the maintenance and replacement costs of durable medical equipment during their anticipated lifetime.

Paralegals working for plaintiffs' firms can help seriously injured clients obtain prescribed medical equipment, by gathering documentation of the medical necessity for the durable medical equipment. Paralegals should request (and then frequently remind) clients to provide treating doctors' written notes or scripts for any prescribed items or equipment after *each* office visit. Many adjusters also want the office note from the date the equipment was prescribed, to see the doctor's reasoning or justification for the equipment. If there is an urgent need for the equipment, a paralegal can contact the doctor's office to request that the office note be dictated as soon as possible. After documentation of medical necessity has been obtained, a paralegal can send a letter or draft a letter for the supervising attorney's signature to send to the carrier/administrator for the approval and purchase of the durable medical equipment, together with copies of the script and the office note. *See Form 8.1, Sample Request for Myoelectric Prosthesis.* If a carrier/administrator has assigned a rehabilitation consultant, medical case manager or nurse case manager to the claim, a paralegal can work with the consultant to make sure the injured worker receives the prescribed items.

Disputes can arise if the carrier/administrator refuses to purchase durable medical equipment recommended by a treating physician, such as a standing wheelchair or a myoelectric prosthesis. *See Form 8.1, Sample Request for Myoelectric Prosthesis.* A paralegal can contact the doctor's office and request a letter of medical necessity from the doctor. Sometimes a medical necessity letter signed by the doctor will convince the carrier/administrator to approve the purchase of the equipment. In other cases, the injured worker's attorney may have to request a hearing before the state agency. At a hearing for durable medical equipment, the worker's attorney may present evidence supporting the need for the durable medical equipment, such as the treating doctor's letter of necessity and/or affidavit, the deposition of the treating doctor, the testimony of the injured worker, and cost estimates for the equipment. The employer's attorney would present contrary evidence for the same equipment.

The kinds of durable medical equipment frequently used in workers' compensation claims includes (but is not limited to):

- Braces for back, leg or arm
- Crutches and canes
- Commode chairs
- Feeding pumps
- Hospital Beds
- Ostomy supplies (following surgery to create an opening to allow stools to leave the body)
- Oxygen equipment
- Prosthetic devices (for lost limbs)

- Pulse ox monitors
- Reachers/dressing sticks (for amputees or individuals who cannot bend over or reach overhead)
- Shoe inserts or orthotics (or special shoes)
- Wheelchairs
- Walkers

A list of the durable medical equipment covered by Medicare can be found at http://www.medicare.gov/Publications/Pubs/pdf/11045.pdf.

7.6 Life Care Plans

7.6(1) Determining the Need for a Life Care Plan

A life care plan is a professional medical expert's estimate of a patient's anticipated medical expenses over the patient's anticipated life expectancy. An estimate of the patient's future medical expenses should be customized for the specific medical conditions and may include (but is not limited to) the following types of medical care:

- Doctor or physician evaluations
- Evaluations by specialists such as orthopaedists, neurologists or urologists
- Physical Therapy
- Psychiatric or psychological care
- Pain management visits
- Diagnostic blood work and other labs such as urinalysis
- Diagnostic imaging, such as X-rays, MRIs or CT scans
- Durable medical equipment (canes, braces) replacement
- Wheelchair maintenance
- Wheelchair replacement
- Catheter supplies
- Surgeries
- Hospitalizations
- Walkers
- Urodynamic studies
- Drugs or medications
- Mileage for travel to medical providers

In workers' compensation cases, life care plans are generally only obtained when injured workers have sustained serious or catastrophic injuries and will need a significant amount of medical treatment for the remainder of their lives. Life care plans may be requested by either party, or both parties may agree to obtain one life care plan. A life care plan may be agreed to by both parties when they are trying to negotiate settlement of a worker's compensation case involving significant future medical expenses. Life care plans may also be obtained in cases where the parties cannot agree on the worker's future medical needs. A life care plan prepared by a reputable neutral professional provides both parties with an objective summary of the worker's anticipated future medical needs and expenses. Sometimes the state agency will order the carrier/administrator to obtain a life care plan if the parties disagree on a plan of care for the worker or payment of long term major medical expenses and request a ruling from the state agency.

7.6(2) Who Pays for the Life Care Plan

Life care plans can cost several thousand dollars or more. If both parties want a life care plan, they may agree to split the cost equally. In many cases, the carrier/administrator will pay for the life care plan if it can choose the life care planner. If the injured worker's attorney disagrees with the life care plan obtained by the carrier/administrator, the firm may decide to advance the cost of obtaining its own life care plan. If the state agency orders preparation of a life care plan because the parties cannot reach an agreement regarding a plan of care or payment of long term medical expenses, it will order payment, usually by the carrier/administrator.

7.6(3) Finding a Life Care Planner

Obtaining a professional estimation of a seriously injured worker's lifetime medical needs and expenses is a major issue, because the parties may rely heavily on a life care plan to assign a numerical sum to the value of future medical expenses. A carrier/administrator will rely on a life care plan to evaluate its exposure to payment of medical expenses over the worker's lifetime. An injured worker may rely heavily on the plan to evaluate coverage from other health insurance providers, including Medicare. An injured worker and the worker's attorney will also rely on the plan to evaluate the worker's risk of paying out-of-pocket for future medical expenses if he or she accepts a lump sum of money and waives the right to receive ongoing medical benefits. If a worker is interested in settling the workers' compensation case, the worker will want to make sure any sum received includes enough money to pay for future medical expenses not covered by other health insurance plans.

Therefore, it is crucial that a reputable and experienced life care planner prepare the report. The firm may have a list of preferred life care planners it uses. If not, a good life care planner can be located in a similar fashion to any other expert, such as attorney referrals, reviewing similar state agency cases where life care planners have testified, and life care planner directories.

7.6(4) Reviewing Life Care Plans

Paralegals and attorneys should carefully review life care plans upon receipt. Many life care plans include spreadsheets which list the type of medical care the patient will need, the number of times the patient will need it in the future, and the average annual costs of the care.[1] A knowledgeable paralegal who has summarized the medical records and handled many of the medical issues in the workers' compensation claim can review a life care plan for accuracy. The paralegal will likely be familiar with the treating doctor's prognosis and treatment recommendations. The paralegal may have drafted correspondence to the treating doctor asking for an opinion regarding future medical treatment and reviewed the doctor's response. The injured worker's attorney should carefully review the life care plan with the injured worker. Paralegals and attorneys working for either plaintiffs' or defense firms should check the mathematical calculations in the life care plan as well, to verify the figures are correct.

7.7 Death Cases

Death cases require additional records to document that the death occurred. Cases involving deceased workers who died on the date of the work accident, or shortly thereafter, may have few medical records, but more factual evidence to obtain. Cases where the injured worker died later from complications of the work injury or occupational disease will involve more medical records and will likely need more causation evidence, especially if the death occurred years after the original injury or onset of illness.

7.7(1) Death at Time of Injury

Some death claims have a less complicated set of facts than others. If the deceased worker died at the time of an obvious accidental injury (or shortly

---

1. Some life care plans may include a separate spread sheet with estimates for anticipated one-time medical costs.

thereafter) while performing job duties, such as being electrocuted while working on power lines, or falling from a ladder on a construction site, then the investigation of the accident facts may be relatively straightforward and causation of death due to the deceased worker's employment may not be an issue in the case.[2] Causation may become an issue if a deceased worker suffers a separate fatal medical condition at the same time as the accidental injury, such as a heart attack. It is not unusual for death cases to be denied by the carrier/administrator if the medical records include a diagnosis of a fatal heart attack or other fatal idiopathic conditions in addition to trauma from the injury. For example, the deceased worker may have been involved in a motor vehicle collision and also had a heart attack or seizure at the same time. It may be difficult for both parties to determine if the motor vehicle collision caused the heart attack or seizure, or if the heart attack or seizure caused the motor vehicle collision. Even the treating doctor may find it difficult to provide an opinion regarding causation of death in these situations.

7.7(2) Death Later from Complications

A worker may survive a serious work injury or illness, but die at a later date from complications due to the work injury or illness. Causation may be an issue if the deceased worker had other chronic health problems in addition to the conditions related to the work injury or occupational disease. It is not unusual for death cases to be denied by the carrier/administrator if the medical records include treatment for other chronic medical conditions. It may be difficult for both parties to determine the cause of death in cases complicated by other medical conditions. Even the treating doctor may find it difficult to provide an opinion regarding causation of death in these situations.

7.7(3) Documentation of Death

The state agency and the carrier/administrator or its counsel will require specific documentation of the deceased worker's death during the course of employment. The requested documentation may include (but is not limited to):

- Death certificate
- Official autopsy report

---

2. Whether the deceased was actually working or performing job duties on behalf of the employer at the time of death may be a disputed issue, especially if the worker died while combining personal and business activities.

- Official incident report showing the death occurred during the course of employment
- Accident report(s) from other agencies, such as the police, highway patrol or state or federal Occupational Safety Health Administration (OSHA)
- Witness affidavits
- Proof of employment at the time of death

7.7(4) Expert Opinion for Cause of Death

If the parties dispute the cause of death and do not agree that it was related to the work injury or occupational illness, the worker's attorney may have to request a hearing before the state agency. Experts will be needed to testify regarding the cause of death. The following types of experts may be asked to review the records and provide expert opinions:

- Emergency room physicians
- Treating physicians
- Medical examiner or coroner (who performed autopsy)
- Hired expert, such as a medical specialist or accident reconstruction specialist

7.8 Death Benefits

Paralegals for either plaintiffs' or defense firms should know where to locate the statutory provisions for death benefits under the relevant state's workers' compensation act and be familiar with the amount of death benefits available, including benefits for funeral expenses and medical expenses. They should also be familiar with the claim forms for death benefits required to be filed by the state agency.

7.8(1) Determining Benefits

There are several kinds of death benefits which may be available when the decedent has died during the course of employment or because of job duties. For an analysis of death benefits provided by each state, see ***Table 12—Benefits for Surviving Spouses and Children in Death Cases by Workers' Compensation Statutes in the U.S.*** at http://www.dol.gov/esa/regs/statutes/owcp/stwclaw/stwclaw.htm.

Death benefits may include:

- **Wage Loss:** Compensation in the form of weekly benefits. *See also Chapter 2.*
- **Medical Expenses:** Reimbursement for medical expenses incurred, even though the worker died (such as the ambulance or hospital emergency room services). Copies of all medical records and bills for services rendered to the decedent, including ambulance reports, should be obtained.
- **Funeral or Burial Expenses:** Reimbursement for funeral expenses up to a set amount. All bills and invoices for funeral expenses, including the funeral service, cemetery plot, flowers and/or grave marker, should be obtained.

7.8(2) Determining Beneficiaries

The relevant state workers' compensation laws will dictate who is eligible to receive death benefits. The most obvious beneficiaries are the decedent's spouse or children, living with and dependent on the deceased worker at the time of death. However, there may be other qualified dependents based on the definition in the relevant state's workers' compensation act. Documentation is required to avoid paying benefits to individuals who are not lawfully entitled to receive them. *See Section 7.8(3).*

7.8(3) Documentation of Beneficiaries

The state agency, as well as the carrier/administrator or its counsel, will require evidence documenting the existence of legal beneficiaries to the deceased worker's death benefits. This evidence of dependent family members as defined by law may include (but is not limited to):

- Affidavit or state agency form executed by the surviving spouse attesting to being married to and living with the decedent for the required period prior to his death
- Marriage certificate for spouse and decedent
- Divorce decrees if the deceased was previously married
- Birth certificate showing decedent is the parent of a child
- Adoption decree (or modified birth certificate) showing decedent is the adoptive parent of a child
- Order of legal guardianship showing the deceased worker is the legal guardian of a dependent
- Legal adjudication or acknowledgment of paternity of illegitimate children
- Order or adjudication of disability for incompetent or incapacitated dependents

- Affidavit from parents or other neutral witnesses attesting that parents or other dependents were totally supported by decedent
- Documentation of appointment of an administrator of decedent's estate
- Answers to written interrogatories and responses to requests for production of documents.

Before it will approve payment of death benefits, the state agency must have sufficient evidence to show that the named beneficiaries are entitled to a share of the benefits, as well as to try to ensure that no other eligible beneficiaries are excluded, such as minor children who did not live with the decedent at the time of death.

7.8(4) Appointment of Guardian Ad Litem and Opening an Estate

If the legal beneficiaries of a deceased worker's death benefits are minors, incompetent or otherwise incapacitated, a guardian ad litem will need to be appointed by the state agency to receive the benefits. In cases involving the spouse and children, the spouse may be named as the guardian ad litem for the children. Paralegals should know the state law and state agency rules and forms for appointment of a guardian ad litem in a workers' compensation case.

State law may require that an estate be established on behalf of the deceased worker if he or she had assets or monies in his or her name, or if the death may result in recovery of monies in excess of a set amount. The paralegal can ask the supervising attorney if an estate is required. If an estate does need to be opened, the paralegal can contact the clerk of the estate division or probate office in the county and state where the deceased worker resided at the time of death to get information and forms.

Form 7.1—Sample Request for Myoelectric Prosthesis

[Insert address of carrier/administrator's adjuster or defense attorney]

Re: File No. 55555, Sally Smith v. Big Corporation

Dear [insert name]:

I am writing to explain why a myoelectric prosthesis is a reasonable and necessary medical benefit which the [state agency] is likely to award my client, Ms. Sally Smith.

As you know, Ms. Smith's treating orthopaedic surgeon, Dr. Robert Jones, originally prescribed the myoelectric prosthesis in June 2006. *See attached copy of June 17, 2006 office note and prescription for a myoelectric prosthesis.* He strongly feels that Ms. Smith needs this type of prosthesis. As you likely already know, the provision of myoelectric prostheses for patients with traumatic amputations of forearms and hands is the norm, not an exception. The body-powered prosthesis is usually considered a temporary prosthesis to get amputees used to using one and to allow the stump to fully heal before being fitted for a myoelectric prosthesis. A myoelectric prosthesis provides greatly improved function and range of functional position as opposed to the heavier body-operated or "hook" prosthesis which attaches with a harness. Unlike a body-powered prosthesis, it only requires the amputee to flex her muscles, eliminating the need for a tight, often uncomfortable harness. Ms. Smith's harness for her body-powered prosthesis is binding and uncomfortable across her shoulders and upper back, and requires frequent adjustment. The harness must also be excessively shortened to reach the furthest distance of the limited range of the hook.

Because a myoelectric prosthesis does not require a control cable or harness, a cosmetic skin can be applied, greatly improving the cosmetic restoration. The patient's range of motion is also greatly increased because the prosthesis can be operated over Ms. Smith's head, down by her feet and out to her side, unlike her current prosthesis. She cannot currently reach over her head or to the side to grasp an object with her hook. In addition, the grip force of a myoelectric prosthesis is significantly improved versus a body-powered prosthesis.

Ms. Smith is a great candidate for a myoelectric prosthesis, according to Richard Wall at Power Prostheses, Inc. He indicates that you have contacted him regarding Ms. Smith's candidacy for the prosthesis, and he has confirmed she is well-suited for this device. In addition to the ease of operation, greater grip strength and increased range of motion described above, Mr. Wall strongly feels that it is a necessary device for upper extremity amputees in the workplace, due to the improved cosmetic appearance and lack of a cumbersome harness. The traditional hook prosthesis is necessary as a back-up for the myoelectric prosthesis in places where there is a lot of water or dirt, such as washing a car or performing yard work, and in the event of a breakdown of the myoelectric prosthesis. If we have to depose Ms. Smith's treating doctor, Dr. Jones, and Mr. Wall, they will confirm that with a myoelectric prosthesis, Ms. Smith can reach a higher level of functionality with her injured right arm, will have greater speed and accuracy when performing activities of daily living as well as work-related tasks, and will experience relief of some of the overuse of her left arm, for which she has already had one overuse-related surgery.

The State Agency has on numerous occasions ordered defendants to pay for extremely expensive adaptive devices, including modified vehicles and homes, and lifetime replacement prostheses. On at least one occasion the State Agency has ordered defendants to provide a myoelectric prosthesis for an amputee, as well as lifetime replacement myoelectric and body-powered prostheses. *[Cite and attach state agency cases]*. The hearing officer states, "Both the hook and the myoelectric hand are reasonably necessary original artificial members."

There seems to be a mind set among insurance carriers that provision of a myoelectric prosthesis makes the amputee whole, in addition to providing some extra "bells and whistles." A myoelectric prosthesis is not an "extra," nor is it the medical equivalent of a luxury sports car. No device, no matter how sophisticated, is going to replicate the function of a lost hand or arm. However, a myoelectric prosthesis comes much closer to alleviating some of the grievous limitations imposed by a lost limb, and that is a State Agency mandate, to give the injured worker reasonable relief and lessen the disability arising out of the compensable injury. I know that you have not had the opportunity to meet Ms. Smith, but she is an incredibly delightful woman with a positive outlook and a desire to live her life as if she had not lost her hand. No hearing officer is going to listen to her testify and deny her a myoelectric prosthesis.

Please contact me at your earliest convenience to discuss the purchase of a myoelectric prosthesis for Ms. Smith. I appreciate your attention to this issue.

[Signature line]

Attachment as stated
cc: Ms. Sally Smith
Dr. Robert Jones
Mr. Richard Wall, Power Prosthesis, Inc.

CHAPTER 8

Mediations and Hearings

Paralegal Practice Tips

Paralegals can perform a number of the tasks which need to be completed to prepare a workers' compensation case for a mediation or hearing. The paralegal should:

- Keep a list of names, contact information and fees for the firm's preferred mediators.
- Enter reminders or "ticklers" on the firm's calender with all state agency mediation deadlines, including the deadline to complete the mediation or request an extension of time, if necessary.
- Explain the mediation process to the client and patiently answer any questions.
- Start preparing for a mediation or hearing well in advance of the date of the mediation or hearing.
- Upon receipt of a mediation or hearing notice, immediately review the injured worker's medical file and request updated or missing medical records and bills.
- Summarize the injured worker's medical records.
- Summarize the injured worker's denied medical expenses, if any.
- Request a printout of all benefits paid by the carrier/administrator, if any.
- Read and follow the hearing officer's pre-hearing instructions very carefully.
- Prepare a witness list for the hearing.
- Take detailed, legible notes at the hearing.
- Carefully enter reminders or "ticklers" of all post hearing deadlines.

* * *

8.1 Mediations

A **mediation** is a settlement conference, essentially a meeting between the parties to attempt to resolve the legal issues in dispute, without having to proceed to a hearing and have the state agency decide how the case will be resolved. The conference is presided over and facilitated by a neutral **mediator** agreed to by the parties or appointed by the state agency. The mediator is usually a licensed attorney experienced in the area of workers' compensation law, and may even be a retired judge or former state agency hearing officer. Mediators charge the parties for their services, usually a lump sum administrative fee plus an hourly rate for the length of time their services are utilized by the parties. Some mediators also charge for their travel time and mileage. Generally, the parties equally share the mediator's fees, although sometimes payment of the entire mediator's fee by the carrier/administrator can be negotiated in a successful settlement resolution. An experienced mediator well-versed in the relevant state's workers' compensation laws is preferable.

All **parties** must attend the mediation. Generally the parties are:

- **The injured worker** (also known as the "claimant," the "plaintiff" or the "employee");
- **The adjuster**, claims handler or representative of the carrier/administrator; and
- **The attorneys of record**, if any, for all parties. Parties who do not have attorneys are called *pro se* plaintiffs or defendants. Most state agencies recommend that a party who files a request for hearing retain an attorney.

The representative of the carrier/employer must have the **monetary authority** (the ability to agree on behalf of the company to settle the case for a certain amount of money). Most representatives of the carrier/administrator have a set **reserve**, or a limit on the amount of money which can be offered to settle the case. The amount of the reserve is rarely disclosed to the other party.

Sometimes a representative of the employer will attend the mediation as well. The attorneys may agree that an out-of-state adjuster with monetary authority can be available via telephone during the conference, instead of appearing in person. In cases involving lifetime disability benefits and/or significant lifetime medical expenses, the parties may invite a representative of an annuity company to attend as well, to calculate the value of monies invested and paid out over different periods of time and to provide reports regarding possible structured settlements.

Mediations can be **voluntary** if agreed to between the parties or **court-ordered** if required by the state agency. Most state agencies require that cases pending on their hearing dockets be scheduled for a mediation conference prior to being placed on an actual hearing calendar. Due to the high volume of workers' compensation claims filed each year, the state agency usually has a large backlog of cases pending for hearing. Mediation is viewed as an opportunity for parties to try to resolve issues between themselves and ideally, if some cases settle via the mediation process, remove a number of pending cases from overloaded hearing dockets.

When a party files a **request for hearing**, the state agency may issue an order requiring a mediation conference to occur within a set time period. Failure to mediate the case within the time period specified may be grounds for the state agency to dismiss the claim and sometimes even impose severe penalties or **sanctions**, such as not allowing the claim to be re-filed for hearing. In cases where the parties cannot schedule mediation within the ordered deadline, one or both parties should file a motion asking the state agency to extend the mediation deadline.

In some cases which are not pending on a state agency hearing calendar, the parties may agree that a voluntary (not court-ordered) mediation conference is a reasonable method to try to resolve the issues in dispute. Rather than exchange correspondence and phone calls between lawyers and/or the adjuster over an extended period of time, the parties may agree that it will be more efficient and might expedite settlement discussions to get everyone together for a voluntary mediation, including the injured worker and the individual with monetary authority for the carrier/administrator.

A mediation gives both parties the opportunity to present their position regarding disputed factual and legal issues in an informal setting. Generally, at the beginning of the mediation, the parties and their attorneys are all present in the same conference room. The mediator gives a brief opening speech or statement, which may include the following statements:

- The purpose of mediation is to give the parties an opportunity to try to settle their differences without going to a hearing.
- The mediator is a neutral party and facilitator of settlement discussions.
- The mediator is not like a judge and has no authority to order a party to settle.
- The mediator's duty is to keep disclosures by either party confidential at the request of the party. The mediator may share any information a party allows him to share with the other party.

Then both parties have the opportunity to present their positions in the case, usually via informal opening statements given by their attorneys. The mediator sometimes includes in the opening statement an invitation to the injured worker, employer representative, or adjuster to talk and present their points of view if they wish to do so. However, some attorneys prefer their clients not to talk during the opening remarks of the mediation, simply because an emotional or upset client may make statements which are not helpful to the case. Many attorneys advise their clients to try to remain calm and simply listen during the opening remarks and save any comments or questions for later in the mediation, when they are alone with the mediator.

During the opening remarks of the mediation, the injured worker's attorney generally explains why the worker should receive workers' compensation benefits and summarizes the value of those benefits. The worker's attorney may give an overview of the evidence and the law which the attorney contends supports the worker's claim to benefits. The carrier/administrator's attorney generally explains why the injured worker should not receive all or part of the workers' compensation benefits claimed and may discuss the evidence and the law which the carrier/administrator contends supports its position. This may be the first time that the injured worker hears the attorney for the carrier/administrator explain why certain benefits are not being paid or why they feel the injured worker is not disabled and may be capable of earning wages. This is sometimes difficult for the injured worker to hear. This may also be the first time the adjuster and defense attorney have a chance to actually meet the injured worker and evaluate his or her disability and/or credibility in person.

Often, after the mediator and the attorneys for the parties give their opening remarks, the parties and their attorneys go to separate rooms, and the mediator moves back and forth between the parties. The mediator relays settlement offers, if any, and often spends time alone with the parties and their attorneys, discussing the pros and cons of the case. An experienced mediator well-versed in the relevant state's workers' compensation laws can give the injured worker objective insight regarding the chances of winning the case. Even if the injured worker has already had similar discussions with the plaintiff's attorney, sometimes it helps to hear from a neutral attorney as well. The mediator can also have a similar effect on an adjuster or representative of the employer, who may have received a recommendation from their attorney to pay some or all of the benefits in dispute, but need to hear from an objective attorney that the evidence and the law favor the injured worker's odds of winning.

At the conclusion of the mediation, the mediator is generally required to submit a report to the state agency regarding the outcome. If the case settled, the mediator will report the terms of settlement, including the monetary amount, who has agreed to pay the mediator's fees, and other specific conditions of settlement, such as a requirement that the injured worker must sign a resignation from active employment with the defendant-employer. If the case did not settle, the mediator will report an **impasse**, meaning the parties could not reach an agreement. In some cases where the parties think they can reach an agreement if given additional time, the mediator may report that the parties have agreed to continue the mediation process.

8.1(1) Documents Needed for Mediation

Well in advance of a scheduled mediation, a paralegal should review the client file and verify that the following documentation is available:

- **Medical Records:** Verify that all of the injured worker's medical records have been requested and provided by the medical providers. The records should be up-to-date and include the most recent date of service. A paralegal can use various sources of information to identify all of the injured worker's medical providers, including medical bills and insurance statements. Also determine whether copies of the injured worker's medical records have been provided to the opposing party, or its legal representative, pursuant to the relevant state's rules or statutes. Failure to provide these records prior to mediation may mean that the opposing party's attorney does not have sufficient information to fully evaluate the case.
- **Written Opinions/State Agency Form Completed by Doctors**: Medical issues are often disputed in workers' compensation cases. The issues can range from whether medical treatment was reasonable and necessary, whether the injury or illness arose out of the injured worker's employment, whether the injured worker is capable of earning any wages, or whether the injured worker has sustained permanent impairment to one or more parts of his body. A paralegal can assist the attorney to gather the treating doctors' written opinions regarding specific medical issues, which can be helpful to present at mediation. The treating doctor may need to complete state agency forms regarding the ability to work or the degree of permanent impairment to a body part. A paralegal can draft the necessary forms for the attorney's review and then provide them to the doctor, as well as follow up with the doctor's office to make sure the completed form is returned prior to the mediation. Sometimes an attorney will want a treating doctor's opinion in letter form. An experienced paralegal can draft correspondence to the doctor, briefly summarizing the injured worker's work and medical history, and ask questions

about specific medical issues for the doctor's review and written response. This kind of letter will often require supporting exhibits, which a paralegal can organize and copy to go with the letter.

- **Medical Bills:** If a carrier/administrator is denying payment of the injured worker's medical expenses, obtain itemized billing statements from all of the worker's medical providers, showing all of the medical expenses incurred by the worker as a result of the alleged work injury or occupational disease. The itemized billing statements should show the cost of the medical services, any payments made on the account, any adjustments to the account, and the unpaid balance, if any. The statements should be current and if possible, include the most recent date of service.
- **Carrier/Administrator Benefits Printout/Itemization**: A printout or itemization of medical and indemnity benefits, if any, paid to date by the carrier/administrator can be requested informally or via formal discovery. Most adjusters will provide a printout upon request.
- **Wage Verification**: Documentation of the injured worker's average weekly earnings should be in the file, preferably on the state agency's wage verification form, if applicable.
- **Complete Discovery Responses**: Make sure that all discovery responses, such as answers to interrogatories and responses to requests for document production from either party have been provided. If either party owes interrogatory answers or documents to the other party, follow-up on those responses. Both parties' discovery responses need to be supplemented with updated medical information or additional factual information. Work with the client and the attorney to prepare a supplemental discovery response prior to mediation. Incomplete discovery responses or responses provided without sufficient time to review them prior to mediation may mean that one or both parties have insufficient information to accurately evaluate the case.
- **All Case Pleadings/Filings**: Verify that the firm has a copy of all pleadings and paperwork filed with the state agency. If not, contact the state agency and request a complete file.
- **Personnel/Employment Records**: Verify that the firm has obtained a copy of the injured worker's personnel file from the employer. If the firm does not have a copy of the file, this information should be obtained immediately. The injured worker's personnel records may obtain crucial information that the attorney should consider when evaluating the case, such as whether the worker was a reliable employee or had a poor employment history. Review the injured worker's employment application carefully. In some states, if evidence shows the injured worker falsified

information on the initial employment application, the worker's claim for workers' compensation benefits may be adversely affected.

- **Documentation of Social Security and Other Disability Benefits:** If the injured worker is receiving Social Security disability benefits or other group disability benefits, such as long or short term disability benefits, information such as the award notices, plan descriptions and a printout of benefits paid to date should be obtained. If the injured worker recently received an award of Social Security disability benefits, a paralegal may be able to contact the local office of the Social Security Administration, if it still has the file, to make arrangements to copy the Social Security file if the attorney needs it. If the local office does not have the file, it can provide the contact information to request it from a central location. If the injured worker's group disability coverage is provided by the employer, a copy of the group disability file can be obtained via formal discovery, such as a request for production of these documents. If the group disability coverage is provided by a separate plan purchased by the injured worker, this information can be requested directly from the plan administrator if the attorney needs it. Proper releases will need to be obtained.
- **Criminal Record Check:** If the firm has not already reviewed the criminal records of the injured worker and witnesses, this is a good time to request the records and review them. An attorney does not need to be unpleasantly surprised at mediation or hearing with negative information about the worker or witnesses. A criminal background can affect the credibility of the injured worker or a witness, which in turn can affect the firm's claim or defense of the case.

8.1(2) Preparation for Mediation

Advance preparation is the key to a successful mediation. Carefully evaluating the injured worker's claim to workers' compensation benefits, as well as obtaining and organizing all of the evidence needed to prove or disprove that the injured worker is entitled to certain benefits, **well in advance of the mediation**, helps ensure that all parties have everything they need to discuss their contentions and to try to work toward resolving their legal disputes during the actual settlement conference. Being fully prepared prevents the mediation process from being a waste of the parties' time and money because necessary documentation is missing or the attorneys have not submitted a summary of their contentions prior to the mediation. Once a mediation has been scheduled, the paralegal should tickle reminder dates in the firm's calendaring system to appear at least several months in advance of the mediation. These ticklers will remind the plaintiffs' or defense firm to take the appropriate steps to review the file and obtain the necessary information to be fully prepared for the actual mediation. Paralegals can perform a great deal of the work to prepare for mediations including (but not limited to) the following tasks:

- **Meet with the attorney to review the file and legal or factual issues in dispute.** The attorney and the paralegal should discuss the legal and factual issues in dispute, as well as the firm's contentions regarding payment of workers' compensation benefits. They should also discuss the necessary evidence needed to prove or disprove the injured worker's entitlement to benefits, and if it has not already been obtained, form a plan of action to get the evidence prior to mediation, if possible.
- **Summarize the medical records.** If a chronological summary of the injured worker's medical treatment to date (including the worker's prior medical history for at least a five-year period) has not already been prepared and updated, prepare a summary or update the existing summary prior to the mediation. A medical summary is helpful to an attorney to provide an overview of the injured worker's medical treatment and to identify key medical evidence the attorney may want to emphasize at mediation.
- **Summarize the denied medical expenses.** The amount of the injured worker's denied medical expenses, as well as the worker's uninsured and unreimbursed medical expenses is necessary information to consider at mediation. Prepare a summary of the total denied medical expenses, including the actual cost of each service, the amount paid by the risk carrier, the amount paid by the group health insurance carrier, the amount adjusted off by the provider, the amount the patient paid and the amount still owed. These figures will not only be included in the valuation of the injured worker's entitlement to unpaid and unreimbursed medical benefits, but if the case settles, the state agency may require this information to be attached as an exhibit to clincher or settlement agreements. Also determine the amount of denied prescription expenses, unreimbursed mileage and other out-of-pocket expenses incurred by the injured worker.
- **Identify any liens against the injured worker's potential recovery.** In cases where the self-insured employer or risk carrier have refused to pay the injured worker's medical expenses, the injured worker may have obtained necessary medical treatment through group health insurance coverage, usually through his or her employment or a spouse's employment. In this scenario, many group health insurance carriers have provisions to be paid back in the event the insured wins the worker's compensation case. Some medical providers with unpaid balances may also have statu-

tory liens against the injured worker's potential recovery. Review the file carefully for any lien notices and make sure the attorney has this information to review, both to determine the validity of the lien and if the lien is valid, factor the amount of the lien into the case evaluation.

8.1(3) Valuing the Injured Worker's Entitlement to Benefits

Experienced paralegals can draft case evaluation forms for an attorney's review. In addition to familiarity with the firm's cases, paralegals who value claims need to know the relevant state's workers' compensation laws and state agency rules regarding the type and amount of workers' compensation benefits available to injured workers. Paralegals should also know how to calculate the different types of benefits. The firm may find it helpful to create a **case evaluation form** which lists all benefits available to injured workers per the relevant state's workers' compensation laws, as well as the method of calculating those benefits. Knowledgeable paralegals can use the form to draft an initial summary of the injured worker's entitlement to benefits. The completed form should be given to the supervising attorney to review and if necessary, amend. *See Form 8.1, Sample Case Evaluation Form.*

Each state workers' compensation act provides its own schedule of benefits and different methods for calculating those benefits. However, there are some similar valuation principals any paralegal can use when calculating the following types of benefits:

- **Outstanding Indemnity (Unpaid Weekly Disability) Benefits:** If the claim is denied or the carrier/administrator stopped paying indemnity benefits after a certain point, the value of these benefits can be calculated by counting the number of weeks prior to the mediation or settlement demand that the benefits are owed and then multiplying them by the weekly compensation rate to get the amount of past due benefits as of the date of mediation or settlement demand. If possible, use a "verified" compensation rate, one either calculated by the state agency or agreed to by the parties. In cases where the compensation rate is disputed, use the rate the firm contends is the correct rate.

  For example, the injured worker's average weekly wage is $1,000.00 and his compensation rate is 66 2/3 or .667 of his average weekly wage, or $667.00. His treating doctor wrote him out of work on February 1, 2007 and his mediation is scheduled for July 5, 2007, a 22-week period. To get the total of his past due benefits, multiply 22 weeks times $667.00 for a total of $14,674.00 in outstanding indemnity benefits.

- **Employer Credits:** The employer may be entitled to a credit for unemployment benefits, salary continuation benefits or for entirely employer funded long or short term disability benefits received by the injured worker while he or she was not able to work due to the injury. The firm can obtain documentation of these types of payments by requesting that the employer or its representatives provide an itemized printout of the benefits paid. For group disability insurance obtained through the injured worker's employment, additional documentation that the employer fully funded or paid for the coverage will be needed. The supervising attorney will review the documentation and make the final decision as to whether these benefits are a potential credit for the carrier/administrator. Any credits should be noted on the case evaluation form and subtracted from any outstanding indemnity benefits owed.
- **Permanent Impairment or Disability Ratings to a Body Member:** If state law allows the injured worker to be compensated for permanent impairment or disability ratings to a specific body member, such as a back, leg or arm, use the method set forth in the state law or state agency rules to calculate the value of these benefits. In some jurisdictions, the injured worker may have options regarding which benefits he selects. The worker's attorney makes the final decision regarding the type of benefit the attorney will recommend that the injured worker accept.
- **Lifetime Indemnity (Weekly Disability) Benefits:** If the injured worker's attorney contends that the worker is entitled to indemnity or disability benefits for the rest of his or her life, the value of those benefits has to be calculated. Paralegals working for defense firms also need to know how lifetime disability benefits are calculated, to help a carrier/administrator access its risk if the injured worker wins the case. The usual method of calculation is to multiply the number of weeks of the injured worker's life expectancy by the amount of the weekly benefit or compensation rate. This will yield how much a carrier/administrator would have to pay each week if the injured worker lives for at least his or her anticipated life expectancy. Life expectancy is based on life expectancy tables, such as the *U.S. Life Expectancy Tables* published by the National Center for Health Statistics, http://www.cdc.gov/nchs/fastats/lifexpec.htm.

  For example, if the injured worker is 44 years old and has a life expectancy of 33.4 years, convert years to weeks by multiplying 33.4 times 52 (the number of weeks in a year) to get a life expectancy of 1,736.80 weeks. The value of the indemnity benefits paid every week over his life expectancy is obtained by multiplying 1,736.80 weeks times $667.00, which equals $1,158,445.60. However, this is *not* the figure that the parties will use to discuss the value of potential lifetime indemnity benefits.

When discussing the value of lifetime indemnity benefits, the parties will use the **present value** of these benefits, or the lump sum amount that the injured worker could invest today in a savings account, certificate of deposit, money market account or annuity plan at a certain interest rate, and then draw a weekly check from the investment over the period of his life expectancy (without ever withdrawing all or part of the principal sum). The parties may agree on a statutory life expectancy table, often the *U.S. Life Expectancy Tables* published by the National Center for Health Statistics. The parties may use different present value calculators[1] or pay an accountant or annuity specialist to obtain the present value of the injured worker's entitlement to lifetime weekly benefits, if he or she received a lump sum of money today and could invest it to yield the same weekly benefit over the same period.

For example, one method of calculating the present value of the 44 year old injured worker's potential entitlement to $1,158,445.60 in benefits paid out weekly over his life, is to first calculate his annual entitlement to weekly indemnity benefits by multiplying the number of weeks in a year, 52 times the compensation rate of $667.00 to obtain the annual yearly benefit of $34,684.00. Assuming that the injured worker will receive an income of $34,684.00 for the anticipated 33 (rounded from 33.4) years of his life expectancy and using 6% as an interest rate, and 14.2302 from a present value calculator for future dollars paid annually, multiply the annual income of $34,684.00 times 14.2302 to obtain a present value of $493,560.26.[2] The parties may calculate different present values by using higher or lower interest rates (depending on the economy, the proposed investment and/or annuity company offers), or by using different (shorter) life expectancies, especially if the injured worker has chronic related or unrelated medical conditions.

---

1. Lawyers & Judges Publishing Company, Inc. publishes an inexpensive ***Future Damage Calculator*** with ***Present Value Tables***, Catalog No. 0615. This is a great tool for each attorney and paralegal to keep at his or her desk to calculate present values quickly. The most recent edition of the calculator can be ordered from the company's website at http://www.lawyersandjudges.com/index.cfm.

2. Present Value obtained from Lawyers & Judges Publishing Company, Inc. ***Future Damage Calculator*** (2003).

8.1(4) Mediation Outline or Case Summary

Once all of the documentation for the mediation has been obtained and reviewed, and the case has been valued, a paralegal can draft a mediation outline or case summary for the attorney's use at the mediation. The attorney can use the case summary to prepare an opening statement. The summary may save the attorney from having to hunt through the paper file for essential information. The outline is basically a summary of the injured worker's medical and vocational background, as well as his or her entitlement to workers' compensation benefits. *See Form 8.2, Sample Mediation Outline.*

8.2 Pre-Hearing Preparations

A paralegal who is familiar with the case facts and has worked extensively on the file can provide a great deal of support to an attorney preparing for a hearing in a disputed case. The paralegal will be familiar with the issues in dispute, as well as the facts and the documents. He or she can draft hearing documents for the attorney's review, as well as assist in identifying exhibits for use at the hearing.

8.2(1) Pre-Trial Agreements

Paralegals should know the state agency rules and/or requirements for pre-trial agreements. The state agency may have a preferred format or form. The pre-trial agreement for workers' compensation hearings may be very similar to the pre-trial agreement used in civil cases. The purpose of a pre-trial agreement is to give the parties a chance to agree or **stipulate** to the admission of as many facts and documentary evidence as possible prior to the hearing and to identify the disputed issues that the hearing officer will need to decide. This can save the hearing officer and the attorneys a substantial amount of time at the hearing.

The firm should have the state agency's mandated or preferred pre-trial agreement form that it can modify in each case set for hearing. *See Form 8.3, Sample Pre-Trial Agreement.* The hearing officer may have a preferred format or language, which is stated in the pre-hearing instructions to the parties. Paralegals can also review state agency decisions previously entered by the hearing officer to see the preferred language or format.

Pre-trial agreements generally contain the parties' stipulations or agreement regarding the following hearing issues:

1) **Jurisdiction:** The parties agree that the state where the hearing is taking place is the proper jurisdiction to file the claim, and that the state's agency has the legal authority to issue legally binding decisions. In some cases, the parties may not agree that the state agency where the case was filed has the authority to oversee the claim and this may be one of the issues in dispute.
2) **Employment:** The parties agree that an employer/employee relationship existed between the injured worker and the defendant-employer at the time of the alleged injury and the parties are subject to the applicable workers' compensation act. In some cases the parties may not agree that an employment relationship existed at the time of the injury and this may be one of the issues in dispute. The employer in particular may allege that the injured worker was not an employee covered by the state's workers' compensation act but an independent contractor.
3) **Average Earnings:** The parties agree to the amount of the employee's pre-injury average earnings over a set period and the subsequent compensation rate allowed by state law. If the parties do not agree with the calculation of the employee's average earnings over a set period, this may be one of the issues in dispute.
4) **Exhibits:** The parties each list the exhibits they may present at the hearing. Listing the exhibits on the pre-trial agreement does not mean they have to be presented at the hearing. However, leaving exhibits out of the pre-trial agreement may mean that the hearing officer will not allow them to be used. The parties may stipulate that certain exhibits can be admitted into the record without presenting further evidence, such as medical records, personnel files and state agency documents. The parties can also identify the exhibits which may be contested at the hearing. In those instances, the hearing officers will decide whether the exhibits can be admitted into the record.
5) **Witnesses:** The parties each list the witnesses they may call at the hearing, including the doctors who may be deposed after the hearing. Listing the witnesses on the pre-trial agreement does not mean they have to testify at the hearing or a deposition. However, leaving witnesses off the pre-trial agreement may mean that the hearing officer will not allow them to testify. Also, if one party lists a potential witness, the other party could subpoena them to testify at the hearing or a deposition. Therefore, disclosure of witnesses on the pre-trial agreement is an extremely important decision to be made by the supervising attorney.
6) **Issues:** The parties generally try to agree regarding the legal issues in dispute. Standard issues listed on pre-trial agreements may include:

- Was the employee injured by accident arising out of and in the course of his employment on a certain date?
- Did the employee sustain an occupational disease because of his employment?
- Is the employee entitled to workers' compensation benefits? If so, to which benefits and in what amount?
- What is the employee's compensation rate?
- Was medical treatment received or is treatment being sought reasonable and necessary, and if so, should the defendants pay for it?
- Is the employee permanently and totally disabled?
- Is the employee able to return to work?
- Did the employee refuse to return to suitable work?

If the parties cannot agree regarding the hearing issues, they can list their issues separately on the pre-trial agreement.

The parties should submit the pre-trial agreement to the hearing officer pursuant to state agency rules and the hearing officer's instructions. Failure to file the pre-trial agreement in a timely manner may result in sanctions against one or both parties, including dismissal of the employee's claim or the employer's defenses.

8.2(2) Subpoenaing Witnesses

Paralegals should know the relevant state law and state agency rules for issuing subpoenas to witnesses to appear at a hearing. Instructions for issuing hearing subpoenas may also come with the hearing calendar or the hearing officer's pre-hearing instructions. The deadlines for issuing subpoenas should be entered in the firm's reminder or "tickler" system. The state agency's subpoena forms should be used and may be downloaded from the state agency's website or sent with the hearing calendar or hearing officer's pre-hearing instructions.

The attorney and a paralegal may work together to review the file and draft a list of proposed hearing witnesses, including a summary of their testimony. The supervising attorney will decide which witnesses are to be subpoenaed to appear at the hearing. The subpoenas should be prepared and served per state law and state agency instructions. The firm should retain a copy of all subpoenas served. Documentary evidence that the subpoenas were served should be obtained and attached to the subpoenas, such as a completed certificate of service if served by a sheriff or process server or the return receipt card if served by certified mail. The attorney may need proof of service at the hearing, if a subpoenaed witness fails to appear.

8.2(3) Scheduling Depositions

Paralegals should know the state law and state agency rules for scheduling depositions before or after the hearing. The state agency may allow doctors to provide testimony via deposition, rather than having to appear at the hearing and wait for an extended period of time to testify. If that is the case, the state agency may also request that the doctors' depositions must be scheduled (if not taken) before the actual hearing and that the dates of their depositions must be listed on the pre-trial agreement. If the firm cannot schedule the depositions in a timely manner, a motion or request for extension of time to schedule and take the depositions should be filed with the state agency. The hearing officer could issue sanctions against one or both parties if the depositions are not scheduled per the state agency rules or the hearing officer's pre-hearing instructions.

8.2(4) Exhibits

The attorney and a paralegal may work together to identify potential exhibits for the hearing. The attorney and/or paralegal should review every single document in the file to determine if it is a viable hearing exhibit. This review can be time-consuming if the paper file is voluminous, but it is necessary. Once the evidentiary record is closed, no additional exhibits may be submitted. The following types of exhibits may be potential hearing exhibits:

- Medical records, including prior and unrelated records if applicable
- Medical correspondence, including medical expert opinions
- Employment records
- Rehabilitation records (vocational and medical)
- State agency paperwork
- Discovery responses exchanged by the parties
- Photographs
- Videotapes
- Expert reports (medical, rehabilitation, ergonomic, accident reconstruction or other)
- Objects (work tools, work materials)

The parties may stipulate to some exhibits and submit a joint exhibit, such as "Stipulated Exhibit 1—Medical Records." The attorneys may want to keep other exhibits out of the record and may prepare arguments, motions or briefs for or against admitting certain exhibits at the hearing.

8.3 Assisting the Attorney at Hearing

A paralegal may be asked to attend the hearing and assist the supervising attorney with witnesses, exhibits or taking notes.

8.3(1) Scheduling Witness Testimony

A witness list should be drafted for the attorney's review in advance of the hearing. *See Form 8.4, Sample Witness List.* For each witness, the list should contain the name, contact information, summary of testimony, and whether or not the witness has been interviewed and/or served with a subpoena. Obtain as many telephone numbers for each witness as possible, especially a number that the witness can be reached immediately preceding the hearing, in case the hearing schedule changes. The list should include witnesses listed by the other party on the pre-trial agreement, even if the firm is prohibited from contacting them or did not subpoena them. The supervising attorney should have a copy of the list, and the paralegal should have his or her own copy to refer to during the hearing. The paralegal may need to leave the courtroom and make phone calls to witnesses during the hearing.

Many witnesses are not enthusiastic about having their lives disrupted to attend a workers' compensation hearing. Some of the witnesses subpoenaed may be reluctant to attend and testify. A paralegal should verify with the supervising attorney when witnesses are needed at the hearing. The attorney may want witnesses present in the courtroom at the time the hearing is scheduled to start, or if the injured worker's testimony is likely to be lengthy, the attorney may want witnesses to come later during the day. The attorney may allow witnesses to be on standby if they can get to the courthouse on short notice. Paralegals should give witnesses as much advance notice as possible of changes in a hearing date or schedule. If the attorney decides to release a witness from a subpoena or the hearing is cancelled or postponed, calling the witnesses to notify them of any changes should be a priority.

8.3(2) Hearing Exhibit Log

A paralegal can draft an exhibit log for the attorney's review prior to the hearing. *See Form 8.5, Sample Hearing Exhibit Log.* A paralegal can also help the attorney complete the log at the hearing. The log is used to record the exhibit numbers assigned to an exhibit when the exhibit is introduced. The log is also used to make sure that all of the stipulated exhibits and the client's exhibits have been presented to the court, and admitted into the evidentiary record, either by stipulation or by order of the hearing officer. The log also helps the attorney keep track of the opposing party's exhibits, including whether he or she has a copy, what exhibit number was assigned, and whether the hearing officer admitted the exhibit into the evidence or sustained an objection to its admission.

8.3(3) Taking Notes

Paralegals can assist at a workers' compensation hearing by taking a good set of detailed (and legible) notes. The hearing officer's statements regarding the pre-trial agreement, stipulated facts and exhibits, and orders regarding post-hearing deadlines should be carefully and accurately noted. Careful and legible notes should be taken during each witness's testimony. In a lengthy hearing, the attorney may ask the paralegal questions about prior witness testimony. The paralegal may have to refer to the hearing notes if he or she does not recall the specific testimony. The hearing notes may also be necessary to refer to when writing post-hearing briefs, if the firm does not order a hearing transcript from the court reporter.

8.3(4) Tickling Post-Hearing Deadlines

The hearing officer may set deadlines for the parties to complete depositions and then file hearing briefs. All deadlines ordered by the hearing officer should be accurately noted and entered in the firm's tickler (reminder) system as soon as possible. The state agency may also send an order containing post-hearing deadlines after the hearing. Failure to complete depositions or submit briefs in a timely manner could result in sanctions against one or both parties by the state agency. If either party believes an extension of time to take depositions or submit briefs is needed, the requesting party should check with the other party to see if they are agreeable to the extension and then submit a motion for extension of time to the hearing officer. However, both sides should be prepared to meet the original deadlines if the hearing officer does not grant the extension.

Form 8. 1—Sample Preliminary Case Evaluation Form

State Agency File No. 555555, Joe Smith v. Big Corporation and Giant Insurance Company
DOI: January 1, 200__
DX: Herniated disc L4-5, status post fusion surgery

Type of Benefit	Value	Status
Outstanding Indemnity Benefit(s): Average Weekly Wage: $1,000.00 Compensation Rate: $667.00	N/A	Accepted claim, via State Agency Form _______
Employer Credits ___ Short Term Disability ___ Long Term Disability ___ Unemployment Benefits ___ Salary Continuation	N/A	
Permanent Impairment or Rating 25% to Back per Dr. Jones on February 1, 2007 = 75 weeks x $667.00 compensation rate =	**$50,025.00**	Do not elect—lifetime disability benefits more valuable benefit
Partial Wage Earning Impairment	N/A	Has not returned to work
Lifetime Disability Benefits (DOB: 02/08/1963) = 44 years old Life expectancy per U.S. Life Tables, White Male = 33.4 years or 1,736.80 weeks x $667 =$1,158,445.60 **Assuming an annual WC income of $34,684.00, the PRESENT VALUE for 33 years is: 6% (14.2302 x $34,684.00) = $**	**$493,560.26**	Claimant is 44 years old and has not been released RTW. ****Claimant has received award of Social Security disability benefits and will be eligible for Medicare within 30 months*****
Outstanding Medical Expenses	N/A	Accepted claim.
Vocational Rehabilitation Expenses	N/A	Has not been released RTW
Unpaid Sick Travel & Prescriptions	N/A	Accepted claim
Future Medicals	**$46,198.25**	**See MSA Report**
TOTAL	$539,758.51	

Notes:

- **Liens:** None known.
- **Financial Goals**: Injured worker wants to pay off mortgage on home.
- **Future Surgeries**: Treating doctor does not anticipate any additional surgeries.
- **Social Security**: Receiving

- **Medicare Set-aside Trust Arrangement:** See report from vendor
- **Realistic Settlement Range of This Case:**

ANALYSIS OF WCMSA REPORT (Rated Age = 25 years)

Total Expenses over LE	**Medicare covered Expenses over LE**
Average annual medical over LE 25 × \$733.29 = **\$18,332.25**	Medicare covered annual medicare over LE 25 × \$698.29 = **\$17,457.25**
Add'tl medical over next year = **\$116.00**	Medicare covered medical over next year = **\$102.00**
Average annual RX over LE 25 × \$1,110.00 = **\$27,750.00**	Medicare covered RX over LE 25 × \$1,110.00 = **\$27,750.00**
Limited add'tl RX = **\$0**	Limited Medicare covered add'tl RX = **\$0**
TOTAL EXP OVER LE = **\$46,198.25**	TOTAL MEDICARE COVERED OVER LE = **\$45,309.25**
	Not covered by Medicare = \$889.00

Form 8.2—Sample Mediation Outline

State Agency File No. 555555, Joe Smith v. Big Corporation and Giant Insurance Company

1. **Employee Information**
   a. Name: Joe Smith
   b. Age & DOB: 44 years old (02/08/1963)
   c. Marital Status: Married 15 years to Brenda, two children, ages 8, 10
   d. Education/Technical Training: High school diploma
   e. Other (i.e, military service, etc.): 4 years Army, honorably discharged

2. **Past Work Experience**
   a. Fork lift operator for 10 years
   b. Machine mechanic for defendant-employer for 15 years

3. **Other Past Significant Experiences**
   a. Coronary bypass surgery in 2002 due to coronary artery disease
   b. Smoker
   c. Per medical records: excessive alcohol use
   d. High blood pressure and high cholesterol treated with medication but occasional periods of noncompliance
   e. Currently taking medication for adjustment disorder with anxiety

4. **Current Job**: N/A, alleges permanently and totally disabled. Not looking for work

5. **Compensable Injury**
   a. Date of injury: January __, 200__
   b. Description of how accident occurred: Herniated disk while attempting to move bin weighing in excess of 100 lbs.
   c. Description of injuries: Herniated disk L4-5, status post fusion surgery
   d. Medical treatment received: Failed conservative methods including physical therapy, epidural steroid injections, and nerve blocks. Underwent fusion L4-5 in 200__. Developed chronic pain syndrome in low back and right lower extremity, currently under the care of pain management facility—monthly medication management visits, prescription opioids and selective nerve root blocks.
   e. Medical treatment anticipated: Continued pain management, including medication management visits, prescription opioids and selective nerve root blocks. Not a candidate for additional lumbar surgeries.
   f. Current Medical Condition and Prognosis: Per treating pain management physician, prognosis is fair, cannot work due to chronic pain syndrome and side effects of prescription medications.

6. **Workers' Compensation Information**
   a. Accepted or Denied: Accepted on State Agency Form ____
   b. AWW $1,000.00—Yields Comp Rate $667.00
   c. Is Hearing Pending—Hearing pending regarding whether Mr. Smith is permanently and totally disabled.
   d. Issues in dispute:

      i. Contested medical treatment: No

      ii. Disagreement over treating MD: No

      iii. Vocational issues: Yes, ability to return to work

      iv. Rating issue: No

      v. Whether claim is compensable: No

      vi. Other: No

7. **Damages**
   a. Ability to RTW: Defendants allege they found him a suitable job working third shift sitting in a guard booth at the entrance of a local express mail company.
   b. Wage earning disability: His doctors say he can work at a sedentary job with no lifting more than 5 pounds but that he cannot work continuously due to chronic pain and medication side effects.
   c. Permanent Physical Impairment: **$50,025.00** (25% rating to back)
   d. Present value of lifetime wage earning disability, using 6%: $493,560.26
   e. Cost of future medical treatment: **$46,198.25**
   f. Demand: $__________ [insert amount per supervising attorney]

Form 8.3—Sample Pre-Trial Agreement

[Insert Case Caption]

PRE-TRIAL AGREEMENT

Pursuant to the Pre-Trial Order of [insert hearing officer's name], the parties state the following:

(1) It is stipulated that all parties are properly before the [insert state agency name], and that the [insert state agency name] has jurisdiction of the parties and of the subject matter.

(2) It is stipulated that all parties have been correctly designated, and there is no question as to misjoinder or nonjoinder of parties.

(3) In addition to the other stipulations contained herein, the parties stipulate and agree with respect to the following undisputed facts:

(a) All parties are subject to and bound by the provisions of the [insert state workers' compensation act]

(b) The employer-employee relationship existed between plaintiff [insert name] and defendant [insert name]. prior to and on [insert date of injury]

(c) [Insert name of insurance company] is the carrier on the risk;

-or-

Defendant-employer is self-insured and [insert name of administrator] is the administrator for the defendant-employer;

(d) The parties agree that medical records or reports and/or itemized billing statements of the following medical providers: [insert names of all medical care providers] may be submitted by any of the parties into evidence, only after the reports or records have been shared with the other counsel, and subject to the right of any of the parties to depose the health care providers;

(e) Plaintiff's compensation rate is $[insert compensation rate] based on an average weekly wage of $[insert average weekly wage];

(f) Plaintiff sustained a compensable injury on or about [insert date of injury], which defendants accepted on a [insert state agency form] dated [insert date of state agency form].

-or-

Defendant has denied liability for the injury on a [state agency form], dated [insert date of state agency form].

(g) The parties agree that the depositions of the following expert(s) may be taken and that the parties have made a good faith effort to schedule said depositions prior to the hearing.

(1) doctor name, M.D. (Deposition scheduled___);

(2) doctor name, M.D. (Deposition scheduled____);

(3) doctor name, Ph.D. (Deposition scheduled____); and

(4) doctor name, M.D. (Deposition scheduled____);

(4) The following is a list of all known exhibits the plaintiff may offer at the trial.

(a) Copies of plaintiff's medical records, employment records and rehabilitation reports;

(b) All pleadings and discovery filed herein;

(c) All [insert name of state agency] forms, orders, notices and correspondence;

(d) Any documents listed by defendants; and

(e) Plaintiff reserves the right to use and enter additional exhibits.

(5) The following is a list of all known exhibits the defendants may offer at trial.

(a) Any documents listed by plaintiff;

(b) Defendants reserve the right to use and enter additional exhibits.

(6) The following is a list of the names of all known witnesses the plaintiff may offer at the trial:

(a)

(b)

(c)

(d) Any witness identified by the defendants; and

(e) Plaintiff reserves the right to call additional witnesses.

(7) The following is a list of the names of all known witnesses the defendants may offer at the trial:

(a) Any witnesses listed by plaintiff;

(b) Defendants reserve the right to call additional witnesses;

(8) There are no motions currently pending.

(9) The parties contend that the contested issues to be tried by the [insert state agency name] are as follows:

(a) Is plaintiff permanently and totally disabled from working?

This the _____ day of _______________, ____.

Law firm name

____

Attorney name
Attorney for Plaintiff
Address of attorney
Telephone:
Facsimile:

Law firm name

____

Attorney name
Attorney for Defendants
Address of attorney
Telephone:
Facsimile:

Form 8.4—Sample Witness List

Witness List (revised 07/01/2007) **Joe Smith v. Big Corporation and Giant Insurance Company**				
Name/Contact	Testimony	Inter-viewed	Subpoe-naed	Served
Edwards, Tom 405 Main St. Raleigh, NC (919) 555-1234	Current EE, **Supervisor in Shipping Department**, has declined to be interviewed but not listed by defendants as witness in pre-trial agreement. Joe and Tamara say they reported injury to Mr. Edwards.		✓	✓
Jones, Tamara	Current EE, **Clerk in Shipping Department**, will testify that she saw Joe slip in puddle of oil and fall in shipping department. She helped him up and called their supervisor, Tom Edwards.	✓	✓	✓
Roberts, Calvin	Current EE, **Plant Manager**, defendants' interrogatory responses say he will testify that Joe hurt his back moving furniture at home			
Smith, Mary	Joe's **spouse**, will testify that he moved some furniture the weekend prior to the injury but did not complain of any back pain. Will also testify that he has suffered from depression since being hurt and unable to work.	✓		
Walters, James	**Private investigator** hired by defendants, took videotape of Joe mowing his grass on a riding lawn mower April 2007.			

Form 8.5—Sample Hearing Exhibit Log

State Agency File No. 555555, Joe Smith v. Big Corporation and Giant Insurance Company

Date of Hearing: [Insert date]

Tab	No.	Exhibit Description	Offered	Admitted
1	Stip. 1	Medical Records	✓	✓
2	Stip. 2	State Agency Claim File	✓	✓
3	Stip. 3	Employment file from Big Corporation	✓	✓
4	Stip. 4			
5	Stip. 5			
6	Stip. 6			
7	Stip. 7			
8	Stip. 8			
9	Plaintiff 1	Photographs of oil on floor	✓	✓
10	Plaintiff 2	Plaintiff's diary entries for month of injury	✓	✓
11	Plaintiff 3	Plaintiff's company physical three weeks before injury	✓	✓
12	Plaintiff 4			
13	Plaintiff 5			
14	Plaintiff 6			
15	Plaintiff 7			
16	Defendant 1	Affidavit of Calvin Roberts	✓	
17	Defendant 2	Surveillance videotapes	✓	✓
18	Defendant 3			
19	Defendant 4			
20	Defendant 5			
21	Defendant 6			

CHAPTER 9

Workers' Compensation Medicare Set-Aside Arrangements (WCMSAs)

Paralegal Practice Tips

Paralegals who work on cases involving injured workers who are also eligible for Medicare coverage need to know basic information about Workers' Compensation Medicare Set-aside Arrangements (WCMSAs). At minimum, a paralegal should:

- Bookmark or save as a favorite to the web browser the CMS Workers Compensation Agency Services website at http://www.cms.hhs.gov/WorkersCompAgencyServices/.
- Bookmark or save as a favorite the CMS "Submissions of WCMSAs" link at http://www.cms.hhs.gov/WorkersCompAgencyServices/05_wcmsa submission.asp.
- Review the CMS Workers Compensation Services Agency website frequently for updates in the law, requirements or submission process for WCMSAs.
- Review the CMS "Submissions of WCMSAs" link frequently to verify that the firm is using the most current version of its "WC Submission Checklist."
- Create form documents or templates for the firm using the sample documents published at the CMS Workers Compensation Services Agency "Submissions of WCMSAs" link.
- Review the CMS "Submissions of WCMSAs" link frequently to verify that the firm is using the most current version of its "Sample Submission" as a model for its form documents.

- Keep names and contact information for individuals at various CMS offices who have been helpful in the past.
- Keep a set of release forms for frequently used WCMSA allocation report providers and check their websites to see if the forms are available online.

* * *

9.1 Basis for WCMSAs in Workers' Compensation Cases

Workers' Compensation Medicare Set-aside Arrangements (WCMSAs) are a complex aspect of workers' compensation practice which can be confusing even to experienced workers' compensation practitioners. Prior to 2001, WCMSAs were not required when workers' compensation cases were settled. In July 2001, the federal government established provisions enforced by The Centers for Medicare and Medicaid Services (CMS) to prevent employers and insurance carriers from shifting responsibility for payment of future work-related medical expenses to Medicare when workers' compensation cases are settled. The provisions include a requirement that injured workers who settle their workers' compensation cases place a designated amount of money, approved by CMS, in a separate interest-bearing account (the Medicare Set Aside account) to pay future work-related medical expenses. The amount of money placed in the separate account is based on the anticipated cost of future medical care related to the compensable injury, which would be paid by the workers' compensation insurance carrier if the case was not settled. The Medicare Set Aside account is used after the settlement to pay for injury-related medical expenses. If the account becomes depleted, Medicare will start paying for treatment related to the compensable injury. If the account is never depleted it passes to the heirs of the injured worker as part of the worker's estate. As of January 1, 2006, the cost of future prescription medications must be included in a WCMSA. This is a relatively new area of federal Medicare law that changes frequently. More changes are anticipated in the future, with legislation pending in Congress at the time of this book's publication.

The process of obtaining the extensive information required by the Centers for Medicare and Medicaid Services (CMS) to approve a WCMSA is time-consuming and document-intensive. The process can become even longer and more frustrating when CMS not only does not accept a proposed WCMSA amount that the parties have all agreed to as a condition of settlement, but then requests that a much larger sum of money be set aside. The process requires paralegals to have a working knowledge of CMS requirements for submission of a WCMSA proposal, even if the firm is not preparing and submitting the proposal. This is an area where paralegals will rely heavily on well-organized and summarized medical documents to review WCMSA proposals from private contractors and to respond to CMS requests for information.

The purpose of this chapter is to provide a very basic overview of the WCMSA process and to direct paralegals to online sources to find the most current CMS requirements for WCMSA submissions (which may have already been updated or changed by the time the first edition of this textbook is printed).

9.2 Key Abbreviations Used by CMS

Centers for Medicare and Medicaid Services (CMS) uses standard abbreviations throughout its Workers' Compensation Agency Services publications. Paralegals who do not know the abbreviations may have a difficult time navigating the CMS website and comprehending its instructions and sample documents. The following CMS abbreviations will also be used throughout this chapter:

CDC—Centers for Disease Control
CMS—Centers for Medicare and Medicaid Services
COB—Coordination of Benefits
DOB—Date of Birth
DOI—Date of Injury
FAQ—Frequently Asked Questions
GAO—General Account Office
GHP—Group Health Plan
HICN—Health Insurance Claim Number (assigned to insured by Medicare)
LE—Life Expectancy
MSA—Medicare Set-aside Arrangement
MSP—Medicare Secondary Payor
PSD—Proposed Settlement Date
SSA—Social Security Administration
SSDB—Social Security Disability Benefits
SSN—Social Security Number
TPA—Third Party Administrator
VA—Veterans' Administration
WC—Workers' Compensation

WCMSA—Workers Compensation Medicare Set-Aside Arrangement
WCRC—Workers' Compensation Review Contractor

9.3 When WCMSAs Are Required

CMS publishes the criteria for cases which require a WCMSA on its website under "Workers' Compensation Set-aside Arrangements CMS Review Threshold" found at http://www.cms.hhs.gov/WorkersCompAgencyServices/04_wcsetaside.asp.

A WCMSA is **not** required when the parties have settled the injured worker's claim to indemnity or wage loss benefits but **left the claim for medical benefits open**. A WCMSA is required when:

- The injured worker is a **Medicare recipient** and the total amount of the settlement of all claims to workers' compensation benefits is **more than $25,000.00**; or
- The injured worker **may be covered by Medicare within thirty (30) months** of the PSD and the anticipated amount of the settlement of all claims to workers' compensation benefits will be **more than $250,000.00.**

However, even when a WCMSA is not required, the parties are required to consider and protect Medicare's interest. Thus, almost every settlement involving an injured worker, who may not return to work and may apply for Social Security disability benefits and Medicare, should include language in the settlement agreement that acknowledges the parties have considered Medicare's interest. The settlement agreement should then state that either the parties have not set aside money and provide the rationale, or have set aside money and provide the rationale.

9.4 Obtaining a WCMSA Proposal

In cases where WCMSAs are required by CMS, the parties will need to provide a written recommendation to CMS proposing a sum of money which should be placed in a separate account or "set aside" in a WCMSA to pay for future Medicare-covered treatment of conditions related to the work injury or illness. This written recommendation may be referred to as a MSA or WCMSA allocation proposal, report, recommendation, determination or in cases of catastrophic injury, a life care plan. WCMSA proposals are similar to life care plans and are generally prepared by an individual, company or contractor with specialized knowledge of the CMS requirements and estimated future medical expenses (both Medicare and non-Medicare covered) for the specified medical conditions.

A plaintiff's attorney or a defense attorney may prepare and submit a WCMSA proposal to CMS. In some cases, attorneys believe they can better represent their client's interest by preparing the proposal themselves. This requires the law firm to gather all of the required documentation and submit requests for the treating medical doctors' opinions regarding future medical care. A paralegal will normally be substantially involved in that process.

However, in many cases, the carrier/administrator pays for the WCMSA proposal and selects a private contractor to prepare and submit it to CMS upon settlement of the workers' compensation claim. The parties can agree on a contractor to prepare the proposal, especially when it is needed quickly to resolve the case, and one contractor may have a better turnover rate. An updated proposal may need to be obtained if the original proposal was prepared some time ago and/or the injured worker's medical condition and projected medical expenses have changed.

The carrier/administrator usually provides information such as medical records and a medical benefits printout to the contractor, as well as Social Security and Medicare releases signed by the injured worker. If the carrier/administrator does not send signed releases with the medical documents, the contractor may send the releases to the parties' attorneys to obtain signatures and return. The contractor may also directly contact the parties' attorneys for missing documentation, such as recent medical records or prescription printouts. Paralegals can assist in gathering this information for the contractor.

In some cases, the attorneys may disagree with the WCMSA proposal obtained by the carrier/administrator. The attorneys may decide to obtain another WCMSA proposal from a different source to present to CMS for consideration. There is no guarantee that CMS will approve any of the submitted proposals. Sometimes CMS rejects the WCMSA proposal submitted for approval and requests that a different sum of money be set aside. However, in cases involving disputed future medical expenses, the cost of obtaining another proposal might benefit the injured worker. Both plaintiffs' and defense firms should maintain a list of reputable contractors who prepare WCMSA proposals.

9.5 Submitting WCMSA Proposal to CMS for Approval

CMS prefers that WCMSA proposals be submitted on a compact disc or CD-ROM. CMS has published instructions for submitting WCMSA proposals via CD-ROM at its website. As of the date of this publication, CMS requests that the documents be saved on the CD-ROM in PDF format and named using its document codes in the prefix. The paralegal should use the instructions, codes submission address(es) and contact number(s) listed at CMS "Submissions of WCMSAs" link.

9.5(1) Required Consent to Release Form

CMS publishes the required release forms on its website in its "Sample Submission" documents located at http://www.cms.hhs.gov/WorkersCompAgencyServices/05_wcmsasubmission.asp.

9.5(2) Rated Age

The WCMSA submission must include the injured worker's life expectancy. In some cases, the life expectancy is given based on a "rated age", the hypothetical age assigned by insurance and annuity companies to individuals with reduced life expectancies due to pre-existing medical conditions (work-related and unrelated) and other documented risk factors, such as smoking or obesity. The "rated age" is used by insurance and annuity companies to evaluate their risk of paying benefits over the individual's anticipated life time.

For example, due to the chronic health problems associated with immobility from spinal cord injuries, such as such poor circulation, skin breakdown and increased pulmonary infections, a 40-year old paraplegic may be treated as having the same mortality risk factors as a healthy 60-year old. If the annuity company uses the most recent *Life Expectancy Tables for the Total U.S. Population* published by U.S. Department of Health and Human Services, National Center for Health Statistics, National Vital Statistics Reports, and finds that a 60-year old's life expectancy is approximately 22 years, it will state the 40-year old's "rated age" as 60 years on its report and forecast the payment of benefits over an anticipated 22-year period.

9.5(3) Settlement Agreement or Court Order

CMS requires that a copy of the parties' final settlement agreement and/or state agency approval or order be submitted for review.

9.5(4) Set-Aside Administrator Agreement

A WCMSA can be self-administered by the injured worker or professionally administered by a medical claims administrator or third party administrator. The injured worker may opt to administer his or her own WCMSA and submit the required annual documentation to CMS.

9.5(5) Medical Records

CMS should review a copy of all medical records the parties have gathered prior to settlement, including but not limited to, records documenting prior or unrelated medical conditions. Paralegals responsible for gathering the medical records should verify that the medical records are complete and well-organized for review by CMS.

9.5(6) Medicare Payment History

CMS may send a letter to the injured worker, or the worker's attorney if it has received confirmation of representation, asking the worker to review a Medicare payment printout for a specific period and stating Medicare should be reimbursed for any **conditional payments** for services related to the work injury or illness. The injured worker has the opportunity to mark any payments the worker contends were not related to the work injury and return it to CMS. A paralegal can review the printout and verify unrelated medical payments by comparing it to the case medical summary and also looking up the diagnosis codes for dates of service not included in the case summary. If the paralegal still has questions about dates of service, the paralegal may need to talk to the injured worker or request medical records for the dates in question. The printout should be carefully reviewed, clearly marked and returned to CMS as quickly as possible. CMS may send repeated requests for the same information, but none of the requests should be ignored, even if it means responding to the request with a copy of information previously sent regarding unrelated payments.

CMS requires that a printout of all medical payments made by the carrier/administrator be submitted with the WCMSA proposal documents.

9.6 Online Sources of Information about WCMSAs

The following websites are useful to review for more detailed information regarding WCMSAs:

- **U.S. Department of Health and Human Services, CMS Workers' Compensation Agency Services,** http://www.cms.hhs.gov/WorkersCompAgencyServices/
- **U.S. Department of Health and Human Services, CMS Workers' Compensation Agency Services "Submissions of WCMSAs",** http://www.cms.hhs.gov/WorkersCompAgencyServices/http://www.cms.hhs.gov/WorkersCompAgencyServices/05_wcmsasubmission.asp
- **U.S. Department of Health and Human Services, Medicare Coverage Section,** http://www.medicare.gov/Coverage/Home.asp
- **US. Department of Health and Human Services, National Center for Health Statistics Life Tables,** http://www.cdc.gov/nchs/products/pubs/pubd/lftbls/life/1966.htm
- **Campbell, John J., The Medicare Set Aside Bulletin,** http://www.jjcelderlaw.com/MSABulletin.htm
- **Merlino, Michael R., Workers' Compensation Medicare Set-Asides,** http://www.wcmsainfo.com/
- **Gould and Lamb, LLC, Workers' Compensation Medicare Set Aside Arrangement,** http://www.gouldandlamb.com/MSA_primer.htm

CHAPTER 10

Miscellaneous Workers' Compensation Issues

Paralegal Practice Tips

Knowledgeable paralegals recognize that other kinds of legal claims may arise out of workers' compensation claims, including civil claims against negligent third parties and creditor claims if a carrier/administrator declares bankruptcy. A paralegal should:

- Treat bankruptcy notices from self-insured employers or risk carriers as a priority.
- Upon receipt of a bankruptcy notice, enter reminders or "ticklers" in the firm calendar of all applicable deadlines, including deadlines to submit proof of claim forms on behalf of the injured worker.
- File any paperwork required by the bankruptcy court, including proof of claim forms, in a timely manner.
- Upon receipt of a bankruptcy notice, enter reminders or "ticklers" of the deadline to file a claim with the state guaranty agency or other state insolvency fund, if applicable.
- If the claim will be administered by a state guaranty agency or other state insolvency fund, immediately research the requirements to submit a claim to that agency, including deadlines and forms.
- Be aware of possible third party claims when reviewing client case files.
- Know the state law and state agency rules regarding carrier/administrator subrogation liens against third party recoveries.
- Request a resume or curriculum vitae from rehabilitation consultants assigned to the injured worker's case.
- Carefully review all rehabilitation reports and documentation, including E-mail, prepared by rehabilitation consultants.

* * *

10.1 Bankrupt Employer or Insurance Carrier

A self-insured employer or insurance carrier's bankruptcy is not a typical issue in most workers' compensation cases. However, it does happen occasionally. Paralegals, at minimum, need to know that this situation may complicate a workers' compensation case considerably, as well as trigger different deadlines and filing requirements outside of the case. Sometimes self-insured employers or insurance carriers declare bankruptcy while injured workers are receiving benefits or have claims pending. Bankruptcy filings have the potential to create serious hardship for injured workers whose only source of income is a weekly indemnity (disability) check and only source of health insurance is the workers' compensation coverage. Receipt of a bankruptcy notice from a self-insured employer or an insurance carrier adds new deadlines in courts outside of the state workers' compensation agency, including the United States Bankruptcy Court and/or the state guaranty fund or other state insolvency fund if applicable. News of large corporations' pending bankruptcies or bankruptcy filings may be published in the media, including the state agency news, or discussed in workers' compensation listservs, before receipt of an actual bankruptcy notice.

10.1(1) State Guaranty Funds

States have laws which protect various types of insurance claims, including workers compensation claims, when eligible insurance carriers declare bankruptcy. In each state, guaranty funds have been established to administer and pay homeowners, automobile and workers' compensation claims for insolvent insurers covered by the fund, including payment of medical or indemnity benefits to injured workers. State guaranty funds do not cover self-insured employers in most cases; however, a separate state insolvency fund may apply for self-insured employers. Assessments from self-insured employers and/or insurance carriers are the main source of funds for these non-profit state agencies.

Sometimes a different company or corporation will purchase or "take over" the bankrupt company and assume payment of benefits. If the employer or insurance carrier is not purchased by another company, and the employer or insurance carrier is not covered by a state guaranty fund or other state insolvency fund, an injured worker's only remedy may be to pursue an unsecured creditor's claim directly through the division of the U.S. Bankruptcy Court which has jurisdiction of the case. If the company or debtor has minimal or no assets for the bankruptcy court to disburse to creditors with valid claims, there may be no other source of payment of workers' compensation benefits.

If a plaintiff's firm receives notice that a self-insured employer or insurance carrier has filed bankruptcy, this should be taken very seriously. The supervising attorney will decide on a course of action to handle the new bankruptcy issue. The paralegal should consult the supervising attorney and enter reminders or "ticklers" in the firm calendar of all applicable bankruptcy deadlines, including the deadline to complete **proof of claim** forms on behalf of the injured worker. Any paperwork required by the U.S. Bankruptcy Court to preserve the injured worker's claim should be filed in a timely manner and on the correct forms as stated by the applicable division of the U.S. Bankruptcy Court. If a state guaranty fund or other state insolvency fund will be administering the workers' compensation claim, then it is crucial to immediately verify and tickle the fund's deadlines to file a claim, as well as filing any required proof of claim forms.

If it is the defense firm's client that has gone bankrupt, the defense attorney and staff will need to work with the attorneys handling the bankruptcy. Paralegals may be responsible for drafting estimates of the bankrupt self-insured employer's or insurance carrier's liability for the claims the firm is defending. The defense attorney or staff will need to notify all parties and the state agency that the bankruptcy petition was filed, resulting in a **stay**[1] against any further proceedings against the bankrupt client. A bankruptcy stay normally stops all mediations, settlement negotiations, contempt hearings and trials until the stay is lifted. On some occasions, the bankrupt self-insured employer or carrier will immediately obtain the court's approval to pay approved claims during the pendency of the bankruptcy.

10.1(2) Submitting Proof of Claim Forms

The bankruptcy court and/or state guaranty fund will require documentary evidence that an injured worker has a valid workers' compensation claim, as well as documentation of monetary amounts owed for weekly indemnity (disability) and/or medical benefits. The following documents may be required by the bankruptcy court and/or state guaranty or insolvency fund to prove that an injured worker has a valid claim:

---

1. An automatic stay by the bankruptcy court protects the debtor by halting or prohibiting any legal actions by the debtor's creditors for 90 days from the date the petition was filed.

- State agency form compensation agreements accepting liability for the workers' compensation claim and agreeing to pay benefits.
- State agency orders finding that the carrier/administrator is liable for payment of workers' compensation benefits and the amount and type of benefits to be paid.
- A printout of benefits paid to date by the carrier/administrator.
- Documentation of unpaid or unreimbursed medical benefits, including medical bills and pharmacy printouts.

In addition, the state agency or other insolvency fund may require a copy of the injured worker's proof of claim filed in U.S. Bankruptcy Court.

10.1(3) Online Sources for Bankruptcy Information

Additional information regarding workers' compensation and bankruptcy may be found at the following websites:

- **National Conference of Insurance Guaranty Funds,** http://www.ncigf.org/guaranty/summary.asp, (summarizes state insurance guaranty fund laws, includes a guaranty fund directory)
- **McKenna, Sue, "The Untold Story: State Guaranty Funds", Insurance Journal**, November 2006,http://www.insurancejournal.com/magazines/southeast/2006/11/06/features/74488.htm
- **"Insolvencies and Guaranty Funds", Insurance Information Institute,** http://www.iii.org/media/hottopics/insurance/insolvencies/
- **United States Bankruptcy Courts**, http://www.uscourts.gov/bankruptcycourts.html

10.2 Third Party Claims

When a worker is injured on the job, in most cases the workers' compensation claim is the only "remedy" or source of recovery for monetary compensation or benefits (unless the worker is eligible for unemployment, group disability or Social Security benefits). State workers' compensation acts limit benefits to medical treatment and indemnity benefits during the period the injured worker cannot earn wages, and may also provide for payment of a limited sum for permanent physical impairment. The injured worker cannot recover compensation for physical and emotional pain and suffering, loss of enjoyment of life or punitive damages from the employer in a standard workers' compensation case.[2] However, if the worker's injury was caused by the fault or negligence of someone other than the employer, the worker might have a **third party claim** for additional damages against the negligent individual or company.[3]

The supervising attorney will evaluate an injured worker's possible third party claims, if any, but paralegals can assist with the investigation of these claims. Potential third party claims should be investigated as quickly as possible because they may have different statutes of limitations than the workers' compensation claim. The supervising attorney will review the facts and decide whether the injured worker has an actionable third party claim in addition to the workers' compensation case. However, while reviewing case documents, paralegals should be aware of and flag information which may relate to possible third party claims for the attorney's review. In some states, the employer and the carrier/administrator may pursue the third party claim (including filing a lawsuit) on behalf of the employee. This allows the employer and the carrier/administrator to recover the costs of the injury from the negligent party.

10.2(1) Identifying Third Party Claims

Paralegals should recognize basic types of third party claims, including but not limited to:

- **Motor Vehicle Accidents**—If a worker is injured in a motor vehicle accident while driving during the course of employment, and the collision was caused by the other driver's fault or negligence, the worker may have a third party personal injury or bodily injury claim against the other driver and/or owner of the other vehicle. For example, a delivery truck driver who is injured when another vehicle rear-ends his truck may have a third party claim against the negligent driver and/or the owner of the vehicle.
- **Violations of State and/or Federal Safety Laws**—If a worker is injured by another company's failure to abide by state or federal safety laws, the worker may have a third party claim against the negligent company. The third party's safety violations may occur on the employer's job site or at

2. In some jurisdictions, the injured worker might be able to recover additional damages from the employer in a separate civil action, if the employer's intentional misconduct caused serious injury or death to the worker.

3. Sometimes referred to as the "tortfeasor"

another site the employee visited due to the job duties. For example, a construction worker who is injured on a construction site due to another contractor's failure to abide by state safety requirements may have a third party claim against the negligent contractor.

- **Product Liability**—If a worker is injured due to a defective product or equipment malfunction during the course of employment, the worker may have a third party product liability claim against entities who designed, manufactured and/or sold the defective product or malfunctioning equipment. Investigating these claims can be difficult, especially if the product or equipment is older. In many cases involving older equipment, the statute of limitations regarding product liability has expired.
- **Professional Malpractice**—The likelihood of an injured worker having a third party claim due to professional negligence or malpractice, in addition to a workers' compensation claim, is unusual but does occur occasionally. During the course of treatment for the work injury, the injured worker may have suffered additional injury due to the negligence of a medical provider, such as a doctor or a hospital. For example, a doctor may have failed to timely diagnose and treat a severe infection while the worker was hospitalized after surgery for the work injury. If a medical provider's mistake harmed the injured worker, the worker may have a professional malpractice claim against the provider.

  Another example of professional malpractice or negligence occurs when an injured worker's attorney makes a critical mistake. Perhaps the injured worker's previous attorney missed an important deadline or failed to file necessary documentation. If the attorney's mistake caused the injured worker to lose benefits to which the worker would otherwise have been entitled, the worker may have a professional malpractice claim against the negligent attorney.

10.2(2) Statutes of Limitations in Third Party Claims

Paralegals should be aware that third party claims have different deadlines or statutes of limitations than workers' compensation claims. The calculation of the statute of limitations depends on the type of third party claim, the state or jurisdiction in which the negligence occurred, the states where the parties reside, and in some cases, whether the worker died due to the negligence. The supervising attorney is responsible for calculating and verifying statutes of limitations in third party claims. Paralegals should work closely with their supervising attorneys to ensure that deadlines and reminders are properly entered into the firm's calendaring system.

10.2(3) Representation in Third Party Claims

In some cases, the plaintiff's firm may be able to represent the injured worker in the workers' compensation claim, as well as the third party claim. If the firm does not handle third party claims (or if it does but does not want to handle this one), it is crucial that the firm advises (preferably in writing) the injured worker to contact a lawyer who does handle these matters in a timely fashion, to avoid legal malpractice issues.

10.2(4) Carrier/Administrator Liens Against Third Party Recoveries

If an injured worker has an actionable third party claim and may recover monetary compensation from a negligent third party, in addition to workers' compensation benefits, state law may give the carrier/administrator a lien interest or "**subrogation lien**" against any third party monies recovered. A valid subrogation lien means the carrier/administrator has the right to be reimbursed from any third party recovery for the workers' compensation benefits it paid to the injured worker. Paralegals should know the state law regarding carrier/administrator subrogation liens against third party recoveries.

A carrier/administrator will usually know if an injured worker may have a third party claim because of its own initial investigation. The carrier/administrator may have even obtained evidence that a third party's negligence caused the work injury. Most carrier/administrators are more than happy to share this information with the injured worker's attorney, in hopes of recovering all or part of the workers' compensation benefits paid. As mentioned previously, if the worker does not pursue the third party claim, state law may allow the employer or carrier/administrator to pursue the claim on the worker's behalf, including filing a lawsuit against the negligent third party. The carrier/administrator will be required to produce evidence of its lien interest upon request, sometimes called a "**subrogation package**," which includes a printout of all workers' compensation benefits paid to date and supporting documentation of the payments, such as billing statements and invoices from medical providers, pharmacy companies and rehabilitation consultants.

State law may limit a carrier/administrator's lien recovery to a percentage of the total third party recovery (such as half) after deduction of attorney fees and costs. In some jurisdictions, an injured worker's attorney may be able to have a state civil court or state agency reduce the lien, depending on the injured worker's injuries and future medical needs, as well as the amount of the third party recovery. In some cases, the parties will negotiate to voluntarily reduce or waive a carrier/administrator's interest in any third party recovery. In order to protect the carrier/administrator's potential lien interest, state law may require that the court and/or the state agency approve third party settlements before the third party monies can be disbursed. Paralegals should know if the state agency has specific formats or forms to use when an injured worker is requesting approval for a disbursement of a third party recovery.

10.3 Working with Rehabilitation Consultants

If a carrier/administrator has accepted an injured worker's claim and is paying medical or indemnity benefits, it may assign a medical and/or vocational rehabilitation consultant (hereinafter "rehabilitation consultant") to the claim. The carrier/administrator pays the rehabilitation consultant to work with the injured worker and manage medical treatment and/or assist in the return to work. The benefit to a carrier/administrator is a potential reduction in the total amount of benefits it is paying to the injured worker, especially if the worker is not earning wages due to the injury. Paralegals should know the state law and state agency rules regarding the use of rehabilitation consultants in workers' compensation cases. A good rehabilitation consultant can provide assistance to an injured worker, especially in the area of medical case management, by attending medical appointments, coordinating authorization of medical treatment, and keeping all parties informed regarding the status of the worker's recovery from the injuries.

10.3(1) Initial Contact

If an injured worker is represented by an attorney when a rehabilitation consultant is assigned to the case, the consultant should contact the plaintiff's attorney's office first to ask permission to contact the worker directly and to schedule an initial meeting between the attorney, the consultant and the worker. This meeting usually takes place at the injured worker's attorney's office. Once the meeting is scheduled, the plaintiff's attorney should send the rehabilitation consultant a letter confirming the appointment time and requesting that the following documents be provided:

- A copy of the rehabilitation consultant's resume and/or curriculum vitae summarizing the consultant's professional qualifications.
- A copy of the forms required by the state agency (if any) to be filed upon the rehabilitation consultant's assignment to the claim.

- A copy of any written documentation from the employer or carrier/administrator regarding the rehabilitation consultant's assignment.

See Forms 10.1 and 10.2, Sample Letters to Rehabilitation Consultants. The plaintiff's attorney may want a paralegal to be present during the initial meeting, to take notes and provide information from the client file as needed. During the meeting, the following issues may be discussed:

- The rehabilitation consultant's role and the nature of the services to be provided.
- The rehabilitation consultant's legal obligations and restrictions.
- The injured worker's medical and vocational background, as well as the worker's vocational goals.
- The attorney's request to be copied on all rehabilitation documents generated or obtained by the consultant, including E-mail correspondence.
- The attorney's request to be immediately contacted by the rehabilitation consultant to try to resolve disputes as they arise.
- The medical or vocational consultant's rehabilitation plan.

Once the plaintiff's attorney, the rehabilitation consultant and the injured worker agree on an initial plan to provide medical case management and/or return the worker to suitable employment, the consultant should document the rehabilitation plan in writing. If the consultant does not document the plan in writing, the paralegal can draft correspondence to the consultant, using the paralegal's or the attorney's notes, summarizing the plan or services discussed at the meeting.

An initial vocational plan may include the following recommendations (in order of preference):

1) Try to return the injured worker to the worker's former job with the same employer, with or without accommodations by the employer.
2) Try to return the injured worker to a different job with the same employer, with or without accommodations by the employer.
3) Direct the injured worker in a job search for a suitable job with a different employer.
4) Arrange for the injured worker to undergo a series of evaluations and/or tests to determine the injured worker's level of education, transferable skills if any, vocational aptitudes and job interests.
5) Arrange for the injured worker to have a functional capacity evaluation (FCE) to determine the appropriate level of work (sedentary, light, medium or heavy) the worker can perform.

6) Enroll the injured worker in a vocational training program or secondary school to obtain transferable job skills.

10.3(2) Physical or Work Restrictions

Injured workers should obtain written work notes at each visit with treating doctors. The note should state whether:

- The patient can return to unrestricted work;
- The patient can return to work with restrictions, such as no lifting over a certain number of pounds, or for only four hours per day; or
- The patient cannot work at all due to the injury.

If an injured worker does not get a work note after an office visit, the worker can often call the doctor's office after the visit to request the note and go back to pick it up or have it faxed to the plaintiff's attorney's office. If the firm has a medical authorization signed by the worker, a paralegal can also contact the doctor's office and ask the doctor to provide a note or disability statement regarding the patient's current restrictions.

10.3(3) Job Search

Paralegals working for plaintiffs' firms should stay up-to-date regarding their clients' medical case status. As soon as an injured worker is released to return to work by a treating doctor, a meeting should be scheduled with the injured worker and the plaintiff's attorney to discuss a reasonable vocational plan, regardless of whether the carrier/administrator has assigned a vocational rehabilitation consultant to the claim. At the meeting, the plaintiff's attorney will explain the injured worker's rights and obligations under state law.

Paralegals working for defense firms should also stay up-to-date regarding injured workers' medical case status. They should notify the supervising attorney of the worker's release to return to work. The defense attorney and the employer can decide on a plan of action based on the worker's employability with the defendant-employer or another employer. If the defendant-employer cannot offer employment to the worker, the plan of action may include the assignment of a vocational rehabilitation to the case to assist the worker in a job search.

If state law requires injured workers to seek suitable employment in order to remain eligible to receive ongoing indemnity benefits, the injured worker will need to make reasonable efforts to find a job. The worker will need to document all job search efforts, in case evidence of the job search is needed at a later date. *See Form 10.3, Sample Job Search Log.* Paralegals working for the plaintiff's firm should periodically contact the worker to discuss job search efforts and request completed job search logs for the attorney's review.

If a vocational rehabilitation consultant has not been hired by the carrier/administrator but the injured worker's treating doctor has released him to return to work, the plaintiff's firm may be in the position of directing the worker's vocational activities. These may include directing the injured worker to:

- Contact the defendant-employer about returning to the worker's former job, with or without accommodations, or a different job, with or without accommodations. If the defendant-employer is placing ads for positions which may be suitable for the worker, but is refusing to offer the worker (assuming he or she is either still employed or terminated but eligible for rehire) a job, the plaintiff's firm should collect documentary evidence such as employment ads placed internally or externally by the employer. The plaintiff's attorney can review this information to see if the worker has any actionable employment claims against the defendant-employer. The plaintiff's attorney can also work with the defendant-employer, the carrier/administrator or its defense counsel to see if the worker can return to work with the employer in any capacity. The firm can also send interrogatories to the defendant-employer or its defense counsel, inquiring about employment opportunities.
- Hire a private vocational rehabilitation expert or consultant to evaluate the worker and make vocational recommendations. However, vocational experts charge substantial fees for their time and expertise, and this may not be economically feasible for the worker.
- Apply for vocational rehabilitation services at the state's division of vocational rehabilitation services. If the state vocational agency finds that the worker is eligible for services but has a pending workers' compensation claim, it may file a notice of lien to be reimbursed for the cost of its services out of any potential workers' compensation recovery.
- Apply for vocational rehabilitation services from a nonprofit vocational rehabilitation agency, such as Goodwill Industries.
- Go to the local state unemployment agency to register to access the job bank and/or talk with a vocational counselor. A directory of state unemployment and other state department of labor services is located at the U.S. Department of Labor's website at http://www.dol.gov/dol/location.htm.
- Search employment ads in local papers or online, place applications for suitable jobs and document all job search contacts, inquiries and responses in a job search log.

- Contact the admissions office of the local community college to investigate certificate, training or degree programs, especially if the worker has significant physical restrictions and few transferable skills. The worker should provide the information obtained regarding specific programs, the length of time to complete the program, and an estimate of tuition and books to the attorney to review. The plaintiff's attorney may ask the carrier/administrator and/or the state agency to approve the worker's enrollment in a certificate or degree program as a reasonable vocational plan and to pay for the cost of obtaining the degree, including tuition and books. If the carrier/administrator is not paying benefits and the case is pending for motion or hearing, the plaintiff's attorney may advise the worker to enroll in the program, if the worker can afford it.

10.3(4) Rehabilitation Reports

Pursuant to state law, state agency rules and/or rehabilitation guidelines, rehabilitation consultants should simultaneously copy all parties with their rehabilitation reports (including attachments). Most rehabilitation consultants prepare status reports on a monthly or bimonthly basis. Paralegals should tickle the due dates of the reports and contact the rehabilitation consultants to request any past due reports. Upon receipt of the reports, the attorney and a paralegal should carefully review them for accuracy and send a copy to the client to review for accuracy as well. "Red flag" items in a report which need to be addressed immediately may include (but are not limited to):

- The consultant states that the injured worker is not attending scheduled meetings or performing agreed upon job search tasks or otherwise not cooperating.
- The consultant states that the injured worker is missing medical appointments or otherwise not complying with medical providers' treatment recommendations.
- The consultant appears to be providing job leads which are outside the injured worker's qualifications or physical restrictions or are otherwise inappropriate.
- The consultant is providing personal opinions regarding the injured worker, which are outside the scope of the rehabilitation services or are not supported by evidence.
- The consultant fails to provide copies of documents referenced in the report.

- The consultant has contacted the injured worker's medical providers without the knowledge and permission of the plaintiff's attorney.
- The consultant is not abiding by the rehabilitation plan agreed to by the parties.
- The consultant is giving legal advice to the injured worker.

Paralegals who are familiar with the case facts and know the state law, state agency rules and rehabilitation guidelines regarding rehabilitation consultants can draft correspondence to the rehabilitation consultant or the other party regarding disputed issues, for the attorney's review and signature.

In cases where the parties are unable to resolve disputed rehabilitation issues or where the carrier/administrator attempts to stop payment of benefits due to the injured worker's alleged non-cooperation or non-compliance with the rehabilitation plan, one or both of the parties may have to file a motion or hearing request with the state agency to review the facts and issue an order regarding the rehabilitation services. If the plaintiff's attorney believes that the rehabilitation consultant is providing inadequate services or violating state laws, the attorney may opt to file a motion with the state agency to remove the rehabilitation consultant from the case. In any case where the parties ask the state agency to resolve rehabilitation issues, extensive evidence to support their allegations regarding rehabilitation issues will be required. Paralegals should document all contact with rehabilitation consultants, preferably in writing. They should also be aware that any information provided to rehabilitation consultants, including E-mail, may be attached to rehabilitation reports or pleading exhibits.

10.3(5) Online Sources for Rehabilitation Consultant Information

Additional information regarding rehabilitation consultants, their qualifications, and ethical guidelines or rules of professional conduct can be found at the following websites:

- **Code of Ethics for Nurses with Interpretive Statements**, http://www.nursingworld.org/ethics/ecode.htm, (For view only online; hard copy may be purchased)
- **Commission on Rehabilitation Counselor Certification**, http://www.crccertification.com/ (Certification process for Certified Rehabilitation Counselor (CRC) and **Code of Ethics**)
- **Certification of Disability Management Specialists Commission**, http://www.cdms.org/ (Certification process for Certified Disability Management Specialists (CDMS) and **Code of Professional Conduct**)

- **Association of Rehabilitation Nurses,** http://www.rehabnurse.org/certification/crrn.html (Certification process for Certified Registered Rehabilitation Nurse (CRRN))
- **Commission on Certification of Work Adjustment and Vocational Evaluation Specialists,** http://www.ccwaves.org/ (Certification process and **Code of Ethics** for Certified Vocational Evaluator (CVE), Certified Work Adjustment Specialist (CWA) and Certified Career Assessment Associate (CCAA))
- **American Board for Occupational Health Nurses, Inc.**, http://www.abohn.org/ (Certification process for Certified Occupational Health Nurse (COHN)
- **Orthopaedics Nurse Certification Board**, http://www.oncb.org/ Certification process for Orthopaedic Nurse Certified (ONC)
- **Commission for Case Manager Certification**, http://www.ccmcertification.org/ (Certification process and **Code of Professional Conduct** for Certified Case Manager (CCM))
- **International Association of Rehabilitation Specialists**, http://www.rehabpro.org/ (Member directory and **Ethics Code**)

Form 10.1—Sample Initial Letter to Medical Rehabilitation Consultant

[Insert Date]

[Insert Address]

Re: [Insert State Agency Case Caption]

Dear [Insert Name]

As you know, I represent the above-referenced worker in his claim for workers' compensation benefits. It is my understanding that you have been assigned to his claim to provide medical rehabilitation.

This will confirm that you are scheduled to meet my client and me at my office on [insert date]. Please send me a copy of your curriculum vitae prior to this meeting. In addition, please divulge any conflicts of interest, or any compensation carrier's or employer's ownership of or affiliation with you. Please be prepared to identify the specific medical case management services you were retained to provide and the information you were provided regarding my client. Finally, please identify the statutes, rules, and code of ethics which govern your conduct and where a copy of each may be obtained.

My client is entitled to a private exam with his treating doctor(s). I am requesting that you honor his request to a private exam at each appointment with his treating doctor(s). If the doctor is willing to meet with you after the private exam, my client wishes to be present at that meeting.

I expect to receive periodic written statements documenting the rehabilitation activity in this claim. I should be provided reports and correspondence, including E-mail, at the same time they are provided to the carrier, employer, or defense counsel. These reports should contain only information relevant and material to my client's medical rehabilitation. Please advise me immediately if you believe that he is not cooperating with the provision of rehabilitative services and describe what cooperative action you seek from him. Your work and your reports should make every effort to avoid undue invasion of his privacy.

Also, you should refrain from advising my client regarding legal aspects of his claim, such as settlement negotiations, investigative activities, or perform any other non rehabilitation activity. If he has any questions regarding his claim, you should refer them to my office, and refrain from commenting.

If you have questions or would like to discuss this further, please do not hesitate to contact me at any time during this process. I would also be happy to meet with you, and/or an employer/carrier's representative, if it would help facilitate the medical rehabilitation process.

[Signature line]

cc: [Client's name]
[Adjuster or attorney's name]

Form 10.2—Sample Initial Letter to Vocational Rehabilitation Consultant

[Insert Date]

[Insert Address]

Re: [Insert State Agency Case Caption]

Dear [Insert Name]

As you know, I represent the above-referenced worker in his claim for workers' compensation benefits. It is my understanding that you have been assigned to his claim to provide vocational rehabilitation.

This will confirm that you are scheduled to meet my client and me at my office on [insert date]. Please send me a copy of your curriculum vitae prior to this meeting. In addition, please divulge any conflicts of interest, or any compensation carrier's or employer's ownership of or affiliation with you. Please be prepared to identify the specific vocational services you were retained to provide and the information you were provided regarding my client. Finally, please identify the statutes, rules, and code of ethics which govern your conduct and where a copy of each may be obtained.

I am requesting that you prepare an ***individualized*** plan designed to achieve the goal of vocational rehabilitation. Therefore, as soon as possible after the initial meeting and prior to initiating any further contact with my client, please:

1. Provide your vocational assessment based on your evaluation of my client's social, medical, and vocational standing, other information significant to his employability, and your initial interview with him, as well as other pertinent information provided by the carrier. This assessment should identify the specific type and sequence of appropriate services, and evaluate any specific requests by the worker for vocational training. It should also identify the worker's need for services, and benefits expected.

2. Provide your proposed individualized plan for vocational services based on your vocational assessment, specifying its goals and return-to-work strategy. Return to work options should be considered in the following priority:

    a. Current job, current employer

    b. New job, current employer

c. On-the-job training, current employer

d. New job, new employer

e. On-the-job training, new employer

f. Formal vocational training to prepare worker for job with current or new employer

g. Self employment

3. Provide a relevant labor market survey which supports the likelihood of success of your proposed rehabilitation plan, based on your vocational assessment.

The vocational plan outlined above should be designed to return my client to suitable employment. It is my position that my client's vocational plan, including any proposed job search, should be directed at restoring him to his pre-injury wage and to a substantially similar earning capacity, including the opportunity for income growth. In order to determine if your proposed vocational plan is directed at restoring my client to his pre-injury wage and to a substantially similar earning capacity, including the opportunity for income growth, please provide as part of your vocational plan a report of what his pre-injury job is currently paying, including the value of all employer paid benefits.

My reasonable expectation is that you will make every effort to return my client to employment as close to his former earnings as possible. He had a position with [insert employer's name] which offered job security and included basic benefits such as health insurance. A minimum wage, "dead end" job will not come even close to restoring him to his former earnings and station in life, or even start him down the road to restoration of income growth. In addition, a temporary job is even less desirable than a minimum wage dead end job. I do not expect my client's employment efforts to be directed to temporary agencies. I am advising you in advance that I will object to part-time or temporary employment as "suitable", unless within 60 to 90 days, it has the strong likelihood of leading to **suitable** permanent full-time employment. Securing a temporary position for my client would not relieve the employer of its obligation to continue to provide vocational rehabilitation benefits and wage loss benefits.

I expect to receive periodic written statements documenting the rehabilitation activity in this claim. I should be provided reports and correspondence, including E-mail, at the same time they are provided to the carrier, employer, or defense counsel. These reports should contain only information relevant and material to my client's vocational rehabilitation. Please advise me immediately if you believe that he is not cooperating with the provision of rehabilitative services and describe what cooperative action you seek from him. Your work and your reports should make every effort to avoid undue invasion of his privacy.

In identifying proposed employment, you should provide me with a copy of the written or videotaped job description, and I will provide any objections in writing within [insert number] calendar days. You should also consider my client's transportation requirements, and should not initiate or continue placement activities which do not appear reasonably likely to result in placement of my client in suitable employment.

Also, you should refrain from advising my client regarding legal aspects of his claim, such as settlement negotiations, investigative activities, or perform any other non-rehabilitation activity. If he has any questions regarding his claim, you should refer them to my office, and refrain from commenting.

If you have questions or would like to discuss this further, please do not hesitate to contact me at any time during this process. I would also be happy to meet with you, and/or an employer/carrier's representative, if it would help facilitate the vocational rehabilitation process.

[Signature line]

cc: [Client's name]
[Adjuster or attorney's name]

Form 10.3—Sample Job Search Log

<table>
<tr>
<td>Name of Business: ______
Address: ______
______
Phone: ______
Contact: ______
Job Applied For: ______
Date Applied: ______
Applied by:
☐ In person application
☐ Online/Internet application
☐ Cover letter/resume via facsimile
Fax number: ______
☐ Cover letter/resume via E-mail
E-mail address: ______
☐ Cover letter/resume via U.S. Postal Service
Results:
☐ No response
☐ Offered Interview
Date: ______
☐ Advised not hiring at this time
☐ Advised not qualified for job
☐ Advised position filled
☐ Other response: ______
______</td>
<td>Name of Business: ______
Address: ______
______
Phone: ______
Contact: ______
Job Applied For: ______
Date Applied: ______
Applied by:
☐ In person application
☐ Online/Internet application
☐ Cover letter/resume via facsimile
Fax number: ______
☐ Cover letter/resume via E-mail
E-mail address: ______
☐ Cover letter/resume via U.S. Postal Service
Results:
☐ No response
☐ Offered Interview
Date: ______
☐ Advised not hiring at this time
☐ Advised not qualified for job
☐ Advised position filled
☐ Other response: ______
______</td>
</tr>
<tr>
<td>Name of Business: ______
Address: ______
______
Phone: ______
Contact: ______
Job Applied For: ______
Date Applied: ______
Applied by:
☐ In person application
☐ Online/Internet application
☐ Cover letter/resume via facsimile
Fax number: ______
☐ Cover letter/resume via E-mail
E-mail address: ______
☐ Cover letter/resume via U.S. Postal Service
Results:
☐ No response
☐ Offered Interview
Date: ______
☐ Advised not hiring at this time
☐ Advised not qualified for job
☐ Advised position filled
☐ Other response: ______
______</td>
<td>Name of Business: ______
Address: ______
______
Phone: ______
Contact: ______
Job Applied For: ______
Date Applied: ______
Applied by:
☐ In person application
☐ Online/Internet application
☐ Cover letter/resume via facsimile
Fax number: ______
☐ Cover letter/resume via E-mail
E-mail address: ______
☐ Cover letter/resume via U.S. Postal Service
Results:
☐ No response
☐ Offered Interview
Date: ______
☐ Advised not hiring at this time
☐ Advised not qualified for job
☐ Advised position filled
☐ Other response: ______
______</td>
</tr>
</table>

APPENDIX A

List of Frequently Used Medical Abbreviations

A	(Assessment)
ABD	(abdomen)
ADCF	(anterior diskectomy cervical fusion)
ADL	(activities of daily living)
AMA	(against medical advice)
amb	(ambulate)
ASA	(acetylsalicylic acid a/k/a aspirin)

B	(bilateral)
bid	(twice a day)
BM	(bowel movement or bone marrow)
BP	(blood pressure)
Bx	(biopsy)

c	(with)
C-spine	(cervical spine)
CA	(cancer)
CAD	(coronary artery disease)
CBC	(complete blood count)
CC	(chief complaint)

C/O	(complaint, complained, complaining of)
CNS	(central nervous system)
COPD	(chronic obstructive pulmonary disease)
CPE	(complete physical exam)
CRIF	(closed reduction internal fixation)
CT	(Cat scan or computerized tomography)
CXR	(chest x-ray)

D/C	(discontinue or discharge)
DDD	(degenerative disc disease)
DJD	(degenerative joint disease)
DM	(diabetes mellitus)
DME	(durable medical equipment)
DOA	(dead on arrival)
DTR	(deep tendon reflexes)
Dx	(diagnosis)

ECG or EKG	(electrocardiogram)
ED	(emergency department)
EENT	(ear eyes nose throat)
EKG	(electrocardiogram)
EMS	(emergency medical service)
ER	(emergency room)
ESI	(epidural steroid injection)
ETOH	(ethanol)
Ext	(extremity)

F	(female)
FH	(family history)
Flex	(flexion)

FU or f/u	(follow-up)
Fx	(fracture)

GCS	(Glasgow Coma Scale)
GI	(gastrointestinol)
GYN	(gynecological)

HA or H/A	(headache)
HEENT	(head ears eyes nose throat)
HEP	(home exercise program)
HNP	(herniated nucleus pulposus)
HO or h/o	(history of)
H&P	(history and physical)
HPI	(history of present illness)
HR	(heart rate)
HS or hs	(take at bedtime)
HTN	(hypertensive or "high blood pressure")
Hx	(history)

ICU	(intensive care unit)
IM	(intramuscular injection)
IV	(intravenous)
IVF	(intravenous fluids)

L	(left)
L-spine	(lumbar spine)
LBP	(lower back pain)
LE	(lower extremity)
LLE	(left lower extremity)
LMD	(last medical doctor)

LMV	(last medical visit)
LOC	(loss of consciousness)
LUE	(left upper extremity)
M	(male)
Meds	(medications)
MMI	(maximum medical improvement)
MRI	(magnetic resonance imaging)
MRN	(medical record number)
MVA	(motor vehicle accident)
MVC	(motor vehicle collision or crash)

N	(normal)
NAD	(no acute distress)
NKA	(no known allergies)
NKDA	(no known drug allergies)
NPO	(nothing by mouth)
NSAID	(non-steroidal anti-inflammatory drugs)

O	(objective)
OOW	(out of work)
OT	(occupational therapy)
OTC	(over the counter, as in medication)
OTJ	(on-the-job)
ORIF	(open reduction internal fixation)
OV	(office visit)

PCP	(primary care physician)
PPD	(permanent partial disability)
PE	(physical exam)
PMH	(previous or past medical history)

PNCV	(peripheral nerve conduction studies)
PO	(by mouth)
POC	(plan of care)
Pt	(patient)
PT	(physical therapy)
PRN	(as needed)

q	(every)
qh	(every hour)
qd	(every day)
qhs	(every night)
qid	(four times a day)

R	(right)
RCT	(rotator cuff tear)
RCR	(rotator cuff repair)
RLE	(right lower extremity)
R/O	(rule out)
ROM	(range of motion)
ROS	(review of symptoms)
RTC	(return to clinic)
RTW	(return to work)
RUE	(right upper extremity)
Rx	(medication or prescription)

s	(without)
S	(subjective)
SI or SIJ	(sacroiliac joint)
SIJI	(sacroiliac joint injection)
SLR	(straight leg raising)

SOAP	(subjective, objective, assessment, diagnosis)
SOB	(short of breath)
S/P	(status post)
STAT	(immediate)
Sx	(symptoms)

tid	(three times per day)
TKR	(total knee replacement)
T-spine	(thoracic spine)
Tx	(treatment)

U/A	(urine analysis)
UE	(upper extremity)
URI	(upper respiratory infection)
US	(ultrasound)
UTI	(urinary tract infection)

VAS	(visual analog scale)
VR	(vocational rehabilitation)

W/C	(wheelchair)
WNL	(within normal limits)

XR	(x-ray)

yo	(year old)

Index